Youth, Education, and Marginality

Youth, Education, and Marginality

Local and Global Expressions

Kate Tilleczek and
H. Bruce Ferguson,
editors

WILFRID LAURIER
UNIVERSITY PRESS   SickKids

Wilfrid Laurier University Press acknowledges the financial support of the Government of Canada through the Canada Book Fund for our publishing activities.

Library and Archives Canada Cataloguing in Publication

Youth, education, and marginality : local and global expressions / Kate Tilleczek and H. Bruce Ferguson, editors.

(SickKids community and mental health series)
Co-published by: Hospital for Sick Children.
Includes bibliographical references.
Issued also in electronic formats.
ISBN 978-1-55458-634-9

1. Youth with social disabilities—Education. 2. Marginality, Social. 3. Educational sociology. I. Ferguson, H. Bruce II. Tilleczek, Kate, 1963– III. Hospital for Sick Children IV. Series: SickKids community and mental health series

LC4065.Y68 2013   371.93   C2012-907132-3
——

Electronic monographs.
Issued also in print format.
ISBN 978-1-55458-654-7 (PDF)—ISBN 978-1-55458-329-4 (EPUB)

1. Youth with social disabilities—Education. 2. Marginality, Social. 3. Educational sociology. I. Ferguson, H. Bruce II. Tilleczek, Kate, 1963– III. Hospital for Sick Children IV. Series: SickKids community and mental health series (Online)

LC4065.Y68 2013   371.93   C2012-907133-1

Cover design by Blakeley Words+Pictures. Front-cover image: *missed-education*, an illustration by Roberto Louis Foz, based on the photograph *Barbed Wire*, by Elliott James Tilleczek. Text design by Brenda Prangley.

This book is printed on FSC recycled paper and is certified Ecologo. It is made from 100% post-consumer fibre, processed chlorine free, and manufactured using biogas energy.

Printed in Canada

Published by Wilfrid Laurier University Press
Waterloo, Ontario, Canada
www.wlupress.wlu.ca

For all youth of late modernity, that they sing
vivacious songs.
And for the adults who continue to sing
with and *for* them.

contents

Acknowledgements   xi

Introduction:
Living Intersections of Marginality   1
Kate Tilleczek and Bruce Ferguson

YOUTH ART: *Marginalized Youth* by Kira Duff   7

Opening Words:
Youth Poetry and Prose
Bloodline by Tammy Lou   9
A Changing World by Selina Jacqueline Peters   10
Because I Am a Survivor by Sabnam Mahmuda   10
Examining Our Environments by Farrah Chanda Aslam   12

Chapter 1: Humanities-Infused Praxis *by, with,* and *for* Youth:
Esoteric Hope   17
Kate Tilleczek and Karima Kinlock

YOUTH ART: *Finding Hope* by Tamir Holder   41

Chapter 2: Young People *Speaking Back* from the Margins   43
John Smyth

YOUTH ART: *Grey Matters* by Zera Koutchieva   59

Chapter 3: The Unique Status of Marginalization: The Birth of
Youth-Empowering Parents   61
Agazi Afewerki and Mohammed Shafique

YOUTH ART: *Hunger* by Sarah Laurin   73

Chapter 4: Marginal Spaces, Disparate Places: Educational
and Youth Practices in a Globalizing World   75
Jean Mitchell

YOUTH ART: *On the Coast 2* by Elliott Tilleczek   91

Chapter 5: A Time for Dreams: The Right to Education for First Nations Children and Youth Living On-Reserve   93
Jennifer King, Chelsea Edwards, and Cindy Blackstock

YOUTH ART: *The Blue Bliss* by Angel Ho   113

Chapter 6: Marginalization Inside Education: Racialized, Immigrant, and Aboriginal Youth   115
Joanna Anneke Rummens and George J. Sefa Dei

YOUTH ART: *Barbed Wire* by Elliott Tilleczek   135

Chapter 7: Marginalized Youth in Education: Social and Cultural Dimensions of Exclusion in Canada and the United Kingdom   137
Andy Furlong

YOUTH ART: *Tears and Fears* by Anwesha Sen   153

Chapter 8: On Being Poor in School   155
Kate Tilleczek

Chapter 9: Still Sleeping in the "Gay Tent"? Queer Youth in Canadian Schools   177
Tom Hilton

YOUTH ART: *Two Young Men* by Elliott Tilleczek   195

Chapter 10: Narrative Understandings of Lives in (and out of) Schools   197
Vera Caine, Sean Lessard, Pam Steeves, and D. Jean Clandinin

YOUTH ART: *The Blue Brain Kid* by Bria Dobson   217

Chapter 11: Does Special Education Marginalize Young People?: The Need for Evidence-Informed Practices   219
Peter Chaban

YOUTH ART: *Pieces of Me* by Andrea Bunnie   227

Chapter 12: Using Visual Arts to Enhance Mental Health Literacy in Schools   229
Katherine M. Boydell

Conclusion:

Moving Forward: *With, For*, and *By* Youth
Kate Tilleczek and Bruce Ferguson   241

Closing Words:

Youth Poetry and Prose
Marginalized by Mallory Goss   243
At Risk by Lishai Peel   244
Forgetting the Meaning of ... by Maryam Sharif-Razi   246
I Am from ... by Alycia Fry   247

Index   249

acknowledgements

This book is a celebration. It would not have been possible without the relentlessly kind vision of Bruce Ferguson, founder and director of the Community Health Systems Group at the Hospital for Sick Children in Toronto. This project, like so many others, bears Bruce's stamp of infectious and sincere optimism for children and youth, of rigour in social science research, and of commitments to share our research with many audiences. It was his idea to launch the Collaborative Research Symposium Series at the Hospital for Sick Children and gather together the scholars, young people, and educators who are part of this book. As Bruce predicted, this effort infected and connected many others.

I would also like to acknowledge and thank all of the young artists and chapter authors. They were unflinching in purpose and a pleasure to work with. In addition, Karima Kinlock (and Sarah Bovaird before her) at the Hospital for Sick Children earned the title *shepherdess from paradise* as did Valerie Campbell, my research manager at the University of Prince Edward Island. It was a joy to be assisted in this book project by these bright and dedicated women. My partner Ron Srigley and my left-handed sons, William and Elliott, help to keep it real. They continue to inspire and critique my work *by, with,* and *for* marginalized young people. It is with them that I write.

Kate Tilleczek

I I want to thank the authors of this volume for bringing breadth and intensity to this important area. I am grateful to my co-editor for creating a
process that was not only always committed to excellence but also edifying and
fun. Sarah Bovaird and Karima Kinlock worked hard to make it easy for me to
contribute to the process. Finally, I would like to acknowledge the members of
the Community Health Systems Resource Group at Hospital for Sick Children
whose passion, focus, and knowledge keep me humble and curious and maintain my conviction that together we can and will make a difference in the lives
of our children and youth.

H. Bruce Ferguson

Living Intersections of Marginality

Kate Tilleczek and Bruce Ferguson

> *First get off the streets, second get a job, third finish your education so you can get a career. So it is like steps at a time. It is like some people have those things already and they are lucky that they have those things already handed to them and they don't have to start at the bottom and work their way up. They don't understand what that is like. Starting at the bottom is ... I am slowly getting there. I'm not there, but I am slowly getting there.* (Max)[1]

This book provides evidence and discussion about the ways in which Canadian schools are not always doing well by young people in late modernity. The contributors of this book provide both local and global contexts, data, experiences, and lessons. This variability has been with us since the early twentieth century when many young people did not attend or complete school in Canada's emerging compulsory education system (Davies and Guppy, 2006). Today too many students are still struggling with schooling and too many schools are still struggling with students. We have commented previously that new understandings about the nuances in young lives have shown that too simple a conclusion cannot be drawn about who is marginalized, how, or what should be done:

> One student's coming out as gay or lesbian may be celebrated in one school and community but lead to violent shunning in another. One Aboriginal community's young people live with a host of positive inspirations while another community continues to mourn the loss of their young. The daily hassles experienced by some youth living in poor families or newcomers to Canada are met with serious concern by one teacher but not by another teacher in the same school. And, the shunning or support is negotiated in one manner by some young people and educators and in a different way by others. (Tilleczek, 2011)

This book jumps off from, and into, these nuances through detailed empirical, theoretical, artistic, practical, and policy discussions of what could be next for marginalized youth in public education. And it includes the artistic experience and rendering about marginalization by some talented young people. Young people and the social process of marginalization are not essential or simple categories. We avoid treating all youth the same or knowing what marginality is or what it means to them. We have invoked an imagination that allows the process of viewing late modernity to be vast, abundant, complex, and strange, and we present work that witnesses how young people understand and negotiate its margins in public education.

The social complexity of these experiences and life stories and the ways in which schools respond to them is the focus of this book. It has been organized to begin and end with the perspectives and voices of young people in order to provide a glimpse into this society that they inhabit. In particular, they are addressing the experiences of being on the outside, traversing liminal spaces, being on the margins, and being made marginal and pushed to the boundaries from which it is difficult to learn, to be taken seriously, included, or heard. They wince from there and offer critiques that educators and policy makers need to hear. We do not agree that "giving voice" is entirely possible as many do not hear or take to heart what is heard.

The book is a moment of making space. The contributors work at the intersections of experiences of social marginalization as it plays out in public education. As a group of scholars, young people, educators, and policy-makers, they make fresh contributions about educational responses to young people struggling to negotiate the identity borders of race, social class, poverty, cultural status, mental health challenges, sexualities, linguistic or literacy challenges, familial chaos, and/or being a newcomer to Canada. The authors attempt to elucidate the abundant folds of experience of these young people and their meanings for educational practice and policy. They also take seriously the narratives, biographies, and life stories that illuminate intersections of identity, experience, and the social worlds of youth. In May 2009, many of us had the fortune to assemble at one of Bruce Ferguson's collaborative research symposia at the Hospital for Sick Children in Toronto. I was thrilled to host the symposium *Marginalized Youth in Contemporary Educational Contexts,* the fifth in a series of seven such events (http://www.chsrgevents.ca/default.aspx). Many contributors to this book took part in this dialogue, and others form an emerging network, some of whom contributed in 2011 to a special issue of *Education Canada* on marginalized youth. This conversation has now landed momentarily in this book.

The book begins and ends with the artistic renderings of young people, and you will find visual art from young people between and among the chapters. Look for the visual works of Tamir Holder (*Finding Hope*), Sarah Laurin (*Hunger*), Elliott Tilleczek (*On the Coast 2, Barbed Wire*), Angel Ho (*The Blue Bliss*), Anwesha Sen (*Tears and Fears*), Zera Koutchieva (*Grey Matters*), Kira Duff (*Marginalized Youth*), Bria Dobson (*The Blue Brain Kid*), and Andrea Bunnie (*Pieces of Me*). It opens with poetry and prose by youth contributors Farrah Chanda Aslam, Tammy Lou, Selina Peters, and Sabnam Mahmuda, who demonstrate the power of art in this conversation. The book closes with poetry and prose that looks towards reflection and suggestion by Lishai Peel, Maryam Sharif-Razi, Mallory Goss, and Alycia Fry. The individual contributions are a gift and the collective contributions provide a dizzying and illuminating effect. Interpretation is left up to you but be prepared for an interior journey.

Chapter 1 follows with Kate Tilleczek and Karima Kinlock's examination of the possibilities and promises of "humanities-infused praxis" with and for young people on the margins. They map out the ways in which the art of the young people in this book has been gathered and interpreted. They open with further youth experiences that set the stage for a discussion on how the humanities and social sciences are being used as a means to better understand and communicate the marginalization of youth. They provide some insight as to how various art media are being used by the community to facilitate conversations of youth life experiences and what it means to do so.

Chapter 2 demonstrates John Smyth's insistence that youth have been, and will continue to be, "speaking back from the margins" if only we are able to engage and decipher. Smyth explores youth perspectives on what is happening when young people from contexts of disadvantage make choices against the institution of schooling, despite possible further exacerbation of their apparent marginalization. Through his research spanning over two decades, he gives voice to how youth go about making lives for themselves while speaking back to notions of mainstream schooling and—in many cases—finding their way into alternative and more amenable forms of learning. And following in step is Chapter 3, in which Agazi Afewerki and Mohammed Shafique demonstrate the ways in which Canadian youth have done just that. They discuss a unique and award winning (United Nations) program—Youth Empowering Parents (YEP)—as born in the belly of Regent Park, Toronto. This is a fascinating community and youth-based project whereby the youth are the service providers and adults receive the service. The chapter narrates how YEP came into being, how it operates, and how it has left its mark on the Regent Park community and the two young authors who founded the program.

Chapter 4 also explores youth community engagement in Canada, but it opens the conversation up to global and globalized youth and education. Jean Mitchell discusses her ethnographic research in an urban settlement in

Vanuatu, an archipelago in the southwest Pacific and in an inner-city neighbourhood of Prince Edward Island, Canada. Both are arguably marginalized
but disparate, and there is much gained by the parallel narratives and anthropological interpretations. This chapter provides insight into the importance in
resisting the treatment, as essential, of concepts or processes such as "youth,"
"marginal," or "global." Nuances in the social process of marginalization are
provided as being crucial to this scholarly and practical field of work. Mitchell
provides glimpses into globalized youth and education systems to explore how
everyday lives are impacted.

Chapters 5 and 6 coalesce around cultural and ethnic status and the ways
in which Aboriginal youth in Canada have been, and continue to be, made
marginal to public education. In Chapter 5, Jennifer King, Chelsea Edwards,
and Cindy Blackstock discuss the marginalization of First Nation youth attending school on the reserve. They provide insight into the disparities of First
Nation students in comparison to students across Canada and discuss important initiatives that the First Nation students have themselves put into motion.
In Chapter 6, J. Anneke Rummens and George J. Sefa Dei discuss various origins and orientations of marginalization and how they affect youth. They provide insight into the intersectionality of exclusion/inclusion and the concomitant devaluation of bodies, experiences, cultures, and histories that take place
within our communities. The focus on racialized, immigrant, and Aboriginal
youth is critical for Canadian public education debates.

Chapters 7 and 8 are equally significant as they attend to growing income
inequality and socio-economic status. Why has socio-economic status fallen off
the practice and policy tables of inclusion so readily when it is a most pervasive
form of inequity? How do these trends in inequity feel in the "daily hassles"
of impoverished youth at school? In Chapter 7, Andy Furlong compares the
United Kingdom and Canada on dimensions of social and cultural exclusion
and what it means for young people navigating school. He explores the ways in
which cultural orientations impact on educational attainment while examining
the extent to which modern educational experiences have affected the patterns
of youth engagement. Furlong also discusses the concept of marginalization (as
do many of the contributors and young artists) while examining the changes
in the relationship between inequality and educational outcomes as well as the
ways in which changing educational structures interface with modern transitions to impact marginalization. In Chapter 8, Kate Tilleczek maps out growing
income inequality in Canada and places young people at its nexus in terms of
growing marginalization. Questions are raised as to the impact that it has on
the mental health and well-being of young people and of the ability for schools
to respond. A new form of "cryptic curriculum" is outlined that moves past the

hidden curriculum now made visible for four decades. The rabid staying power of the initial social reproduction of schooling is re-examined in light of shifting social, political, and economic trends. The chapter attends to narratives of young people from working class and impoverished families as they attempt to navigate public education.

Chapters 9 and 10 provide further critical narratives of marginalization from gay and lesbian youth and from a range of young people who have left school before graduation. Tom Hilton addresses queer youth in Canada through historical narratives about human rights and personal narratives of youth and their families. This current work is crucial for Canadian public education as it provides a critical reflection on the policy and practice that frame "gayness" in education by working through comparisons of historical voices. Vera Caine and her co-authors Sean Lessard, Pam Steeves, and Jean Clandinin also place narrativity front and centre as they describe how the lives of youth both affect and are affected by the phenomenon of early school leaving. Powerful youth narratives are successfully engaged to open into youth experiences on early school leaving. The work exposes and interrogates moments of marginalization and how schools might be more responsive to the life composing of all youth.

The final chapters also portray suggestion and directions for shifts in evidence-based practice in public education. In so doing, they address two further groups of young people who experience social marginalization in public education. In Chapter 11, Peter Chaban addresses youth in special education. Katherine Boydell posits ways forward with and for young people with mental health challenges in Chapter 12. Chaban demonstrates how high school special education classes have managed to segregate youth. He specifically shares important work relating to the graduation rates of students with attention deficit hyperactivity disorder (ADHD) and argues that programs and practices such as "graduation initiatives" have served only to aid in the further marginalization of youth in special education. Boydell discusses mental health literacy in public education in a contemporary context. She amply highlights the context of youth mental health and the importance of enhancing mental health literacy in school settings. Like many other authors and young artist contributors in the book, Boydell uses innovative arts-based research methods and processes to create awareness, understanding, and dialogue in secondary schools. Indeed, the work provides fine samples of humanities-infused praxis offering a way into nuanced and esoteric understandings and hopes. The book then closes with youth art that similarly resonates.

Taken as a whole, we hope that the book provides glimpes into local and global expressions of youth, education, and marginality. As we struggle to come to terms with the future of public education and the place of equity within it, the book means to impress upon the reader the nuance and complexity of young lives.

Notes

1 "Max" (pseudonym) is a student who left school prior to graduation and is working to return (Tilleczek, 2008).

References

Davies, S. & Guppy, N. (2006). *The schooled society*. Toronto: Oxford University Press.
Tilleczek, K. (2011). *Approaching youth studies: Being, becoming and belonging*. Toronto: Oxford University Press.

Marginalized Youth, **multimedia drawing by Kira Duff**

T he artwork I have created represents a girl who is being separated (marginalized) from others in society. The hands surrounding her are those of faceless people that represent society itself. The hands are separating her from everyone else and controlling her, pulling, grabbing, and trying to tell her what's right and wrong. They also represent exclusion. By not having faces, it's as if the girl is alone and can't talk to anyone about her issues. The barcode on her head represents how society puts "labels" on certain people due to their differences. She is categorized and labelled by people that have no right in doing so. Lastly, the black paint around the edges is there for contrast and value. It also represents her being swallowed and overwhelmed by an unknown darkness or fear of not fitting in.

YOUTH POETRY AND PROSE

 # Bloodline

Tammy Lou

You told me I couldn't stay
So I paid my way in.
Now you tell me, it's amazing
To see someone like me
Be someone like you.

But let me tell you,
I had to reach up to touch
Rock bottom.
What I couldn't break through,
Broke me.

I came out of the ghetto,
Don't you put me back in.
Back up, hold up.
I'm back on track.

I am what I am
What I am.
A product of my mother's
sacrifice
And my father's reprise.
To cut ties,

And patch together
What was left with
Darkness.

But in a dark room,
Who can see what it is,
For what it is?

Did I forget to mention,
The reason for my dissention,
The object of my contention,
Is that you forgot to mention …

That my father's father,
And my mother's mother,
My very own blood line,
Climbed up the ladder
And got kicked back down.

Down from the A line,
To the B line,
To the C line

9

A Changing World

Selina Jacqueline Peters

My world is changing day by day,
Ever changing like moulding clay.
Days are becoming so long,
I barely even take hits from anyone's bong.
Not sure how I got here now,
But I'm here, And living somehow.
I still walk around with a smile on my face,
Even though I'm sketchy at times in this place.
I found someone I rather like,
Together we smoke, hike, and bike.
We always go on a run around town,
It's rare we get to cuddle and settle down.
Life is not close to anything before,
We often sleep on our buddy's floor.
Nowadays there's not a lot of money to spend,
So instead, we go get high with our good friends.
My life goes up, down, all around,
So this I ask, Please return my brain if found.
I find my mind growing wild,
My actions more free like a child.
Heads turn whenever we walk by,
But we're too busy looking around and into the sky.
My friends just look at me and know,
Others assume it's just our flow.
The way we walk, The way we talk,
The way our lips and jaws either ramble or lock.
So the circle came and the seasons passed,
And I'm here again, just like the past,
But also a new way,
So Fuck it, Get Fucked, And Let's Play.

Because I Am a Survivor

Sabnam Mahmuda

I am a victim,
A victim of our society's expectations.

I am a victim,
A victim of circumstances.

I am haunted,
Haunted by the ghosts of a future unknown.

I am haunted,
Haunted by the terrifying nightmares of growing up too soon.

I am trapped,
Trapped within the walls of fear of making the wrong choices.

I am trapped,
Trapped in the vicious cycle of need to belong and to be someone.

Whenever I close my eyes,
I face the pictures of helpless faces of children in poverty,
I read the silent plea for help in their shadowed eyes.

I face the pictures of soldiers losing their lives fighting for power,
I see their faces colored with courage and blood.

I face the pictures of others like me wielding weapons of self destruction
to escape their troubles,
I hear their voices rising in anger, in pain and in regret.

I face the pictures of smoke from factories clouding up the sky until,
It's all dark.

In the dark I wonder what I am meant to be, what I am meant to do,
where in this maze I belong.

And in the dark, I can't feel anything,
Other than the sharp claws of fear of facing the consequences of my actions.

I can't hear anything,
Except for the sound of my own ragged breathing and a desperate cry
for help.

I can't see anything,
Other than the dark hatred which fills my mind and surrounds my heart.

In the darkness I hide,
I hide deep in the hole I dug,
To shelter myself from the beating of my own emotions.

But amidst the chaos raging in the dark part of my mind,
I know there are others like me,
Who are victims of society's expectations; of circumstances.

Who are haunted by the ghost of a future unknown; haunted by
the terrifying nightmares of growing up.

And I know somewhere deep inside me
I know that I will survive.

That I am not alone in this world fighting to hold onto the innocence
of childhood a little longer.

I take courage from others, who have survived,
To accept my losses, to fight my own demons, to stand for my beliefs
I believe in them and I believe in me
And I know I will survive
Because I am a survivor.

Examining Our Environments

Farrah Chanda Aslam

The ways in which I understand myself are inextricably linked to the social environments I live in, including my community[1] and dominant society.[2] In this paper, I critically examine these environments and the ways in which social relations, identities and inequalities are produced and how they impact my life. More specifically, I analyze my personal experience of choosing to wear the hijab[3] and the role it plays in shaping my lived experiences.

When examining the environmental issues I encounter in my community and in dominant society, I realized that I am in the middle of a tug-of-war between Orientalism on one end and Islamic Fundamentalism at the other end. To begin with, Edward Said (1978) coined the term "Orientalism" as an ideological construction by European-Westerns that create, recreate and reinforce the "free," "civilized" and "progressive" West (Occident) in a binary or above the "primitive," "static" and "barbaric" East (Orient). In turn, this construction facilitates the legitimization of the Occident's imposition over the Orient to "help" with civilizing or overcoming the supposed irrationality exhibited by those in the East (Said, 1978).

Consequently, from an Orientalist standpoint, the hijab is a patriarchal representation of women's oppression that denies women the right to control their bodies and to choose what to wear. Thus, the hijab is seen as an image of the "inferior" Muslim women who is constructed as needing liberation, by the rational, progressive and civilized man because of the oppression imposed on her in the Orient

(Muslim countries) (Tahmasebi, 2008). On the other hand, Islamic fundamentalism views the West as the "problem" and the focus of this discourse is associated with attempting to cleanse Islam of any Western values (i.e., modernity). The rise of Islamic fundamentalism encourages the literal interpretation of the Quran where misogynists have used the hijab as a tool to impose patriarchal laws on women to preserve their own privileges (Tahmasebi, 2008).

I believe that both discourses work simultaneously in shaping my everyday experiences, especially since I identify as a Muslim woman who has chosen to wear the hijab. I find that I am criticized for *why* I even wear the hijab and being told that I wear the hijab the *wrong* way because I do not always align with the conventional norms of how women are considered to wear the hijab.[4] The Orientalist gaze is reflected by my own community when I am told that the hijab is not "modern." It becomes evident that the Western ideas associated with Muslims and Western norms of assimilation are internalized and imposed on me by people who are also targeted by the Orientalist gaze. Furthermore, the criticism I encounter by fellow Muslims about the *way* I wear my hijab, for me illustrates elements of fundamentalism because my wearing of the hijab is not respected and instead is reduced to traditional ideals of Islamic dress code.

Therefore, both discourses exhibited are by my "own people," which does not even begin my exploration of Orientalist ideologies I deal with, especially when I *do* wear my hijab conventionally, from people who do not identify with Islam or Muslims. Some of the reactions I have encountered range from people ignoring my existence, to speaking on my behalf, to telling me that I look as if I am oppressed by my father, to being told that I look too religious and to being asked if I will be forced to marry a cousin who lives "back home." As a result, the Orientalist lens used by people who do not identify as Muslim or with Islam is often put aside for the time being, while I battle or resist the conflicting views of Islamic fundamentalists first.

Furthermore, I believe that the social environments that I live in are affected by the media's representations of Muslim women. The media (i.e., newspapers/magazines, television, films and so forth), operating within the Orientalist and Islamic fundamentalist discourses, are key players in normalizing the essentialization and homogenization of Muslim women. For Islamic fundamentalists, the diversity of Muslims is generally ignored and is narrowed to the traditional roles associated with the family, procreation and dress code ascribed to Muslim women. From the Orientalist view, the homogenization of Muslim women is achieved, as Narayan (2000) describes the "package picture" of Muslim culture, where only certain elements (i.e., Muslim women who are forced to wear the hijab) are selected to represent and label cultural complexities. As a result, the Muslim woman is constructed as ahistorical and static, which normalizes the differences between women in the East and West without considering the complex differences among each category of women. To me, this Islamophobic process works to reinforce the binary between the East and West and prevents analysis by both the key agents in the media and readers/viewers that are Muslim and non-Muslim of the geopolitical issues/struggles at hand.

As a reader/viewer myself, I find that I too, to an extent, internalize the images and columns I am exposed to without realizing the impact they have on my livelihood as a Muslim woman. As a consequence, distorted images and understandings of both the East and West multiply the oppression and dehumanization of anyone who is not "us" is justified, whether we live in Toronto or Iraq, for example. In other words, Islamophobia shapes and is shaped by society because the same individuals that perpetuate Islamophobia also make up the institutions of our society that have the power to illustrate how we *should* understand Muslims. More significantly, I understand that because individuals and social institutions work simultaneously, representing Islam or Muslims in ways that are flawed becomes easily normalized, which prevents consideration of Islamophobia as a crucial form of oppression that needs to be deconstructed by the environments that I live in, in order to understand my experiences of wearing the hijab.

In order to overcome the environmental issues that women who wear the hijab encounter, living in Western societies, I find that many of them stop wearing the hijab for a variety of reasons. I am aware and I understand that wearing the hijab is very difficult for some, compared to others, especially when we experience interlocking systems of oppression, where race, class, gender, sexuality, age, ability, geographical location and so forth are implicated in every experience and work together to mutually reinforce one another in the different environments we live in. This often results in acts that cause pain, inferiorization and exclusion for Muslim women wearing the hijab.

Taking off the hijab may be an option, but I do not believe one has to in order to support Western ideas of what it means to be an empowered, autonomous and a "beautiful" woman. Muslim women can be and are Western women who can wear the hijab, be "fashionable," pursue an education, maintain a career, get married and have children. Thus, I do not believe that I have to solely conform to a single interpretation of each society, showing the fluidity of my identity.

Notes

1   I define "my community" as a social structure founded on shared interests and social characteristics. It includes people, like my parents, who immigrated to Canada from Pakistan 35–40 years ago, with religious and cultural values that shape how they raise their children, who are born and raised here, in Canada.

2   I define "dominant society as mainstream Canadian society—the dominant society based on set of common values and beliefs shared by most people in a given society—which includes my social network of friends and acquaintances and the school I attend.

3   I believe that the hijab has more than one definition because it varies based on the individual, their experiences, understandings of Islam and cultural background. I also believe that it is a state of mind, behaviour and a lifestyle based on dressing/behaving in a fashion that does not provoke uncalled attention and lowering one's gaze, which all also applies to men.

4   When I refer to not wearing my hijab conventionally I mean I often only wear my hijab where the scarf wraps around my hair in the shape of a bun, instead of the "conventional" manner, as seen most commonly in the media, where women use pieces of material to cover their hair, neck and chest area.

Work Cited

Narayan, U. (2000). Undoing the 'Package Picture' of Cultures. In *Women Living under Muslims Laws* (pp. 1–4). Dossier.

Said, E. (1978). Introduction. *Orientalism*. New York: Vintage Books. pp. 1–28.

Tahmasebi, Victoria. (2008, January 14). *The Production and the Representation of Muslim Women: Caught between Two Discourses.* Presented at a WST C30- Gender and Islam lecture at the University of Toronto—Scarborough.

chapter 1

Humanities-Infused Praxis *by, with,* and *for* Youth: Esoteric Hope

Kate Tilleczek and Karima Kinlock

> I thought how unpleasant it is to be locked out; and I thought how it is worse, perhaps, to be locked in and thinking of the safety and prosperity of the one sex and the poverty and insecurity of the other and of the effect of tradition and of the lack of tradition on the mind of the writer, I thought at last it was time to roll up the crumpled skin of the day with its arguments and its impressions and its anger and its laughter and cast it into the hedge ... One seemed alone with an inscrutable society. (Woolf, 1929, p. 31)

In this chapter, we begin in that inscrutable society in which the liberal arts and humanities are under attack in public education. This criticism has been well documented recently by philosophers, social scientists, film makers, and journalists (Collini, 2009; Nussbaum, 2009; Srigley, 2012). While we will not trace this decline here, we lament it deeply and urge readers to track that sinking ship and weigh in on what this attack has meant for the education of our young. There is a curious and contradictory movement however towards the re-emergence of arts, humanities, and social science in forging this critique. A small pocket of writers are pushing back against prevailing reduction and fracture of understanding and experience. Most often referred to generically as "qualitative research" in the social sciences, this shift in ways of seeing and knowing is also referred to as "arts-based" research. However, when the humanities re-collided with the social sciences in this interpretive turn, analysis was more profound than either term suggests, and the situation began to improve for perceptive witnessing of the lives and times of young people. Art and experience flowed into the dismal fact-value void. To see just how true this is, try to imagine a prosaic North American youth voice without J.D. Salinger, Janis Joplin, Bob Dylan, TuPac, Nirvana, and so forth. The confines of abundant experience were freed up, and social/political analysis became increasingly possible.

We see this move as humanities-infused praxis to suggest the deeper influence of the full range of philosophical, artistic, theatrical, photographic, linguistic, visual, literary, and narrative gifts that the humanities have begun to bestow upon a few renegades in social sciences. The academic study of young people is moving nicely towards this influence, and thus these improvements are taking hold. The offerings are endless: anthropology and fine art/film have presented the power of the visual; philosophy, english, theatre, and psychoanalysis the strength of the story; and sociology the dance between human experience and its social/political meaning and organization. And then there is music and dance and so on.

This kind of study *with*, *for*, and *by* young people provides a space to illustrate their abundant lives and the concerns they hold and negotiate in public education and wider society. The reasons for the paradoxical encounter between the death of liberal arts alongside a growth of humanities-infused praxis are unclear and perhaps unimportant for this chapter. Rather, we stridently use this space to invite young people into the conversation. This chapter, like the book, floats through the re-collision of humanities and social sciences to make more evident the esoteric hope and liminal experiences of youth in a public educational system in decline.

> *Sometimes it's hard for me to tell my parents how I feel going through my*
> *everyday life; they have their own problems and I don't want to burden them …*
> *but it's true, I never feel good about keeping things in, that's why I tell my*
> *stories through dance.* (Sandeep, 19)[1]

> *Honestly, when I write poetry, yeah it's art, but really it's like my diary and*
> *if I'm moved to, I can share, and that's how I talk about it or whatever …*
> *usually that's enough for me.* (Wennie, 18)

These lives are brought to bear by the humanities and liberal arts traditions, and these disciplines coalesce in youth studies. We argue that humanities-infused youth studies have the same power and place to make plain, and "trouble up," experiences and witnessing of social marginalization. Historically, art has been reputed to uncover and expose more readily the many layers residing within any given subject—in this case, the strata of youth-lived experiences. Theatre, music, dance, poetry, graphics, paintings, and visual art are but a few art forms that are being recognized in the community as a means to teach and learn—in short, to communicate with the youth of today. Grounding research in the everyday worlds of young people, especially those who have been made socially marginal, is an epistemological approach where knowledge is grounded in mutually determined experience and conversation. Carroll (2006) suggests that youth studies could itself be *praxis*:

> Such a critical perspective proceeds from the recognition that social life as we know it is marked by inequities that are deeply structured yet contingent features of human organization. As a systemic knowledge of the social, sociology is inevitably caught up in these inequities ... As praxis, sociology makes a commitment to understand the deeper, systemic bases of the problems we face, whether social, psychological or ecological, which often means understanding the interconnections between allegedly separate issues and problems as in the intersections of race, class and gender that constitute lived realities. (As cited in Frampton et al., 2006, p. 234)

Youth studies are emerging in this way, and both lived realities and social/political analysis are incubated in arts-infused ways of knowing. Such methodologies are critical in the sense that the work implies "a sort of critique, is democratic in nature, and can root out the underlying connections, issues, joys, and troubles as experienced in many contexts by youth" (Tilleczek, 2011, p. 40).

> The current complication of structural inequalities, and of the forms of self-narration through which they are actively contested and reproduced, clearly requires more sophistication and empirically grounded accounts ... If we are to do justice to what is at stake in young people's lives, we have to find new ways of integrating empirically grounded and dialogical strategies of youth research within interdisciplinary and theoretically sophisticated frameworks of comparative analysis. (Cohen & Ainley, 2000, p. 242)

In this book, as in our research and community work, we have reached out past academic texts to invite and hear from young people about the nuances and complications of social marginality. The process of individualization for young people demonstrates a "progressive weakening of social bonds due to growing social diversity of life experiences" (Furlong & Cartmel, 2007, p. 143), but it is not advisable to overemphasize individual reflexivity and thus miss the modern context. It is unwise to separate youth experiences from social and political contexts and to over or underestimate the extent to which individuals construct their own identities. While social and political landscapes have changed, young people remain tied to marginal social locations, divisions, and inequalities. Methods and tools for witnessing and telling these tales are those that allow for the exposition of sources of inequality and the range and depth of experiences invoked therein:

> [B]iographical and narrative tools are becoming important in that they do not require the abandonment of examinations of structural inequalities in schools, communities, leisure pursuits and so forth. They suggest that mediated experiences remain important for examination but mainly because they *distort reality*. [In] many ways, these difficulties are being worked through very effectively by social scientists studying youth. The development of biographical perspectives, that draw on interpretations of lived experiences, while showing how structures are recreated both through actions and interpretations, offers an appropriate tool that can be used to understand modern life contexts. (Furlong & Cartmel, 2007, p. 143)

Cohen (1999) has proposed youth studies with a mind to autobiography and context. According to Griffen (2001), the emphasis on social, cultural, psychological, and economic processes through which ethnicity, class, gender, dis/ability, and sexuality are produced and reproduced *in practice* by various groups of young people is an important shift. She makes the important point that current and critical youth research engages with globalization theory to "speak about the complex relations between diverse youth cultural practices, discourses of youth, and discourses of pathology that map onto one another in complex and contradictory ways" (p. 161). We would add, however, that humanities-infused praxis makes possible a visibility not just of these discourses but also of the social organizations and interactions of marginalization and freedom. In the book, *In the Country of the Blind: Youth Studies and Cultural Studies in Britain,*

On the Coast by William Tilleczek

Cohen and Ainley (2000) develop an analysis of gender and class formations in which structuralism is not lost altogether but, rather, transformed through a more critical engagement with postmodern frameworks providing a detailed history of the emergence of youth studies and cultural studies. They outline, on the one hand, the ways in which certain strands of cultural studies have over-theorized their work and lost the detailed analyses of practices and experience. On the other hand, they outline how some youth studies research has been too focused on economic and class-based structuralism and empiricism. We dance between them in an esoteric hope for better understanding humanity's offerings for its young people.

Youth Art and Youth Talk

> No other kind of relic or text from the past can offer such a direct testimony about the world which surrounded other people at other times. In this respect, images are more precise and richer than literature. To say this is not to deny the expressive or imaginative quality of art, treating it merely as documentary evidence; the more imaginative the work the more profoundly it allows us to share the artist's experience of the visible. (Berger, 1972, p. 10)

There is a variety of art dispersed throughout this book, and it has been created by young people to illustrate their points of view and experiences *vis-à-vis* the social processes of marginalization. Creative expression was chosen as a vocal medium because, in addition to leisure and expression, youth are using this method as a form of coping and communication.

> *For me, it's not that deep. Honestly, my writing just helps me cope, man. I'm able to put things down on paper and see it for what it is, then I imagine what it could be, write it down and experience an alternate ending for a while ... and it's like ... I have control over that.* (Jackson, 22)

We have chosen creative expression as a fulcrum in this chapter to highlight the role that it plays in inter- and intra-generational communication; in bringing awareness to the gaps between marginalized and privileged populations; and in giving youth the opportunity to express themselves beyond the borders of societal pressure and censorship. To invite young people into our conversation, we held a contest that requested youth to share their definition, perspective, and/or experience of marginalization through their artwork. In addition to being published in this book, ten youth were awarded $100 for articulating their story through artistic expression.

Besides an email blast to organizations across Canada, we visited a number of organizations and met with youth in order to encourage them to document their experiences. A wide range of informal conversations were held surrounding the topic of marginalization, covering topics and lived experiences ranging from educational contexts to instances of social exclusion. The commonality was that youth who had been subjected to marginalization maintained that they had been prejudged and felt unsupported within the context of the relationship they held with society. They were cognizant that they were not afforded the same opportunities as some of their peers and asserted that most of these injustices were not due to anything that they had done. Their unjust treatment stemmed from preconceptions associated with their accent, culture, sexual orientation, and/or socio-economic circumstance—essentially, the characteristics that contribute to how they are perceived by others. We wanted to engage in solidarity with young people by also creating a space for others to get to know them beyond these preconceptions. Underneath the labels, the prejudice, and the marginalized treatment, there exists a young person striving under the pressures of society.

We received 21 contest submissions from young people across the provinces of Ontario and Prince Edward Island.[2] Submissions came in the form of poetry, short essays, paintings, collages, scripts, sketches, and mixed media. Some artwork spoke to the youth's personal experiences, while other entries either disclosed observations of immediate environmental contexts or shared perspectives on how solidarity could be reached with youth from environments that were less familiar to them. Together with their perspective and artistic expression, these youth portray and theorize the experience of social marginalization.

School Lessons in the Community

Youth at Toronto's Alexandra Park Community Centre collaborated with a number of community agencies in order to access various workshops.[3] After an arts workshop geared towards youth expression regarding issues of equity and marginalization, we were able to host a focus group of 21 youth with the help of Olu Quamina.[4] The aim was to invoke discussions on marginalization within educational contexts and uncover the place of art in the exploration of hopes and fears. The focus group's discussion lasted for one hour and thirty-three minutes and introduced a space that provided youth the opportunity to have their perspectives listened to. Class structure, the inability to relate to/ connect with teachers, the pros and cons of school cliques, the notion of being "different," the desire to be treated like everyone else, and artful coping mechanisms were some of the themes that emerged.

> It's not that I want the whole world to cater to me or anything, I just see it catering to everybody else ... and don't get me wrong, I don't need charity or anything, all I want is an equal shot. (Melissa, 22)

Well, good luck, 'cause if there's anything that school has taught me, it's that if you come from the 'hood, everyone treats you like you're from the 'hood ... No matter what happens, they're always looking at you like you did something or like you're going to do something wrong. (Shawn, 18)

Yeah, but look at you ... you've got all these tattoos, tons of piercings, PLUS you got cornrows ... who do you think is going to give you a shot? I wouldn't! You're already Black, dark-skinned at that ... you're not helping yourself! (Jalisha, 18)

It shouldn't matter what I look like ... it should only matter that I want to learn. Period. (Shawn, 18)

Stereotypes and stigmas have impacted these youth, and some were affected to the point of perspectival mimesis whereby their definition of "acceptable" was congruent with that which society deemed "acceptable," despite what their own experiences had already taught them. For example, we noted that throughout the focus group discussion, Jalisha admitted to being subject to marginalization due to her ethnicity and emphasized that her experiences have only taught her to value people for who they are and not for what they look like. However, during the exchange between Jalisha and Shawn (see earlier quotations), we see that Jalisha has evaluated that being Black, in addition to having excessive tattoos and piercings, are all perceived as disadvantages according to society. She then admits that she would not have given Shawn a shot either based solely on his appearance. Her contradiction suggests a congruency with society's definitive description of "acceptable" appearances, even though her very own personal experiences have taught her quite the contrary. She has internalized society's definition of what it means to be "within the margins."

Persons belonging to different racial groups are made aware of their social and academic stereotype differences early on. Simmons, Lewis, and Larson (2011) argue that school serves as a societal marker for racial identity formation and marginalization such that by junior high students have deciphered which stereotype belongs to which group and have conceptualized what it means to belong to each group. Hudley and Graham's (2001) work illustrates this phenomenon. Their study involved African-American, Latino, and Anglo junior high students who had to match photographs of unknown individuals from various ethnic origins to hypothetical scenarios. They all frequently chose photographs of ethnic minority males for scenarios of academic disengagement, consistent with the cultural stereotypes of these young men. Kao (2000) identifies what "acting Black" or "acting White" means to adolescents and how it is associated with academic achievement. He "argues that adolescents define their goals primarily in terms of the stereotypical images attached to their ethnic group" (p. 408). Black students were stereotyped as being less likely to be in honour classes, not doing well in school, and less likely to do homework. Aronson and Inzlicht's (2004) study demonstrates the negative effects of impairment that stereotype vulnerability[5] and stereotype threat[6] have on one's self-knowledge about one's own intellectual abilities. When self-knowledge regarding one's own intellectual ability is altered, it results in the variance of self-confidence, which can affect levels of performance. As the discussion of these youth continued, they disclosed more of their experiences within the classroom context, which included stereotype-related incidences applied both horizontally and vertically.

> *No, I NEVER raised my hand in class! I did it once to ask a question, teacher humiliated me, everybody laughed … and that was the end of that! I feel stupid … I mean, teachers have always told me that I wasn't good enough.* (Melissa, 22)

Melissa's statement was then probed to confirm whether or not she had experienced a teacher who had actually verbalized that she "wasn't good enough." She responded:

> *No in different ways … like giving me "the look" when I raised my hand to ask questions, rushing me when I talked … all the other kids would get "That's a good question!" or "Did everyone hear that answer?" or something … I just never felt like what I had to say mattered in class.* (Melissa, 22)

> *Yeah, I'm back in school now and it's like I won't even raise my hand because I know people don't think I have anything intelligent to say or that I may know the answers to anything … I mean if I'm right and I don't say anything, I feel good about that on the inside … but if I raise my hand and answer something wrong, I don't want to give anybody the satisfaction of proving them right or anything.* (Raheem, 19)

> *That's funny, for me it's the opposite! I raise my hand ALL of the time, just to prove that I do know the answers and that it doesn't matter where I come from, what I look like or where I live, because none of that defines me. And usually I get good reception from teachers and they're supportive. The thing that I don't like is that I'd always hear from all the other students, and it didn't matter if they were White, Chinese, Indian, whatever, they'd always say, "you're not like the other Black people" … and I would always think, "why, 'cause I'm good in school?" More than anything, that always bothered me. Just when you think we're coming to some sort of acknowledgement of equality, it's the people who see you everyday, you share jokes with and whatever, and in the back of their minds, their first instinct is to define you by your stereotype—and when you don't fit, YOU'RE the exception.* (Heather, 21)

The youth continued to illuminate the literature and describe circumstances in which they or their peers had been unable to fit into designated societal moulds. They discussed their feelings regarding the lack of support from role models such as teachers, coaches, and sometimes community or political leaders. The discussion revealed insight into their current marginalized experiences and, subsequently, into their observations of a world governed by stereotypes. Many of these youth have concluded that society remains ill equipped to understand and interact healthfully with them. They described how some youth succumb to the pressure, while others fight it; how some are compliant while others rebel. Yet through the discussion, it became apparent that the definition of rebellion and compliance were both derived by personalized experience-coloured lenses and, thus, always justified. The goal for these youth has been to create their own communities governed by rules that they can comprehend—in effect, a society to which they can freely belong.

> I mean, in a perfect world, it would be great to be embraced without question, but the truth is accents, skin colour, your name even, the way you wear your clothes ... my hijab for example, makes people automatically look at your differences right away ... not fitting into a specific mold automatically means "you are not like me" and "if you are not like me, it must be a bad thing." (Ameya, 20)

> I'm all for multiculturalism and all, but seriously, at the end of the day, that's why I stick to my people ... and at the end of the day, they understand my struggle, they get it without me having to explain everything and I am not alone. (Su-Ling, 22)

> Yeah, it's like creating and living in your own world, a family who's loyal to you ... at the end of the day, that's what really matters, loyalty. (Jalone, 22)

> It's funny though, 'cause everybody has their clicks right? But if you see a group of Black people roll, it's like "Careful now, that's a gang ... ridiculous!" (Shawn, 18)

> But loyalty is BIG! My ex was in a gang because loyalty was so important to him. And he's not a bad person; he was just tired of people telling him that he wasn't good enough. He would always say "Loyalty is rare, you can't find it everywhere" ... but seriously, with his dad dealing, and his mom raising his sisters, I guess he figured he had to do his part and he needed people around him who had his back and would help. (Erin, 22)

> Yeah, that's like Kyle. Remember him from school? He used to write the craziest freestyle poetry and stuff! Anyway, he used to talk about how no one really cared if he failed or passed, especially the teachers 'cause they expected him to fail anyway. I remember teachers used to pretend to listen and then

*would always say that he just wanted attention ... he even got suspended
for it and it was a big deal. Anyway, he always said he was going to make
it regardless ... so I guess he was tired of seeing his family struggle so he
dropped out ... I think he still deals drugs to this day.* (Randy, 19)

*Yeah, but did you see his ride, though? It's hard, 'cause you see that and
sometimes I can't help but to think, you know, like am I doing the right
thing, here? Trying to make it in a system that doesn't really want me.*
(Ahmed, 18)

*Anyway, I agree with not putting up with that ... I mean that's why I stopped
going ... I've watched my family struggle to make it and you're trying to tell
me that I should spend my time fighting teachers and principals and stuff,
trying to convince them that I'm worth it?? I don't have to prove anything to
anyone but myself, and trust me, I do that everyday when I go to work and
make enough money to help my family! I'm worth it and I make a difference.*
(James, 20)

*Yeah, for real! I'm nothing like they think I am! I work hard, I'm not in any
gang, never was; I don't spend my day smoking and drinking, I don't steal ...
I may have dropped out of school, but I'm no idiot ... I'm going back! Just
need to make sure my daughter has what she needs first ... she doesn't need
to go through what I had to ... can't control everything that happens to her,
but I can control this!* (Tye, 21)

Many of the youth voiced frustration from feeling a lack of control and
support. They admitted to not wanting to burden family with their personal
struggles about the education system or how they fit, or did not fit, into it. The
group of youth that shared their perspectives belonged to families whose parents
were receiving employment insurance or who worked two jobs. Such experiences, however, are not limited to this group of youth alone. In 2005, immigrant
women living in Toronto were earning 56 cents for each dollar that a Canadian-
born woman earned. In 2008, half of the students from the Toronto District
School Board were from lower income families, and, in 2009, the number of
employment insurance recipients had increased by 88% from the preceding
year (Toronto's vital signs, 2009). Some of the youth in the group discussion
deduced that their struggle could not compare to that of their parents, and,
as a result, they often felt trapped in their circumstances and their inability to
access resources to help alleviate their frustration. Our discussion gradually
progressed to how the youth were utilizing the resources that they found within
themselves as a means to vent, explain, and explore their circumstances.

*English is not my first language and I don't feel comfortable always talking ...
my painting tells stories. Colour, brush strokes, what I paint will tell you*

how I experience life, and sometimes I just want to know that someone "gets it" ... someone gets me. (Su-Ling, 22)

Me? Well, I just sing ... and I love to sing ... it is so soothing ... I feel that everything washes away and gets drowned out by the harmony of my heart, spirit, mind ... whatever happened during that day no longer exists after I finish a song. (Anwala, 19)

These youth adopted various art forms as coping mechanisms to invoke esoteric hope. Free-style, spoken word, music, singing, writing songs, creating beats, poetry, and dance were just some of the streams that they used to communicate their frustrations, explore their emotions, and advocate for themselves through creative expression. The following are snippets provided in writing.

when I walk into your store
I know exactly what I'm going for –
I just want some milk and on occasion, maybe a bag of bread,
but instead,
you thinking that I want your money,
but I don't want your money,
in fact I wanna give you mine,
and if you allowed me the proper time,
like if your eyes weren't busy chasing my colour out the door
me and my colour probably would have stayed and given you
a whole lot more
More of the clocked time from 8 to 5
In exchange to feed my belly so's I could stay alive
But more than all of that, you would have gotten my respect
A commodity in this world that is absolutely, positively priceless.
(Jalone, 22)

Look at my face, look into my eyes
I am human just like you ...
It's not called a "veil," and no, my hijab's not a disguise
I would never ever hurt you
We are all born, and one day we'll all die
But in between can we be friends
Because I'm so tired, of shielding myself from you
Let's put our differences to an end.
(Ameya, 20)

Was this affinity to creative expression unique to this group of youth or was it something observed in and by the larger community? Would people respond solely to the artistic talent of the individual or would they contemplate the experiences that inspired the art pieces themselves? If the art was isolated within the confines of communities—akin to the group of youth who shared their experiences—how could it be possible for these messages to be brought to the spaces where their challenges and issues could actually be addressed?

Connecting the Community in Art-Full Conversations

Humanities-infused programs have the ability to extract and refine the important roles that creative expression plays in community. Visual art, performance art, music, poetry and prose, and dance are a few media through which we can examine dominant society (Hardee & Reyelt, 2009). Creative expression is a valuable tool, although its value is not always reflected. In 2009, Toronto counted 200 performing arts companies and more than 65 community arts organizations (Toronto's vital signs, 2009). In 2012, Toronto will see a decrease in these programs as tentative budgets describe the "savings of $2.1 million as a result of discontinuing programming at 12 of 29 Toronto District School Board (TDSB) locations … as of March 2012 … Each location offers a mix of programming such as arts, camps, fitness, dance, sports and leadership" (City of Toronto, 2011, p. 3). As a result, Toronto's arts-focused programming and/or the possibility of art integration within already existing youth programs are being threatened.

Harmony Movement, in Toronto, Ontario, is one of the many organizations that promote and encourage arts-infused programs[7] Cian Knights is the manager of community projects and strongly believes that

> [a]rt is about provoking, pushing the limits—bringing people's varying perceptions to light in every way; and because of the freedom that art affords, it's used as a medium to talk about subjects that would otherwise be difficult to approach- youth identity, racism, oppression for example … That's why organizations and programs like Harmony Movement and Arts.for.Equity[8] are important. It brings these types of conversations into the schools as well as in communities and attempts to bridge the gaping hole between education and some of the unspoken truths that take place in schools. As a society, it is important that we strive to encourage these types of conversations with each other and with our youth, both in and out of the classroom. (Cian Knights, personal communication, November 2011)

The Arts.for.Equity event (2011) showcased 54 youth who used four artistic media to communicate their views on marginalization: performance arts, dance, visual arts, and photography. Besides being swept away by the enormous talent of these youth, audiences were awed by the capacity in which they conveyed the layered messages embedded within each of their marginalized experiences.[9] The youth opened the stage with a verbal barrage of apologies set to music. We watched and listened to the youth apologize for things such as being Asian, or young, or short, or original, or clumsy, or gay. They followed this introduction with a string of skits that captured different points in time in which they had been marginalized. Each skit was acted out so well that the crowd could not help but label the scenarios. The crowd's whispers gathered momentum and grew louder with every sketch: "That's ageism!" "sexism!" "racism"—and there were many more "isms" to follow. The youth demonstrated that feelings of marginalization and "un-belonging" were (and are) not exclusive to the context of the incident but that it could be carried over to affect other environmental contexts. We see these correlations in research studies such as Mitchell's (2005), who has illustrated that relationships exist between lowered academic achievements, academic self-concept, and environmental factors. Her research acknowledges that both educational achievement and academic self-concept are affected by occupational, economic, familial, and community stability. The youth portrayed this relationship beautifully as they acted out how marginalization affected their school life and home life and the opportunity and potential for success in educational achievement.

The youth's sketches continued along to portray how unhealthy relationships between teachers and newcomer youth could potentially result in lowered expectations and self-fulfilled prophesies. Cohen, Steele, and Ross (1999) note that minority students are aware of those in their school environment (e.g., teachers, guidance counsellors, peers, and so on) who may doubt their ability and belonging and whose message could be emphasized in critical feedback, resulting in diminished efforts in academia. Results from a study in Finland by Laukkanen, Shemeikka, Notkola, et al. (2002) shows that poor success in school is associated with both externalizing and internalizing problems. Externalizing problems is related to health-damaging behaviour and bullying, while internalizing problems is associated with poor perceived health and a low level of exercise, mental systems, and challenges in social relationships. This study also correlated "dropping out of studies" with educational or social exclusion as well as an exclusion from the labour market (Laukkanen et al., 2002, p. 140; see also Caspi et al., 1998; Taskinen, 2001). The Arts.for.Equity youth elaborated on these themes by introducing a variety of graphic comic strips that articulated how being subjected to exclusion by teachers, parents, and peers could result in gang membership, violence, drug addiction, and, at its worst, even suicide. As the performance came to an end, the youth left the audience with esoteric messages of hope. The dim room was illuminated by a spotlight that shone brightly on the entire youth performer collective. They danced their experiences on stage to the compelling vocal harmonization of two peers who sang Sam Cooke's classic "A Change Is Gonna Come."

One could not help but wonder: Can change really come when there is a consistent history of overlooking the obvious relationships and overlaps between school experiences and societal life? Contrary to how we approach community and education, life is not compartmentalized, and what youth experience in school is visible in how they carry themselves outside of school and vice versa. Is creating an environment that is conducive to learning not a contributing factor to a youth's overall academic achievement? And if this premise is true, should we not make efforts not only to listen to youth and their challenges but also to accommodate their navigation through the system? Angelides and Michaelidou (2009, p. 17) argue that "many researchers have reached the conclusion that if we are really interested in improving schools, then the voices of children who attend those schools should be heard and be taken seriously into account in the discussions for change in education" (see also Ainscow, Booth, & Dyson, 1999; Nieto, 1994; Qvortrup, 1994; Rudduck, Chaplain, & Wallace, 1996; Wallace, 1996).

After the dance, performance, and visual arts portion of the evening, the audience was encouraged to walk around the room to look at the youth's photography. Techniques that included blurring effects, black-and-white photography with partial colour, and images that played with spatial elements such as distance were unique ways in which the youth were able to communicate their experiences and points of view. As one meandered through the auditorium framed with time-distilled stories, one could hear snippets of conversations from other spectators. Some had come to the realization that the marginalization of youth was indeed a social problem that needed to be addressed; some spoke about a new-found awareness regarding the roles that they themselves play in the lives of young people; and others spoke about how the art and performances helped them to actually "get it." What stuck out the most that evening, however, was not so much what people were saying but, rather, the fact that people were able to receive the messages that the youth were disseminating. The humanities–infused praxis by and with youth was vibrating towards esoteric hope.

Simular process have permeated the margins in the boroughs of Montreal, Quebec. Prévention Côte-des-Neiges and Notre-Dame-de-Grâce (CDN-NDG) is an organization that has been active in the community for over 25 years. It caters to these communities by offering outreach programs. They also host youth-focused events such as the Hip Hop You Don't Stop Urban Arts Festival, which is geared towards positive youth engagement and self-expression. Hip hop's influence is pervasive and transcends racial affiliations and geographic barriers, and it has gained popularity around the world, significantly influencing the values and ideologies of many contemporary urban youth (Irizarry, 2009; see also Dolby, 2003; Duncan-Andrade, 2002; Flores, 2000; Newman, 2001; Taylor & Taylor, 2004). Hip hop itself originated in the mid-1970s as an artful "response to many of the social ills experienced by urban youth" (Irizarry, 2009, p. 496), and it is interesting to see how the youth of today still refer to this method of expression to address their disenfranchisement. On the weekend of 24-25 September 2011, Prevention CDN-NDG held their sixth edition of the Hip Hop You Don't Stop Urban Arts Festival. They welcomed approximately 1,000 participants comprised of youth and their families, politicians, school principals, and other community stakeholders who supported the initiative, celebrated youth expression, and enjoyed the festivities. In November 2011, we spoke with both Prevention NDG's executive director, Terri Ste. Marie, and Marc Pagliarulo-Beauchemin, the co-ordinator of the festival. During our conversation, Pagliarulo-Beauchemin, stated:

> It's a great event because the youth see their families, the local schools, politicians, and organizations come together to support them in their element where self-expression is celebrated—and they appreciate that society is acknowledging that they exist. They don't always get to see that in schools. (Pagliarulo-Beauchemin, personal communication, November 2011)

The festival incorporates the four central pillars of hip hop: deejaying, dancing, rapping, and graffiti art. Terri Ste. Marie, director of Prevention CDN-NDG, admitted that graffiti art has gotten a bad name: "The word 'graffiti' itself is generalized by society and people often feel that graffiti art is synonymous with vandalism" (Ste. Marie, personal communication, November 2011). She explained further that graffiti art becomes vandalism when the graffiti artist does not attain permission prior to using public property as their canvas. Due to society's dubious interpretation of graffiti, it has been a controversial subject for years. Prevention CDN-NDG approaches the subject by delivering impactful graffiti art programs that discuss vandalism and alternative ways to legally channel creativity. Pagliarulo-Beauchemin believes that

> [s]ociety really needs to start looking at graffiti vandalism for what it is. It is a bunch of youth who go around tagging their names everywhere as if to say, "I'm a part of society too ... I am here; I exist; and this is my name." (Pagliarulo-Beauchemin, personal communication, November 2011)

It becomes apparent how marginalization can pervade the borders of silence to vocalize its otherwise unspoken existence. Marginalization does not remain self-contained as the youth's problem. It becomes society's problem as well. Pagliarulo-Beauchemin incorporates graffiti in the Hip Hop You Don't Stop Urban Arts Festival by having youth actively participate in painting murals with, and under the supervision of, a professional graffiti artist. He feels that, besides graffiti art being a part of hip-hop culture, it is a good way to relate to youth and harness their energy for positive expression. The graffiti art competition portion of the festival features ten trucks (donated by ten companies) on which ten groups of youth were able to work together cohesively to conceptualize, plan, and creatively express themselves through painting these mobile canvases.[10] Bates, a world-renowned graffiti artist and legend, was one of the personalities who judged the competition. Bates has been creating graffiti art since 1984, using his home of Copenhagen, Denmark, as a canvas. Aside from being commissioned to create art for countries all over the world, he is endorsed by a number of paint companies, has designed for some clothing companies, and has been featured in books.

The festival also features another fundamental aspect of hip hop: the dance component. Break dancers had the opportunity to "battle" and be judged by Stephen Leafloor (also known as Buddha), who is the founder of Canada's oldest b-boy crew, "The Canadian Floor Masters." Besides having established himself as a legend in the b-boy world, Stephen Leafloor has since gone on to complete his Masters in Social Work and has founded Blue Print for Life, an organization that uses hip hop to address social issues in First Nations schools and communities. The festival also featured acts from local and international hip-hop artists, who, in addition to their performances, spoke with youth about the "behind the scenes" of being a successful artist. Pagliarulo-Beauchemin explains that

> [i]t's important for them to know that the lifestyle isn't just the shows, the fame and the fortune ... there is a lot of hard work that goes into it and they can't just rely on their talent. For some, they think that it's a way out—many of their excuses for not doing well in school revolve around "having to work hard," but the truth is, you have to work hard at something if you want to be successful ... they don't necessarily see that side of things when it comes to the arts. Youth categorize the "working hard" aspect with academic-based careers ... but really, "working hard" is necessary if you want to make it, regardless of your career of choice ... it's a universal phenomenon. (Pagliarulo-Beauchemin, personal communication, November 2011)

In summary, these young people and arts programs demonstrate that: (1) youth ideas and experiences can be conducted via arts-infused programs to the greater community; (2) arts-infused programs serve to educate youth beyond institutionalized standard courses; and (3) arts-infused programs are a vehicle that communicates hope for inclusivity, even beyond the margins. As Pagliarulo-Beauchemin explains,

> don't get me wrong, the adolescents don't chase me down to say, "I'm so very happy that society is finally including me and considering what

I value as important, so thank you so much for doing this!" No, not at all. But they do say, "Yeah, that's cool," and then I see them participating in the activities, watching the performances all day alongside teachers, police and politicians, laughing and just being themselves ... and to me, that conveys the same message. (Pagliarulo-Beauchemin, personal communication, November 2011)

Coming Full Circle: Humanities-Infused Praxis *by, with,* and *for* youth

I hate it when you say my name and then you laugh
I hate it when you think we're only good at math
I hate it when you act like it's the first time you've seen someone
with my slanted eyes
The truth is they're large enough to see right through your lies.
(Shen, 19)

Jason Promesse is a Montreal-based drummer, producer, and musical director who has worked with reggae artists across Canada, the United States, and the Caribbean. He has been a part of Montreal's urban music scene for almost two decades and has played in the world-renowned Montreal Jazz Festival. During our conversation in 2011, Jason disclosed that he first discovered his musical abilities during his adolescence. He explained that his relationship with music first began as a means to escape his environment while providing a distraction from the social barriers he faced as an Anglophone Black male growing up in Montreal, Quebec: "I learned how to play the drums to stay out of trouble" (Promesse, personal communication, November 2011). Two decades later, in addition to helping youth with self-expression, he uses his musical talents to help them address their challenges. The programs that he offers are atypical in that there is not any formal structure—it is the youth who decide the direction. Although the groups have fundamental discussions pertaining to the youth's relationship with music and their various types of inspiration, the topics that are addressed during the course of the program emerge from the act of creating music together. They discuss how art, experiences, education, politics, and role models (or lack thereof) relate to their lives as youth, in addition to exploring what elements of themselves are most influential in the creation of their own unique reverberations.

Promesse feels that reaching out to youth and encouraging their individuality is very important because society teaches them to hide certain parts of themselves. Many marginalized students adopt masks that serve as a façade of normalization, yet their identities are in contradiction to the norms by which society expects them to abide (Hardee & Reyelt, 2009, p. 30). Thus, "[r]ather than helping youths navigate the turbulence they experience growing up in the current social order, society quickly labels [them] as undesirable troublemakers and perceives them as disposable commodities" (Pomeroy & Browning, 2010, p. 197). Hardee and Reyelt (2009, p. 32) document through their study that "many students felt that they had to develop two different identities, one for school and one for outside school walls, and the arts enabled them to reveal these feelings."

This understanding parallels Promesse's experiences with the youth as he reveals that as his program progressed he was able to see them emerge from hiding, "but the process is usually the same. There is always some initial resistance from the youth" (Promesse, personal communication, November 2011). He has observed that they present themselves as being guarded until they are certain that the environment is safe and receptive to the uncovering and sharing of their experiences. Hardee and Reyelt (2009, p. 33-34) argue that "if given the chance to examine themselves and the pressures put upon them, students can learn to form a strong sense of identity that does not need to fit into any specific molds." Promesse has seen how that music and art can present the space and opportunity for youth to develop in this way, and he adds that the facilitator plays a large role in their development. He has deduced from conversations held during programming that they have grown accustomed to not having anyone really listen to them or offer them the support that they need:

> I never push anyone to talk, or to open up to me. I want [youth] to be able to build trust from their level of experience and pace; not mine. The youth that I've interacted with have expressed that either people don't listen, or if they do listen—it is only to the extent to which their organizational mandate stipulates. Youth are smart and they can sense where your time, your concern and your support are coming from ... Most of the youth that I have interacted with are used to it not coming from a genuine place, so most of the time they don't bother to engage, and that's why there's that resistance at first. (Promesse, personal communication, November 2011)

He affirms that by the time they have finished composing their music and are well into "jamming" together, there is an observable openness that accompanies the musical harmonization: "The youth aren't as guarded and they are quite comfortable being themselves, whatever that means to them." Promesse believes that youth need a space for self-expression and an outlet for coping with the challenges that they face everyday. Hardee and Reyelt (2009) refer to this space as the "borderland" and believe that the arts can facilitate its existence. They argue that in providing youth with borderlands marginalized youth are able to question dominant ideologies and attain a space to freely grow without having to assimilate. Promesse concludes: "It's always so amazing to arrive at the end of the program and see how the young people have transformed their negative experiences into positive ones. In the end, I am so humbled. I am made the student and they have taught me so much" (Promesse, personal communication, November 2011).

The art of music is capable of opening up what the pressures of society have tried to close. Sheldon Pitt, better known by his fans as Silver (and formerly known as Solitair), is a Toronto-based, Juno-nominated hip-hop artist and producer who also believes that music transcends the walls of resistance. When he is not in the studio, on tour, or producing for other international artists, he uses his celebrity as an avenue for youth mentorship towards academic persistence and also addresses the art of balancing academia with creative expression: "I have been doing workshops in schools and communities for years. I started it because I had been approached by a number of teachers who had asked me to speak to their students because they were facing challenges engaging them in the classroom" (Pitt, personal communication, November 2011).

Teachers have reported that economically disadvantaged students in urban and rural schools are in the minority of students who come to school "motivationally ready and able to learn" (Adelman & Taylor, 2002). To face these challenges, some teachers have solicited help and support in order to encourage their students (Adelman & Taylor, 2002). Many feel that a crucial aspect of their role as teachers is making the curriculum content relevant to the students with whom they work (Irizarry, 2009). This idea is reflective in Pitt's report as his access and proximity to the hip-hop culture has been solicited in the classroom as a tool of relativity. There is a wealth of research that explores various ways in which teachers are able to use hip hop as a bridge to help students engage in the standard curriculum (Irizarry, 2009; see also Duncan-Andrade, 2002; Duncan-Andrade & Morrell, 2000; Ginwright, 2004; Stovall, 2006). Using these as references, Irizarry (2009, p. 490) affirms that "the potential of using urban youth culture to engage students in more formal learning processes aimed at acquiring academic skills and critical literacies has been well documented."

During the summer of 2011, Pitt's workshop challenged 15 youth participants to consider concepts that had long ago been abandoned. The importance of school, taking negative school experiences and using them as inspiration for writing or music, and the possibility of a healthy co-existence between academics and a passion for creative expression were subjects that he touched on. It was not at all surprising that with such ease, Pitt had managed to garner their attention, encourage participation, and create an environment in which they felt comfortable enough to ask questions and engage in experience sharing.

Despite the workshop's success, however, Pitt still believes that as a society, we should be doing more for youth:

> Workshops are great because youth are able to approach subjects from a different perspective and it gets their juices going … it's exciting for them. Long-term, though, "workshops-on-occasion" is not enough to offer young people the support that they need. More cooperation needs to happen between community and schools to provide consistency for these youth, especially if we are trying to encourage and motivate them to consider something they fundamentally are having reservations about doing. Community programs approach engaging youth in a different way and it has been my experience that the class rooms seem to benefit from these approaches. (Pitt, personal communication, November 2011)

Experience tells us that Pitt is not alone in his conclusions. After holding discussions with a number of youth, listening to the secrets held hostage within their art, visiting with a number of youth-focused community organizations, reading the decades of social science literature, and speaking with various stakeholders in the community, one may conclude that there are strong shared messages to take away: (1) marginalization exists in the school system and young people are subject to this marginalization; (2) there is a relationship between the experiences that youth internalize in schools and what manifests outside of their academic lives (and vice versa); (3) young people who are exposed to marginalization will require the appropriate supports necessary for successful navigation; and (4) humanities has a critical role to play in the expression, understanding, and redressing of youth marginalization in public education.

Despite the deterioration of liberal arts in public education, humanities-infused praxis exhibits force in understanding, or approaching the social process of marginalization. We invite you to recognize the esoteric hope made visible by humanities-infused praxis as you read through the book and encounter the artistic expressions of marginalized youth throughout. The liminal experience, the complexity and abundance of life, and the contradictory ways in which is it is being lived are made visible. This perspective allows a space not only to make problematic the struggles of youth but also to record and diarize the actions against them. The diversity of knowledge attained from humanities-infused praxis highlights that youth marginalization can be addressed from a multitude of angles: from creating new policies, learning more effective ways in approaching and communicating with youth, developing new programs that aim to support youth, and so on. After combining youth and researcher perspectives, in addition to observing how marginalization affects youth development, education, and life outcomes, we can either ask: "When is *society* going to do something about this?" or we can be empowered by the roles that we play within society and decide to ask ourselves: "What can *I* do about this—*right now*?" How can we open spaces, whatever our locations, to engage and diarize the esoteric hopes and fears of youth?

Notes

1   All quotations of young people are demarcated with a pseudonym.
2   Contest winners featured in this volume include Alycia Frye, Lishai Peel, Farrah Chanda Aslam, Mallory Goss, Elliott Tilleczek, Anwesha Sen, Zera Koutchieva, Angel Ho, Sabnam Mahmuda, and Kira Duff. Art submissions from other youth were also published here.
3   The Alexandra Park Community Centre is located in the downtown core of Toronto, Ontario, and caters to the Atkinson Co-op Housing and Alexandra Park Community population.
4   Olu Quamina is the founder of Concrete Roses Youth Services, a non-profit organization that aims to create healthy sustainable urban communities by engaging youth in social, educational, and employment opportunities.
5   Stereotype vulnerability is the tendency to expect, perceive, and be influenced by negative stereotypes about one's social category (Aronson & Inzlicht, 2004).
6   Stereotype threat is the apprehension one feels when performing in an area in which their group is stereotyped to lack ability (Aronson & Inzlicht, 2004).
7   Harmony Movement (http://www.harmony.ca) is a not-for-profit organization founded in 1994 to promote diversity and combat all forms of discrimination that act as barriers to one's full participation in society.
8   Arts.for.Equity was a one-week program that was part of a three-year initiative entitled Project Peace, which was supported by a grant from Citizenship and Immigration Canada.
9   To see Harmony Movement's 2011 Arts.for.Equity: Summer Series video, visit http://www.youtube.com/watch?v=iOb_igaeRlk.
10 The youth were professional artists.

References

Adelman, H. S., & Taylor, L. (2002). School counselors and school reform. *Professional School Counseling, 5*(4), 235-248.

Ainscow, M., Booth, T., & Dyson, A. (1999). Inclusion and exclusion in schools: Listening to some hidden voices. In K. Ballard (Ed.), *Inclusive education: International voices on disability and justice* (pp. 141-154). London: Falmer Press.

Angelides, P. & Michaelidou, A. (2009). Collaborative artmaking for reducing marginilization. *Studies in Art Education, 51*(1), 36-49.

Aronson, J., & Inzlicht, M. (2004). The ups and downs of attributional ambiguity: Stereotype vulnerability and the academic self-knowledge of African American college students. *Psychological Science, 15*(12), 829-836.

Berger, J. (1972). *Ways of seeing*. London, UK: Penguin Books.

Caspi, A., Wright, B. R. E., Moffit, T. E., & Silva, P. A. (1998). Early failure in the labour market: Childhood and adolescent predictors of unemployment in the transition to adulthood? *American Sociological Review, 63*, 424-451.

City of Toronto (December, 2011). *Released confidential information: Parks, forestry and recreation service change locations.* Online: http://www.toronto.ca/budget2012/pdf/pfr_service_locns.pdf.

Cohen, P. (1999). *Rethinking the youth question: Education, labour and cultural studies.* Durham, NC: Duke University Press.

Cohen.P., & Ainley, P. (2000). *In the country of the blind: Youth studies and cultural studies in Britain.* London: Cavendish Publishing.

Cohen, G. L., Steele, C. M., & Ross L. D. (1999). The mentor's dilemma: Providing critical feedback across the racial divide. *Personality and Social Psychology Bulletin, 25*(10), 1302-1318.

Collini, S. (2009). Impact on humanities: Researchers must take a stand now or be judged and rewarded as salesmen. *Times Literary Supplement* (pp. 1-8). Online: http://www.the-tls.co.uk/tls/.

Dolby, N. (2003). Popular culture and democratic practice. *Harvard Educational Review, 73,* 258-284.

Duncan-Andrade, J. (2002). Why must school be boring: Invigorating the curriculum with youth culture. *Teaching to Change LA, 3*(3). Online: http://www.tcla.gseis.ucla.edu/reportcard/features/3/andrade/youthculture.html.

Duncan-Andrade, J., & Morrell, E. (2000). *Using hip-hop culture as a bridge to canonical poetry texts in an urban secondary English class* (paper presented at the annual meeting of the American Educational Research Association, New Orleans, LA).

Flores, J. (2000). *From bomba to hip-hop: Puerto Rican culture and Latino identity.* New York: Columbia University Press.

Frampton, C., Kinsman, G., Thompson, A., & Tilleczek, K. (Eds.). (2006). *Sociology for changing the world: Social movements social research.* Halifax: Fernwood Press.

Furlong, A., & Cartmel, F. (2007). *Young people and social change: New perspectives.* Bershire, UK: Open University Press.

Ginwright, S. A. (2004). *Black in school: Afrocentric reform, urban youth, and the promise of hip-hop culture.* New York: Teachers College Press.

Griffen, C. (2001). Imagining new narratives of youth: Youth research, the new "Europe" and global youth culture. *Childhood, 8*(2), 147-166.

Hardee, S. C., & Reyelt, A. (2009). Women's well-being initiative: Creating, practicing, and sharing a border pedagogy for youth. *Perspectives on Urban Education, 6*(2), 29-45.

Harmony Movement (Producer). (2011). Arts.for.Equity: Summer Series (Youtube video). Online: http://www.youtube.com/watch?v=iOb_igaeRlk.

Hudley, C., & Graham, S. (2001). Stereotypes of achievement striving among early adolescents. *Social Psychology of Education, 5*(2), 201-224.

Irizarry, J. G. (2009). Representin': Drawing from hip-hop and urban youth culture to inform teacher education. *Education and Urban Society, 41*(4), 489-515.

Kao, G. (2000). Group images and possible selves among adolescents: Linking stereotypes to expectations by race and ethnicity. *Sociological Forum, 15*(3), 407-430.

Laukkanen, E., Shemeikka, S., Notkola, I., Koivumaa-Honkanen, H., & Nissinen, A. (2002). Externalizing and internalizing problems at school as signs of health-damaging behavior and incipient marginalization. *Health Promotion International, 17*(2), 139-146.

Mitchell, N. (2005). Academic achievement among immigrant adolescents: The impact of generational status on academic self-concept. *Professional School Counseling, 8(3)*, 209-218.

Newman, M. (2001). "I represent me": Identity construction in a teenage rap crew. *Texas Linguistic Forum, 44*, 388-400.

Nieto, S. (1994). Lessons from students on creating a chance to dream. *Harvard Educational Review, 64*(4), 392-426.

Nussbaum, M. (2009). Education for profit, education for freedom. *Liberal Education, 95*(3), 6-13.

Pomeroy, E.C., & Browning, P. (2010). Youths in crisis. *National Association of Social Workers, 55*(3), 197-201.

Qvortrup, J. (1994). Childhood matters: An introduction. In J. Qvortup, M. Bardy, G. Sgritta, & H. Winterberger (Eds.), *Childhood matters: Social theory practice and politics* (pp. 1-23). Aldershot, UK: Avebury.

Rudduck, J., Chaplain, R., & Wallace, G. (1996). Pupil voices and school improvement. In J. Rudduck, R. Chaplain, & G. Wallace (Eds.), *School improvement: What can pupils tell us?* (pp. 1-11). London: David Fulton.

Simmons, C., Lewis, C., & Larson, J. (2011). Narrating identities: Schools as touchstones of endemic marginalization. *Anthropology and Education Quarterly, 42*(2), 121-133. doi: 10.1111/j.1548-1492.2011.01120.x.

Srigley, R. (2012). If I didn't laugh, I'd cry: An essay on happiness, productivity and the death of humanities education. *Education Canada, 52*(4), 18-22.

Stovall, D. (2006). We can relate: Hip-hop culture, critical pedagogy, and the secondary classroom. *Urban Education, 41*(6), 585-602.

Taskinen, S. (2001). *"Poor Prognosis": Social exclusion among children and young people*, National Public Health Institute Publication no. 10. Helsinki, Finland: National Public Health Institute.

Taylor, C. S., & Taylor, V. (2004). Hip-hop and youth culture: Contemplations of an emerging cultural phenomenon. *Reclaiming Children and Youth, 12*, 251-253.

Tilleczek, K. (2011). *Approaching youth studies: Being, becoming, and belonging*. Toronto: Oxford University Press.

Toronto's vital signs. *Toronto Star* (6 October 2009) R1-R8.

Wallace, G. (1996). Relating to teachers. In J. Rudduck, R. Chaplain, & G. Wallace (Eds.), *School improvement: What can pupils tell us?* (pp. 1-11). London: David Fulton.

Woolf, V. (1929; reprinted 1992). *A room of one's own*. Oxford, UK: Oxford University Press.

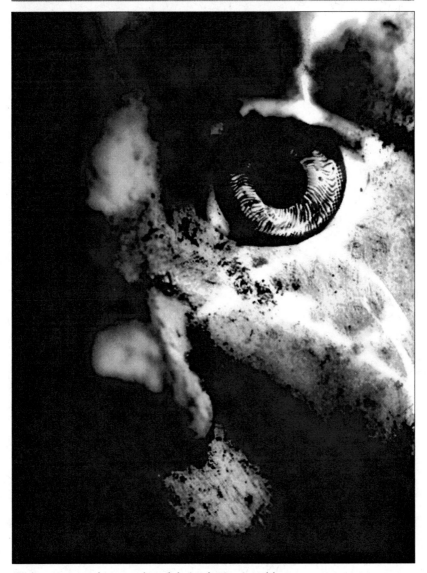

Finding Hope, a photograph and design by Tamir Holder

It is a photograph and design combined, telling the story of why one should not give up. The charred doll represents the pain and torment or "darkened past," while the bright shining lights in the eye represent breakthrough and new-found change.

chapter 2

Young People *Speaking Back* from the Margins

John Smyth

The line I want to take in this chapter is that the way we position young people has a profound bearing on how we deal with them, both in terms of policy and practicality. In taking this line, I want to draw upon some of the issues that have emerged from my own research with young people in Australia over the past two decades or so. The young people I have worked with are predominantly from backgrounds where they, their families, and their communities have been put at a disadvantage through the effects of social, economic, and political forces and by the flow-on effects of globalization that have effectively devastated their communities and lives. Their diminished educational opportunities and subsequent life chances have been dramatic, even to the point of being catastrophic. Having said that, these young people are not hapless victims nor are they passive recipients of deficit categories such as "at-riskness," which are placed upon them by the media, politicians, agencies, and some academics. Rather they are active agents exercising choices and making decisions about their lives in situations that amount to "speaking back."

As Black feminist bell hooks (1990, p. 149) puts it in her essay "Choosing the Margin as a Space of Radical Openness," for people whose lives have been diminished and impoverished, their ability to live "depends on [their] ability to conceptualize alternatives." In a sense, it is their having been pushed to the margins by social and political forces that provides them with the "space of radical openness [as] a margin—a profound edge" (p. 149) from which to construct alternative counter-hegemonic cultural practices—and the experience of education is certainly one of these practices! In essence, hooks (1990,

p. 149) is at pains to make the point that marginality is "much more than a site of deprivation … [rather] just the opposite … [a] site of radical possibility, a space of resistance." For her, "spaces can tell stories and unfold histories" (p. 152). It is when marginality is chosen as a "site of resistance," as distinct from being "imposed" by "oppressive structures" (p. 153), that "we move in solidarity to erase the category colonized/colonizer" (p. 152). She invokes the lines from singer Bob Marley: "We refuse to be what you want us to be, we are what we are, and that's the way it's going to be" (p. 150). In other words, it is from this "space of refusal" (hooks, 1990, p. 150) that alternatives are constructed—which is a most apposite place for me to begin to invoke the voices of young people who have been "exiled" from schooling (Fine & Rosenberg, 1983, p. 257).

In this chapter, I want to explore what is happening when young people from contexts of disadvantage adopt a position of making choices against the institution of schooling that appear to be against their own long-term economic interests and that may have the effect of further exacerbating their apparent marginalization. I want to reflect upon how they go about making lives for themselves while speaking back to notions of mainstream schooling and—in many cases—finding their way into alternative and more amenable forms of learning. Another way of putting this idea is to ask the question: what are the conditions around schooling that young people speak back against and what are the alternative conditions that they argue need to be brought into existence for them to reconnect to, and become re-engaged with, learning?

Positioning Young People in Schooling

Invoking Lakoff and Johnson (1980) in their book *Metaphors We Live By*, Shaker (2010) reminds us that the metaphors we allow to infiltrate our public discourses profoundly affect the positions and policies that are subsequently adopted. In regard to young people and their experiences of schooling, we have allowed all manner of "unwanted visitors" to monopolize and invade our speech (Shaker, 2010). As Shaker (2010) puts it—and this applies to all Western countries—both the politics of education and the public discourses around it have become "choked" by metaphors in which "economic advancement and material productivity are the entire scope of our national purpose."

In the rush to further the problematic metaphor of the economy, markets, business, the military, and international economic competitiveness, we have allowed inappropriate and unhelpful heuristics to dominate, distort, and corrupt the way in which we deal with young people, especially in the context of schools. The problem becomes even more exacerbated when we factor in young people from urban and disadvantaged contexts and when notions of "deficit thinking" are allowed to underpin and powerfully reinforce the already inappropriate images and metaphors of individual meritocracy (Valencia, 1997, 2010).

Since the discourses of schooling and young people have been allowed to be invaded and colonized by corporate and military interests—with their celebration of the virtues and supremacy of big business—then our political masters and the duplicitous media (none of whom have ever practised in the field of education) need to be robustly confronted and told in no uncertain terms that their distorted ways of thinking about young people and their so-called "educational reforms" are no longer acceptable or appropriate. It is against this background that young people have quite literally been shoved to the margins, and it is from here that they are positioned as having to interrupt and "speak back" to these alien and interloper discourses.

What Is Going on in Young Educational Lives?

One thing that gets conveniently overlooked when schools are prevailed upon and assailed by so-called "reforms" from outside and driven by external agendas is that the young people whose lives are most closely and directly affected, and who are the most intimate witnesses of schooling, are the group (along with their teachers) who are the most actively denied an official voice. There is an irony in this situation because in almost all other aspects of their lives these young people, who are from the most complex of backgrounds, are involved in making all kinds of decisions around their own identity formation. They are often significant figures in holding families together economically through part-time work and in dealing with the complexities that come with family dysfunction and wider social fragmentation and disintegration. A number of themes come through repeatedly and consistently with respect to what repels these particular young people from school and turns them into exiles from the social institution of schooling. They are best expressed through the voices of the young people themselves (with acknowledgements to Smyth & Hattam, 2004, in each instance).

School Treats Them as Immature

> I was only 6 months off of being 18 ... and they treat you like little primary kids and I couldn't go back to that environment where they like tell you what to do and treat you like little tiny kids. I just couldn't do it now. I just, I mean, ... I wouldn't go back to like a normal, you know, high school.
> [No. 016] (p. 181)[1]

> [I]n high school you are treated like you are a child, so you act like a child.
> [No. 093] (p. 180)

This line of thinking is often accompanied by confused and mixed messages.

> *[T]hey are told they have the freedom to do whatever you want, while keep[ing] a firm clasp on you, treating you like you are a year 8, saying, you can't do this, do that. [No. 093] (p. 181)*

Not Being Treated Respectfully or Having Their Lives Acknowledged

> *I don't think I'll ever go back to school. I mean, the teachers have got to learn to treat you fairly. If you're going to respect them, they've got to respect you. Like they need to speak to you properly like you're not dirt or trash. They need to let you give your opinions on the work. They need to understand you and not turn their back on you. [No. 104] (p. 184)*

After a period of suspension and having "served their time," others responded in this way.

> *[S]ome [teachers] were really nice and understanding and did their best to try and help me catch up, but one teacher held it [my suspension] against me and called me a "waste of space" and that [I was] "taking up space in the classroom. [No. 015] (p. 176)*

Inconsistency of Treatment and One-Size-Fits-All Policies

> *There was one incident where I got in trouble for my uniform ... I had to go home, change my uniform and then go back to school and there were two other students in the class who basically had the same thing wrong with their uniform, but they didn't get into trouble for it and I thought that was unfair. I could never understand why I'd get in trouble for something but yet someone else would have the same thing wrong and they wouldn't get in trouble for it, then you'd try and say something to the teacher, "how come I'm getting in trouble and that person's not" and they turn around and say "you're back chatting." [No. 025] (p. 177)*

Inability to Flex around the Complexities of Young Lives

> *They'd say "no way, you've had plenty of time like, four weeks, three weeks, and you've left it to the last minute, that's not acceptable" ... Why can't they just give it all to you at the start ... so you know what you're looking at in advance. [No. 009] (p. 176)*

Lack of Opportunity to Meaningful Own Their Learning

> *Most people hate getting told what to do, and that's what teachers do, just tell you ... [I would] just snap and couldn't handle being told what to do. [No. 151] (p. 179)*

No Room for Students' Sense of Justice and Somewhat Exaggerated Sense of What Is Fair

> [I]t's basically "them and us," like there's teachers and there's students and a lot of the friction in the discipline that they try to give us. Like, our school didn't use to have a school uniform and they brought in a school uniform, well that was that. And they just took it way out of proportion ... it's just little things that teachers do ... Like I mean, you're allowed to wear plain blue tracksuit pants but if they've got a little Nike or something, you get detention. [No. 027] (p. 169).

Boring and Irrelevant Curriculum and Learning

> [H]e would actually like write up on the board and as he was writing he would be talking to the board and teaching the board and we'd be sitting there like, yeah okay, and you'll go through it and the next thing you know you're lost ... So that's when you start talking to your friends because he's actually like talking to the board ... so you just lose him and then if you don't understand a problem you put your hand up and he can't see you so he just keeps going so you miss that part, miss that part, you just give up. You just don't worry about it ... like throwing it up on the board and it's so boring ... Teachers treat you like you're a child and like I wasn't allowed to do nothing and like if you're late they would spew at you and it was just full of pressure. [No. 083] (p. 178)

No Relationship to Lives They Wanted to Live beyond School

> It has nothing to do with your life [#062]. I think it is better to leave school ... school's over now ... You can get on with the real stuff or whatever. [No. 059] (p. 170)

Stifling and Uninspiring Teaching

> [T]eachers, they don't explain it to you properly. They explain bits and pieces, then if you put your hand up and ask, they say, weren't you listening? You should listen ... It's like, well, I was listening (but you don't get a chance to say), but I still don't understand. So, they go off their head, and you say, what a waste of time, why am I here, and you just get up and walk out, go home, and forget all about school. [No. 153] (pp. 178-179)

> Teachers just chilled me out ...and the school just gave up on me in the end ... When I left, they just said "see you later." [No. 152] (p. 179)

> I need things explained again ... with maths, do an example for me, then I understand. When I don't understand, I just leave it behind. [No. 151] (p. 179)

Switched-Off and Burnt-Out Teachers

> But the real problem in year 12 was the maths ... I just couldn't do it. I
> needed a lot of help because maths 2 is a really hard subject. And my maths
> teacher at school wasn't any help. He had lots of other jobs around the
> school, and he wasn't much of a teacher anyway. I mean, I'd go see him at
> lunch time, and he'd have students that would show up about uniform or
> something, and I'd have to come back. So basically I'd sit outside his office
> all lunchtime, which is forty minutes, and get five minutes worth. And then
> he'd make mistakes all the way through the problem. And if I asked help
> from other teachers they'd refer me back to him. So I was just pretty much
> depressed, and I was unhappy going to school, and I was just skipping more
> and more days. [No. 093] (p. 159)

A Narrow Vocationalism

> [T]hey should be teaching more about life and about things that you actually
> really do need [to] know to be able to be successful in life as a person ... they
> skip out all, the like, the important stuff, like about, you know, how to deal
> with different things that happen in your life and about, you know, what
> things are open to you to help you along. [No. 087] (p. 143)

> [M]ajority of stuff that you learn ... you don't need it and you know you're
> learning all this stuff and it's like, ok, I'm learning this, ok, I have an under-
> standing of it, but where am I going to use this in real life, you know, every
> day life. [No. 002] (p. 148)

None of this commentary is intended to excessively pillory teachers or castigate schools for the predicament they find themselves in with these young people. The picture is much larger and more complex than apportioning blame in such a simplistic way. As Gibboney (2010, pp. 223-237) has argued recently, these are all artifacts of the way in which "an undemocratic capitalism has brought public education to its knees." What Gibboney is referring to is the unremitting ideo-logical onslaught of neo-liberal policies over the past three decades or so, espe-cially as it has been visited on education in ways that effectively position young people as the objects of "policy hatred" (Hattam, 2001). These young people, their families, neighbourhoods, and lifestyles have been unfairly targeted and blamed for all manner of social and economic ills and dysfunctions that have occurred to them. This whole approach of "blaming the victim" (Ryan, 1976) has been a convenient scapegoat for flawed policies that have wreaked untold havoc and systemic violence through the imposition of a particular universe of meaning on the way we treat young people educationally (Žižek, 2009, p. 1).

The upside to all of these difficulties is that, when asked, young people are very insightful and eloquent in describing the recuperative conditions that have to be created for them to re-engage with learning—and these conditions are demonstrably different from the ones that repelled them in the first place.

How Can We Bring Young People in from the Margins?

One of the perplexing ironies in all of this situation is that the same young people who are ignored, silenced, and marginalized, whose lives are ridden over, and who either self-exile from schools or are propelled out of them are the same young people who have some extremely perceptive views on the very different conditions that can and need to be created for them to learn. Again, there are some consistent themes in what they say:

- When the learning culture of the school is not one of fear, intimidation, punishment, and retribution, young people who often find schools to be hostile and alienating places find they can learn.
- When schools welcome these young people for who they are, where they come from, and the strengths and assets they bring with them, rather than labelling them according to their past histories, then learning occurs.
- When the adults who are charged with assisting them are prepared to reveal something about themselves and their own lives as human beings, then a relational basis that is crucial to learning is created.
- When their teachers convey a sense of genuinely liking these young people for who they are, regardless of perceived imperfections attaching to individuals, family, or social class background, then learning becomes possible.
- When the institutions in which they are required to learn are able to flex around their lives—which is to say, to acknowledge in practical ways the complexities of their lives—then an essential foundation for learning is brought into existence.
- When learning experiences are built around issues that are of interest to these young people, then learning is re-ignited around their passion and desire to learn. They need to see this connection to their lives and the fact that they have genuine space in which to negotiate their learning.
- There need to be non-authoritative ways of resolving interpersonal differences that do not paint young people into corners. This effort involves providing dialogical approaches to the resolution of differences.
- Above all, there needs to be a genuine atmosphere of trust that these young people are indeed capable of learning and that the role of adults is to provide the necessary support.

Below are some heavily edited extracts from over 100 interviews conducted with young people who had "dropped out" of school (it reads more like them having been "shoved out") and who had re-engaged with learning as a result of finding their way into alternative learning programs. These are fragments that are taken from much larger ethnographic interviews and that we have converted into portraits of young people who are speaking back (see Smyth & McInerney, 2011). We provide them (with all identifying features removed) without interruption or interpretation in order to honour the voices of these courageous young people who are far from victims in the ways they are exercising active agency in reconstructing an aspect of their lives. They stand in dramatic contrast to the universally depressing, distressing, and despairing accounts provided by their peers in the earlier part of this chapter.

> *I think [this] is a good program because you come here to learn and most people wouldn't come if they didn't want to.* (Male, 18 years, 9 March 2010)

> *Here I've got the freedom to do things myself.* (Female, 19 years, 9 March 2010)

> *Trust me: if you went to school and had to learn and then you came here you'd see the difference.* (Female, 17 years, 9 March 2010)

> *They (teachers) become more of your mates than your enemy.* (Male, 14 years, 10 March 2010)

> *They don't force me to do stuff.* (Male, 15 years, 10 March 2010)

> *It's an okay place where you can do some work but hang out most of the time.* (Female, 15 years, 10 March 2010)

> *It was my decision to come here. (Male, 14 years, 10 March 2010)*

> *You get more help here.* (Male, 14 years, 10 March 2010)

> *You can do your own things instead of what they tell you.* (Male, 15 years, 10 March 2010)

> *It's easier and the teachers understand you more.* (Male, 14 years, 10 March 2010)

> *I've grown up a fair bit. I'm actually trying to get myself on track and make myself stronger. If I hadn't come here I would be dead or in the gutter.* (Male, 17 years, 11 March 2010)

> *[This] is a great place to just chill.* (Male, 17 years, 11 March 2010)

> *If I stick my head down I can do whatever I want.* (Male, 18 years, 11 March 2010)

> *School should be heaps more like this.* (Female, 17 years, 11 March 2010)

> *If I wasn't here my life wouldn't be so good. I would have quit school.* (Male, 17 years, 11 March 2010)

Here they cut out a lot of the bullshit and just teach you about the things you need for life. (Female, 17 years, 10 March 2010)

I wasn't doing anything with my life. (Female, 17 years, young parent, 12 March 2010)

My life's back on track. (Female, 15 years, young parent, 12 March 2010)

I finally discovered my real self. (Female, 23 years, young parent, 12 March 2010)

[It] has given me control over my life. (Female, 17 years, young parent, 12 March 2010)

You get what you give. (Female, 16 years, 19 April 2010)

We give our teachers respect and they give it back. (Male, 16 years, 19 April 2010)

This place has given me a new lease. It has given me amazing opportunities. (Male, 18 years, 19 April 2010)

The people here are bloody awesome. (Female, 14 years, 20 April 2010)

If I wasn't coming here, I would probably be sitting at home. (Male, 14 years, 20 April 2010)

If I hadn't found this place, I would be into drugs and drinking heavily. (Female, 19 years, 22 April 2010)

There's not the distance between teachers and students that there is at school. (Male, 15 years, 22 April 2010)

I don't experience racism here. (Female, 15 years, 22 April 2010)

Smaller is better. We actually do things that are interesting. Here we choose what we learn. (Female, 17 years, 22 April 2010)

I'm a completely different person. [On the possibility of going back to school] You'd have to chop my leg off! (Female, 15 years, 22 April 2010)

Life before this was crap; [here] you are treated as a person. (Female, 15 years, 7 June 2010)

It's gross, awesome, cool; [dismisses misinformed] outsiders' view of [it] as "bullshit." (Female, 16 years, 7 June 2010)

This has been life saving and life changing for me. (Female, 21 years, young parent, 8 June 2010)

I'm getting to be the person that I want to be. (Female, 18 years, 8 June 2010)

I just got lost in the crowd at school, but here it's more like home.
(Female, 15 years, 9 June 2010)

It's still school but you are learning. (Female, 17 years, 10 June 2010)

If I didn't have this class I would be a mess. (Female, 16 years, 10 June 2010)

*This place has a completely different feel to traditional school. It's more
relaxed. It's not fearful.* (Male, 17 years, 10 June 2010)

In these incredible ethnographic fragments or "slices of life," we can see the
recurring themes around which young people who have been shoved out
(pushed out or eased out) of school have re-assessed the terms and conditions
upon which they are prepared to re-engage with learning—which is markedly
distinct from "schooling" (Green, 2002). Prominent among these is the issue
of having a significant degree of ownership over what they learn, when, how,
and with whom. In addition, they are most vociferous in ensuring that there is
a high degree of congruence with, and relevance to, their lives and aspirations
for the future. There is also the repeatedly recurring theme of being treated with
respect—as quasi-adults, in terms of their class backgrounds, and an acknowl-
edgment that many of these young people have had life experiences way beyond
their years. In particular, there is a strong resonance with the notion that all of
these young people have found pedagogical respect, or what Hult (1979, p. 243)
refers to as "pedagogical caring," which was mostly sadly and abysmally lacking
in their experience of conventional schooling the first time around.

The issues being foregrounded by these young people—of being given
space, afforded respect, consulted about their learning, provided with a measure
of control, while being allowed to socialize as they learn—are all obvious
enough qualities, so much so that it would be easy to over-romanticize them.
However, the overarching point to be made is that these are a constellation or a
mindset of ideas that have to demonstrably be present or brought into existence
in the educational rehabilitation of deeply damaged young lives. The tantalizing
question, therefore, still remains—if these are such self-evident ideas, then how
come they are proving to be so elusive in mainstream schooling?

What, Then, Are the Impediments to This Occurring?

Everything I have said so far sounds eminently reasonable and hardly contest-
able—and herein lies the major problem. There are several obstacles that
present as barriers that result in significant slippage between a reasonable set of
propositions and the reality of ensuring that they become deeply embedded in
educational practice. These obstacles go something like this:

- Schools and teachers need to have ways of interrupting their habituated practices to critically reflect upon, and question themselves about, how they are travelling in respect to the issues noted so far. Put another way, they need ways of doing a collective audit on how they are doing from the vantage point of young people.
- They need to do these collective self-assessments in a climate of non-retribution and a context in which there is a genuine preparedness to challenge the status quo and to change.
- They need to be prepared to foreground the issues of advancing young people's lives as non-negotiable core issues. This action requires considerable courage and leadership, especially in a climate and an ethos that celebrate decisiveness, managing people and outcomes, managing image and impressions, and fixing things through approaches that name, shame, and expose the recalcitrants.

Courage can be in very short supply when those in ascendant positions have to be prepared to jettison their accustomed role, which requires them to demonstrate that they have "solutions," that they have "can-do" policies, and that they are "results-driven"—many of which may be demonstrably wrong-headed approaches. It requires incredible courage to hold to the line that those in subaltern positions might just have important knowledge worth listening to. Approaching complex, multi-faceted questions in the more democratic and inclusive way being suggested here requires more time, can be considered to be more tedious, can appear more untidy, and may not always appear to be moving in a desirable linear direction. Anything less than the kind of political and policy realignment being suggested in this chapter, can only result in young people continuing to be sold short—and that is not a viable long-term option.

On Pushing Back against the Refusal to Listen ... to Young People!

A convincing argument can be made regarding the existence of increasing deafness at a number of levels—by schools and other social institutions, by the media, by the economy, and by policy regimes—that amounts to a consistent refusal to listen to young people—their lives, social class backgrounds, cultural and life experiences, and visions and aspirations for the future. As Tilleczek (2011, p. x) argues, "[t]he social and political inclusion or exclusion of young people is an important development to track in the coming years." As she points out, the irony is that

> [a]t the very time that young people are actively negotiating [the] modern world, their elders are taking up a complex and contradictory stance on youth ... [On the one hand] an appropriation of youth and "being young"

and an unmistakable clamour to look and act youthful ... [while on the
other hand] marginalizing actual young people and creating a climate of
increased dependence. (Tilleczek, 2011, p. x)

What needs to change, Tilleczek (2011, p. 132 [emphasis in original]) argues, is
"the commitment to attempt to share and use ... new knowledge *with* and *for*
young people at multiple levels."

Coming from the vantage point of young people's health and well-being,
Wyn (2009, p. xii) asserts "the importance of understanding young people's
experiences and perspectives ... [by placing] young people's lives ... in the foreground of discussion as much as possible." Notwithstanding, Wyn admits that
"there is a dearth of research on the ways in which wellbeing is managed and
experienced at the local level by young people" (p. xii).

Illustrative of the nature of the problem and the troublesome mismatch
between young people's lives and the way schools try to construct them in particular ways that are demonstrably at odds with one another, are the comments
of 16-year-old Jack from the Brotherhood of St. Laurence's *Life Chances* study:

> Listen! That's what they have to do most and they don't. They're too
> focused on trying to get the kids in line and make sure they wear their
> bloody uniform. They don't ask why they are not wearing their uniform,
> like they got kicked out of the house. They just go "Here's an exemp-
> tion note for today and if you do it again you get suspension." (Taylor &
> Helms, 2008, cited in Wyn, 2009, p. 120)

Similarly, from our own research (Smyth & McInerney, 2007), young people
who have opinions, are analytical, and who do not hold back in voicing them are
labelled "disruptive" elements (McGregor, 2000) and are dealt with harshly—as
in the case of 15-year-old James, who at the time we interviewed him had been
expelled from two high schools:

> No one at our high school wants to be there and that's why the truancy
> rate is so high, that's why the grades are so low, that's why you've got peo-
> ple misbehaving, "undermining teachers' authority"—as they would have
> you believe. That's why they've got people leaving early—because they
> don't want to be there but still the teachers don't see that as being their
> problem, it's the students' problem and there's nothing wrong with the
> system. I think they're scared to say: "Well we were wrong, we failed these
> kids." The biggest problem isn't that students are failing schools and get-
> ting Es, it's that the school is failing the student but they don't want to see
> it that way. The student failed school; the school never fails the student.
> The system is always right. The system is never wrong. That's the problem!
> (James, 25 February 2003, cited in Smyth & McInerney, 2007, pp. 41-42)

I can best round out this chapter and the somewhat despairing portrayal sketched out by these young people in their allusion to the policy indifference and "hatred" noted by Hattam (2001) by invoking the more democratically nurturing relationships that characterize what we have referred to elsewhere in our work as the *active school*. As Hattam describes, "*active* in the sense of reaching out to the lives of young people, and not merely responding to them" (p. 384).

> An active school culture presents itself as stepping out and working reciprocally with students to create an environment in which, regardless of background, all students have the opportunity to succeed. Student voice is the pre-eminent theme within these cultures, which is used to construct rigorous curriculum and pedagogy around the lives and experiences students bring with them to the school. Rather than deny popular culture, or relegate it to the realm of "outside of school," this was seen as an important facet around which curriculum is actively constructed. (Smyth & Hattam, 2002, p. 384)

The active school, while still an archetype in the sense of being an aspiration and a project to be continually worked towards, is to an extent an already existing reality in many contexts (for an extended discussion of of these examples, see Smyth & McInerney, 2007; Smyth et al., 2008, 2009; Smyth, Down, & McInerney, 2010). As we argue, this kind of more inclusive school (Clark et al., 1999) is illustrative of what Anderson (2000, p. 10) calls "some message of hope." Accordingly, the active school:

- does not individualize responsibility and blame students for their own failures;
- does not label students who "speak back" as disruptive cases to be handled through "muscular" behaviour management policies;
- does not tolerate a situation in which some students are allowed to uncaringly "fall through the cracks";
- does not turn its back on "uninspiring pedagogy"; and
- above all, it does not send out a signal to young people that in coming to this school they will be "treated like small children."

The final point with which I want to conclude is that, in respect of schooling as well as other aspects of their lives, young people deserve to be accorded no more than what is encapsulated in that typically Australian idiom of "a fair go"! (Smyth, Hattam, & Lawson, 1998).

Notes

The primary source of ideas that form the major part of this chapter come from a project funded by the Australian Research Council (ARC) (2010-12) entitled *Re-engaging Disadvantaged Young People with Learning*. I have also drawn in a secondary fashion from another ARC-funded project (1996-99) that had the working title *Listen to Me, I'm Leaving: Early School Leaving in South Australian Secondary Schools* (Smyth et al., 2000). I wish to express my appreciation to the ARC for its funding support, to the South Australian, Victorian, and Western Australian Education Departments, the Senior Secondary Assessment Board of South Australia, and, most of all, to the young people concerned for their honesty and generosity in sharing their stories. A shortened version of this chapter was published in *Education Canada 50*(5), 2010, pp. 23-26.

1   The names of the participants were not recorded. They were all between the ages of 13 and 17.

References

Anderson, P. (2000). Editorial: Renewals. *New Left Review, January-February*, 1-20.

Clark, C., Dyson, A., Millward, A., & Robson, S. (1999). Theories of inclusion, theories of schools: Deconstructing and reconstructing the "inclusive school." *British Educational Research Journal, 25*(2), 157-177.

Fine, M., & Rosenberg, P. (1983). Dropping out of high school: The ideology of school and work. *Boston University Journal of Education, 165*(3), 257-272.

Gibboney, R. (2010). Why an undemocratic capitalism has brought public education to its knees. In J. DeVitis & L. Dirwin-DeVitis (Eds.), *Adolescent education: A Reader* (pp. 223-237). New York: Peter Lang Publishing.

Green, P. (2002). *Slices of life: Qualitative research snapshots*. Melbourne: RMIT University Press.

Hattam, R. (2001). *Nurturing democratic relationships in schools against policy "hatred"* (paper presented at the annual meeting of the American Educational Research Association, Seattle, 10-14 April).

hooks, b. (1990). *Yearning: Race, gender and cultural politics*. Boston: South End Press.

Hult, R. (1979). On pedagogical caring. *Educational Theory, 29*(3), 237-243.

Lakoff, G., & Johnson, M. (1980). *Metaphors we live by*. Chicago: University of Chicago Press.

McGregor, G. (2000). Kids who "talk back"—critically literate or disruptive youth? *Journal of Adolescent and Adult Literacy, 44*(3), 220-228.

Ryan, W. (1976). *Blaming the victim*. New York: Vintage Books.

Shaker, P. (2010). Fighting the education wars, metaphorically. *Teachers College Record* (12 November 2010), No. 16232. Online: http://www.tcrecord.org.

Smyth, J., Angus, L., Down, B., & McInerney, P. (2008). *Critically engaged learning: Connecting to young lives*. New York: Peter Lang Publishing.

Smyth, J., Angus, L., Down, B., & McInerney, P. (2009). *Activist and socially critical school and community renewal: Social justice in exploitative times*. Rotterdam, The Netherlands: Sense Publishers.

Smyth, J., Down, B., & McInerney, P. (2010). *"Hanging in with kids" in tough times: Engagement in contexts of educational disadvantage in the relational school*. New York: Peter Lang Publishing.

Smyth, J., & Hattam, R. (2002). Early school leaving and the cultural geography of high schools. *British Educational Research Journal, 28*(3), 375-397.

Smyth, J., & Hattam, R., with Cannon, J., Edwards, J., Wilson, N., & Wurst, S. (2004). *"Dropping out," drifting off, being excluded: Becoming somebody without school.* New York: Peter Lang Publishing.

Smyth, J., Hattam, R., Cannon, J., Edwards, J., Wilson, N., & Wurst, S. (2000). *Listen to me, I'm leaving: Early school leaving in South Australian secondary schools.* Adelaide, Australia: Flinders Institute for the Study of Teaching, Department of Employment, Education and Training; and Senior Secondary Assessment Board of South Australia.

Smyth, J., Hattam, R., & Lawson, M. (Eds.). (1998). *Schooling for a fair go.* Sydney, Australia: Federation Press.

Smyth, J., & McInerney, P. (2007). *Teachers in the middle: Reclaiming the wasteland of the adolescent years of schooling.* New York: Peter Lang Publishing.

Smyth, J., & McInerney, P. (2011). Whose side are you on? Advocacy ethnography: Some methodological aspects of narrative portraits of disadvantaged young people, in socially critical research. *International Journal of Qualitative Studies in Education iFirst,* 1-20.

Taylor, J., & Nelms, L. (2008). *Life chances at 16.* Melbourne, Australia: Brotherhood of St. Laurence.

Tilleczek, K. (2011). *Approaching youth studies: Being, becoming, and belonging.* Toronto: Oxford University Press.

Valencia, R. (Ed.). (1997). *The evolution of deficit thinking. Educational thought and practice.* London: Falmer Press.

Valencia, R. (2010). *Dismantling contemporary deficit thinking: Educational thought and practice.* New York: Routledge.

Wyn, J. (2009). *Youth, health and welfare: Cultural politics of education and wellbeing.* South Melbourne, Australia: Oxford University Press.

Žižek, S. (2009). *Violence.* London: Profile Books.

Grey Matters by Zera Koutchieva

"I am a stud. And I am beautiful. I think."

I 've attempted to write this piece so many times, so many different ways, repeating the title out loud, the topic over and over. And still nothing, just a weak intro, mediocre body, and lame conclusion. "Studs and beauty—what lies beneath?" Half the time I'm wondering if people are wondering what's beneath my clothes, "Hey, don't even dare," I say with my body as I slouch over, trying my best to keep my 36D breasts from looking too inviting. He walks over, "You're beautiful, even in your boy clothes." Even in my boy clothes? I think half insulted and half stunned. Why would he think I was beautiful? How can I be beautiful? I'm not wearing skin-tight clothes, no makeup on, sneakers instead of heels. Then it hits me; this is my inspiration! I've never confronted my own ideas around beauty and how I did or didn't fit into them. Where they came from or how they were constructed. I just always accepted for myself that I wasn't beautiful and that to be such would threaten my gender performance on a whole. It would, undoubtedly, make me less dominant, if I were beautiful. Beauty was the girl in the magazines, on TV, models, and actresses. I've never seen a stud cover of Vogue, or in a Disney movie, no stud princesses, I was more like the prince. Prince Charming, handsome and saves the day, like I'm supposed to for my damsel in distress. I allow my gender performance to silence my natural beauty that comes with being a woman of any shape, size, or colour. That in my womanhood I can be anything I want, including beautiful. Beauty isn't limited to what I'm wearing or how I walk or talk or whom I talk to. Just because of the divinity inside me that gets eclipsed by the term STUD. I may not have all the answers yet, but I'm asking the right questions. I am a woman who identifies as a stud and I am beautiful, all in one. One doesn't cancel the other out. I'll try not to forget.

Kiana Eastmond

chapter 3

The Unique Status of Marginalization:
The Birth of Youth-Empowering Parents

Agazi Afewerki and Mohammed Shafique

It is a routine phenomenon in neighbourhoods such as Regent Park. Hassan returns home after a seven-hour shift, opens and reads the mail, arranges to pay the bills, and decides which mobile phone, television, and Internet service to subscribe to.[1] In essence, Hassan makes most of the major financial decisions in the family. The conclusion one would draw is that Hassan is like most Canadians—however, that would be far from the truth. Hassan does not have any kids, he does not have a wife, nor does he have a job. At the moment, he is not even sure about what type of career he wants to pursue.

That is because Hassan is only 13 years old. He is not an orphan, nor is he eager to move out on his own. Rather, Hassan lives happily at home with his parents. His parents do not disappear from time to time, nor do they have any serious physical ailments preventing them from performing day-to-day routines. On the contrary, Hassan's parents are healthy, caring, and they are raising him well. His parents do not require him to carry out these tasks as some sort of punishment or as a way of exposing him to the responsibilities of an adult. Instead, Hassan does these things out of necessity. He does them because he has to do them. And the reason is because of something that is widely apparent in marginalized communities such as Regent Park—his parents speak very little English and they are technologically illiterate. It is an experience shared by many youth living in Canada, including the authors of this chapter.[2]

Critics may say that if we attempted to get the reader to sympathize with Hassan and his family by telling his story, then we have failed because one could easily ask: "Why have his parents failed to learn English?" "Why have his parents refused to assimilate and become knowledgeable about their society?" "Why do some Canadians continually and generationally reside in these marginalized communities?" and "Why should resources be invested to make the lives of Hassan and his parents easier when there are other issues that deserve more priority?"

Whatever the answers to these questions may be, they are not questions that we are well equipped to answer. One of us now has a degree in law, and the other a degree in business. We are not experts in scrutinizing why the conditions are what they are. What we are well equipped with, however, is our experiences—that is, we share the same story as Hassan. We read and translated mail, handled financial matters, and taught our parents the basics of computers. Ultimately, we elected not to ask ourselves *why* these conditions exist but, rather, *how* our experiences can improve the learning of others in our neighbourhood.

Like Hassan, we grew up in Regent Park, which is considered to be Canada's oldest public housing complex. It was built in the 1940s and is located near the heart of downtown Toronto, occupying a three-block radius in the area south of Gerrard Street East to Shuter Street, and east of Parliament Street to River Street. It is a densely populated community, comprising approximately 7,500 residents in 2,083 households squeezed into 69 acres of land.[3] Fewer than 150 of those households have annual incomes above $30,000. The average income for residents of Regent Park is approximately half the average income of the rest of Toronto.[4] Adult-youth interaction is lacking in Regent Park, where 37% of the population is under the age of 14 years (compared to the city average of 17.5%), and 56.4% of the population is under the age of 24.[5]

For many, these are the statistics that stand out when they hear the phrase "public housing." It evokes a particular image—one of welfare dependency and low levels of education. Our goal was to utilize this situation for a positive benefit—one in which the tasks that Hassan performs would not be seen as a deterrent but, rather, as a set of skills that could be refined and managed for progressive youth and community development. The outcome was a program called Youth Empowering Parents (YEP).[6]

YEP

A typical community program aimed at youth has one or more adult instructors providing the service to them. This is where our program differs since instead of youth being service receivers, they become service providers. We titled the program Youth Empowering Parents because that is precisely what occurs—it is youth who are given the responsibility to ensure the achievements of adults, either their own parent(s) or other adults from the community.

At present, YEP offers computer and English classes to non-fluent English-speaking adults in the Regent Park community. To best explain how the YEP model works, and what makes it different from others, it is best to contrast YEP with other programs offering the same service. A typical computer and English class usually functions as follows: there is one instructor and a group of students; classes operate sometime between Monday to Friday during the daytime; and everyone follows the same module outline at the same pace, regardless of each student's individual skill level. A few obvious concerns are that many adults who need access to these programs are at work when classes are being offered, the pace at which the curriculum progresses is either too slow or too fast for many students, and the language of instruction, English, is not their native language, which causes difficulty in understanding the instructor. These concerns can be dealt with by means of private tutoring, however, such a service is simply a luxury many Regent Park residents cannot afford. Yet what if private tutoring was free? What if low-income residents could receive one-on-one tutoring to assist in their learning?

YEP provides this very service by engaging community youth to deliver that free tutoring. A youth volunteer, such as Hassan, is assigned an adult—either his own parent or another adult from the community who speaks the same language as he does. For the entire semester, Hassan is tasked with teaching that person English and/or computer skills.[7] It might seem odd that these youth are engaging in this type of service without prior training, but the reality of the matter is every single youth volunteer at YEP will tell you that they actually have the necessary experience required. This practice comes from many years of teaching their parents basic computer and English skills. We do not exaggerate when we say that every single youth volunteer at YEP has this experience. During our recruitment of youth, it is the first question we ask them, and the answer is always in the affirmative. In essence, this program takes what already happens naturally at home and aims to mirror that same interaction in a classroom.

From Service Receivers to Service Providers

There are numerous benefits of youth being service providers. Most crucial, perhaps, is the lack of financial dependence to operate YEP. When it launched in September 2010, we purchased standard curricula from our local bookstores, and it quickly became apparent that these texts were not suitable for this type of program. The intention was to operate a classroom where youth tutors would conduct the teaching as opposed to a professional instructor. However, an instructor's manual was often too complex for youth to follow, and a self-study text was far too explanatory and did not have the effective guidelines for a tutor on how to teach the material. More importantly, youth rarely, if ever, referred to such texts when teaching their own parents at home. This is because youth have an adequate understanding of basic English and have sufficient familiarity with computers. There is no purpose then in having a detailed set of instructions that explain, for instance, why we use quotation marks in English grammar or how to italicize words in a word processor. Instead, we found that the only instructions required were as simple as "explain to your student how to highlight text in a document" or "explain to your student the meaning of the following phrase: *I'll see you around*." Very little training is required, and each youth, over time, uses their creativity to develop their own unique way of teaching.

Moreover, a simple cost-benefit analysis can illustrate the number of participants who can benefit from this program. Suppose that the equivalent quality of private tutoring can be had for the Ontario minimum wage of $10.25 per hour and that the cost for a staff member to facilitate a YEP classroom was $20 per hour. It means that if there is one facilitator and four participants—two youth each teaching one adult—the cost would nearly break even in terms of social return. Likewise, the higher the number of participants, the greater the social return because the facilitation cost remains fixed. At the time of writing, three YEP semesters have been completed in which a total of 60 students have received private tutoring. With each semester consisting of 36 hours, a total aggregate value of $22,140 in private tutoring fees was realized for only a staffing cost of $2,160.

YEP Participants

Youth (Tutors)

HOORE is a 13-year-old honours student. Her family immigrated to Canada in 2003 from Bangladesh. She is a YEP tutor and has been with the program since it began in September 2010. She was 12 at the time.

Table 1: Youth enrolment at YEP

	Number of participants	Age range	Median age	Diversity
YEP semester Fall 2010	10	12-16	13	Bengali (8), Tamil (2)
YEP Semester Winter 2011	18	12-17	15	Bengali (10), Tamil (2), Somali (2), Vietnamese (2), Mandarin (1), Cantonese (1)
YEP Semester Summer 2011	32	12-19	15	Bengali (14), Tamil (2), Somali (4), Hindi (2), Urdu (2), Vietnamese (2), Amharic (1), Cantonese (1), Farsi (1), French (1), Mandarin (1), Spanish (1)

JAYBAD is a 15-year-old tutor, also from Bangladesh. His parents came to Canada 18 months before he was born. When he first joined the program in January 2011, he frequently arrived late, was an introvert, and seldom gave answers longer than five words. By the time he finished his first semester in April 2011, he was punctual, active, enthusiastic, and regarded by our professional English-as-a-second-language instructor as one of the best tutors in the program.

THEHAN is a 13-year-old from Sri Lanka. He joined YEP in September 2010, not because of a desire to help adult residents in the community but because he thought it would propel his academic career. He aspires to be an aeronautical engineer and initially seemed to have very little interest in helping the Regent Park community. After being exposed to YEP and seeing the struggles that parents in the community go through, he has become highly engaged in the community and aspires to create his own social program one day.

Adult (Students)

MARIA is a 67-year-old single mother of four. She grew up in Somalia, attended college there, and graduated as a medical life technician. She worked for 15 years in a hospital in Saudi Arabia and another 7 years in a Mogadishu hospital as a laboratory technician. Like many in Regent Park, Maria left her homeland because of war and immigrated to Canada in 1991. And like many adults in Regent Park, she has had to hear the phrase: "your degree is not recognized here," leaving her to surrender her educational qualifications and ambitions to work in low-paying labour jobs in order to support herself and her children. Maria smiles continuously, volunteers a lot in the Somali community, and encourages others to do the same. You would never know based on her behaviour that she recently lost two of her children to medical complications and that she carries an insulin pump with her at all times for her Type-1 diabetes. She would make a great role model for community youth if they got to know her. Maria has been a YEP student since January 2011 and, within 12 weeks, three YEP youth had proclaimed her as their role models. Maria is an excellent storyteller and gives many of the YEP youth advice about education, careers, and life in general.

SHULEY immigrated to Canada in 2007 from Bangladesh. Shuley is only 31 years old and is a stay-at-home mother, caring for her two children while her husband works. She is not well educated and speaks very little English. Her social networks are exclusively within the Bengali community. She does not socialize with persons from other cultures, not because of some sort of personal preference but, rather, because her lack of English inhibits her from doing so.

SHAHEEM arrived from south India with his family in 2009. He is 52 years old and has worked in varying parts of the world as a mechanical engineer. Shaheem is an analytical thinker and appears to be in deep thought in any conversation he engages in. He will easily admit to his technological illiteracy when it comes times to use the computer, and he hopes YEP will accelerate his learning so that he can start thinking about his career options in Canada.

The Importance of a Program Such as YEP

My mother used to go to ESL classes a few years ago. She would listen to whatever the teacher said to her, and when the teacher asked her if she understood the lesson, she would just nod her head and say "yes." But the truth was she didn't understand it at all. And when she got home, she would ask me and my sister to explain it to her. We would explain it to her over and over again, even in our own language if we had to, until she understood it. She was too shy to ask for help during class. There were so many other people there and she didn't want to be embarrassed by not learning the material as quickly as the rest of them. (Jaybad)

There are numerous computer and English classes in the Greater Toronto Area that YEP students can otherwise attend. YEP is distinct in that its aim is to expedite students' learning by establishing an environment that is more comfortable for them—one where the tutor speaks the same language; one where asking questions is highly encouraged; and one where the curriculum progresses at the adult/student's pace. All 60 adult students thus far have indicated that having a tutor who speaks the same language as them is the primary reason they joined YEP. The student does not fall behind because the tutor is able to provide timely responses in their native language.

I tried to register for other ESL [English as a second language] classes but they always say my English is too advanced. But I know my level of English and I know what I need to learn. (Maria)

Maria had difficulty finding a program where she could improve on her deficiencies. She wanted to learn and expand her knowledge on particular components of a standard curriculum rather than sit it in its entirety, the vast majority of which she was already proficient with. YEP offers her that type of flexibility. A standard classroom often does not. Our curriculum aims to be as far removed from rigid as possible. For instance, those who want to improve their vocabulary are given lessons that focus on improving vocabulary.

I am busy on the weekdays so the class times are very important to me. (Shuley)

During our initial assessment of the community, we found it odd that many programs that offered English and computer classes had already existed in Regent Park. However, a majority of adults who desired to learn these skills could not access these programs. The adults and parents had other commitments on weekday mornings and afternoons, which are the times when those community programs were being offered. As such, we found it odd that Regent Park, a neighbourhood with an abundance of computer labs and indoor community space, appeared to have an absence of such programs operating on the weekends—times when many adults who seemingly desire to attend these programs can actually do so. In other words, 28% of the community resources in Regent Park—two of the seven days per week—were not being utilized. We wanted YEP to make effective use of these resources.

YEP began with 10 adult students and 10 youth registrants. 100% of those registrants identified weekend afternoons (1 p.m. to 5 p.m.) as their availability.[8] Since this was a common time slot for all of the respondents, and because youth would not be attending school or afterschool programs during those times, we elected to operate classes on weekend afternoons. If time was an important barrier, YEP has removed it.

At present, YEP is still very much in an exploratory stage.[9] We do believe that this model works, but we cannot yet measure how effectively it works because the YEP curriculum has undergone many changes since its inception, making it difficult to conduct research that would produce reliable data. Nevertheless, we expect that we have observed that the main resources—community space and youth volunteers—are widely available. Thus, we consider the YEP model to be scalable to any area where there is an abundance of families such as Hassan's and by any organization willing to take on the project. The YEP program is currently being hosted at a local community centre, which provides the necessary facilities and equipment free of charge.

At this time, our quantitative data is only being used for internal evaluation purposes. However, one area we are comfortable with sharing is the growth in enrolment. We started with 10 youth and 10 students in the Fall 2010 session. Although one person from each group did not return for the second semester due to external commitments, we still received an additional 9 youth and 9 student registrants, resulting in 18 youth and 18 students for the Winter 2011 session. For the Summer 2011 semester, there were 32 youth and 32 students admitted to YEP, with an additional 26 interested youth placed on a waiting list. Only three youth and two adult students from the previous semester did not return due to other commitments. All three adult students who have left YEP have expressed their satisfaction with the program. Two of those three have expressed their desire to return. At the time of writing, the Fall 2011 semester is nearly under way. There are currently 73 youth and 52 adult students interested in joining.

Table 2: Number of participants

	Total number of students	Number of returns from previous semester (students)	Number of new students admitted	Total number of youth admitted	Number of returns from previous semester (youth)	Number of new youth
Fall 2010	10	—	—	10	—	—
Winter 2011	18	9	9	18	9	9
Summer 2011	32	16	16	32	15	43

Community Engagement

Jaybad enrolled in YEP in January 2011 only after his mother, who was enrolled in YEP as a student, suggested to him that it would be a convenient way to complete 40 hours of volunteer service. Thehan accompanied his mother to an open house in September 2010 because his mother wanted to register. When he learned of the program, he decided to register as a tutor. Another YEP tutor, Jarin, registered during this same open house. She only entered our offices because she did not want to stand outside to wait for her friend, so she came inside to sit down. Like Thehan, she thought YEP would be an interesting experience. Of the 32 youth from the first three semesters, YEP was the first volunteer experience for 26 of them. Many of the youth who enrolled for the Fall 2011 semester have completed the 40 hours of volunteer service required to graduate from an Ontario secondary school, yet they continue to enroll in YEP.

At the end of one of the YEP English classes in the Winter 2011 semester, Jarin and her student Shuley entered the computer lab on their own volition. Shuley had asked Jarin for assistance in filling out a job application. They stayed there for 45 minutes. Shuley said she did not find it odd asking someone who is more than half her age for help. By this time, they had conducted YEP classes together for more than 7 weekends and a relationship had developed whereby a 31-year-old mother willingly trusted a 14-year-old youth.

I see her as more than a tutor but also as my friend. (Shuley)

A Unique Status of "Marginalization"

Youth such as Hassan may be regarded as having a more difficult life compared to other youth whose parents do not have the same challenges as his. For example, if Hassan needs help with his English school work, he cannot ask his parents. Or if Hassan has to translate a government document, he would need to take time and educate himself first as to what the technical terms in the document mean. However, if you ask the youth at YEP if they consider these additional responsibilities to be a deterrent to their lives, their answers are consistent: Hoore—no; Thehan—no; Jaybad—Hell no.

Their reasoning is also identical. Each will refer to their ability to mature at a younger age and to their ability to teach and explain things more clearly. They consider YEP to be a program that helps further their development in these categories. Hoore went on to say that her so called "marginalized status" is something that she considers to be a privilege: "*I know that the struggles that I go through now will only build my character in the future.*"

Limitations of the YEP Model

After one year of YEP, there remain lingering, but by no means fatal, limitations. First, YEP requires extensive co-ordination. Not every youth or parent can be expected to attend every single class. At times, a youth will arrive late or not attend a class without giving prior notice, leaving his/her student without a tutor, and vice versa. Second, the vast majority of students enrolled in YEP are female. Of the 60 students from the first three semesters, 53 are female; of the 60 youth, 46 are female. Third, the YEP model is based on how many adults decide to register. For the Fall 2011 semester, there are currently 73 youth and 52 adult students interested in joining. These numbers mean that 21 youth will have to be put on reserve for the next semester. And, fourth, the YEP model is language specific—often, there needs to be an adult who speaks the same language as the youth. This is not an issue with a language such as Bengali since there is an abundance of Bengali-speaking youth and adults living in Regent Park. However, suppose there is an adult who speaks Amharic—it may be very difficult to find an Amharic-speaking youth to join YEP as a tutor since there are so few of them in Regent Park.

Concluding Comments

Our expectation is that the YEP program will have, at minimum, the following effects on any community in which it operates:

- increased community inclusion—within the program, adults can interact with other adults and with youth from the same or different cultural backgrounds. Outside of the program, those same adults will be equipped with enough English skills to maintain and increase their interactions with other ethnic groups in Regent Park.
- reducing the language barrier—the YEP program aims at improving the English and technology fluency of adults at a very low cost to society. Improving these tangible skills will empower the parents to become more

independent when seeking information and increase their opportunity for future employment.

- closing the generational gap—as technology and communication evolve, there continues to be a growing generational gap between newcomer adults and their children. YEP attempts to close this gap using its innovative method of grassroots education.

- promoting lifelong learning—the YEP program intends to change the culture of the community by promoting the concept of lifelong learning. Once a youth sees the dedication and commitment that their own parent or even another adult is making towards education, we can expect to see a significant shift in culture within the Regent Park community.

It is crucial to note that some marginalized communities possess the very resources required to address pressing social needs that exist in those same communities. Moreover, we frequently use the YEP model for much more than teaching English and computer skills. We partner with local agencies to disseminate information about health and finance; we work with employment agencies to create employment-related activities, such as completing job applications; and we work closely with social housing to circulate any relevant information to YEP adults. More importantly, it is more than just a source of education and skills development. It is also a place for intercultural and intergenerational socialization, two types of interaction that do not occur frequently in highly diverse and marginalized communities such as Regent Park. The YEP program has recently received an award for intercultural innovation, bestowed jointly by the United Nations Alliance of Civilizations and the BMW Group. With this support, it can be expected that YEP will strive to grow and operate in multiple geographies, both nationally and internationally.

Notes

1   The names of the people mentioned in this chapter have been changed to preserve anonymity.
2   It should be noted from the outset that this chapter will not provide much statistical data from which you can derive pedagogical inferences. The intention is to provide you with a broad introduction to our program rather than with a scholarly article.
3   Toronto Community Housing, *Regent Park Social Development Plan* (2007), online: http://www.toronto.ca/revitalization/regent_park.
4   Ibid.
5   Ibid.
6   Although Youth Empowering Parents (YEP) was established by three youth, we would like to thank all of the people who, at the time of writing, have thus far offered us their assistance: Alfred Jean-Baptiste, Aziza Farah, Baillie Zheng, Carolyn Acker, Carrie Hantash, Colin Lynch, Diana Moeser, Dinny Biggs, Esra Shafique, Faisal Miah,

Irene Parvin, Kadijo Afrah, Molly Andrews, Moureen Khan, Peter Nakamura, Sarah Goel, Selim Berbatov, Sufi Mohamed, Tarak Ahmed, Therjo Balasubramaniam, and William Hanchareck.

7   For the remainder of the chapter, "student" will refer to adult participants.

8   Three of the adult students also included weekday hours. One respondent added 2 p.m. to 5 p.m. each day of the week, another respondent added Friday from 5 p.m. to 7 p.m., and the remaining respondent added Tuesday from 5 p.m. to 7 p.m.

9   We are currently engaging in research in the broad areas of skills development, youth leadership, community engagement, cultural integration, and independence, among others. All research, once complete, will be published at http://www.yepeducation .com.

The rich swell up with pride,
The poor from hunger.

Hunger, a multimedia piece by Sarah Laurin

Marginal Spaces, Disparate Places: Educational and Youth Practices in a Globalizing World

Jean Mitchell

Arriving in an urban settlement in Vanuatu, an archipelago in the southwest Pacific, I was immediately struck by the large numbers of energetic out-of-school children and youth who announced with strong conviction that they had "already failed." They were alluding to their failure to pass the examinations needed to move through the various levels of formal education in Vanuatu. With a rapidly growing population, competitive exams were the means "to win" the highly coveted seats in middle and senior school in Vanuatu. As a result, large numbers of young people who wanted to continue their studies were "pushed out" of school. During several years of ethnographic research in the settlement located on the outskirts of the capital, Port Vila, I came to know many of the young people who spent their days "killing time," excluded as they were from the economies of school and work in a settlement where livelihood was precarious for most of the migrants from the island villages.[1] The young people whom I met were profoundly disappointed with their educational experiences and their inability to find employment. Their representation of themselves as having "failed" and been "pushed out" of school underlined the urgency of confronting what it means to be young and marginalized in a globalizing world.

My research with youth suggests that the pursuit of formal education not only features prominently in the lives of young people and their parents but also is central to "globalization and integral to Western and non-Western accounts of modernity" (Jeffery & McDowell, 2004, p. 132). Formal education based on Western models and introduced around the world through missionary and colonial practices has signified and defined what it means to be modern. Education with its promise of cultural capital and its instrumental links to the formal economy compels people to migrate within and between nations in hopes of finding increased access to, and a better quality of, education. With so much invested in education—at the individual, community, national, and international levels—failure or perceived failure in the school system is a critical site for investigating what it means to be marginal in a globalizing world. There are currently more than one billion youth between the ages of 15 and 24 years and more than 85% of them live in "developing" nations that are negotiating a changing global order in which economic restructuring, government disinvestment in social measures, intense global competition, high rates of unemployment, and economic recession are adversely affecting their everyday lives and aspirations (Lloyd et al., 2005). Vanuatu, like many of these formerly colonized nations, has inherited and continued to maintain a system of education that excludes many and erodes local knowledge and epistemologies (Niroa, 2004). Pacific Island educator and poet Konai Thaman (2007, p. 12) insists that "[w]e need a new way of seeing and talking about education and globalization," which challenges the "hegemonic discourses" that are embedded in both of these powerful processes.

This chapter draws on my experiences with young people in the urban settlement of Blacksands and my work with the Vanuatu Young People's Project at the Vanuatu Cultural Centre. This project provides young people with basic tools to conduct research with their peers and the opportunity to present their views about the situation of youth through various media. The project has undertaken two major research projects with youth in Port Vila. I also draw upon my research in an afterschool project for young people in a low-income urban area in Borough, Prince Edward Island. In both places, education and, more specifically, failure at school emerged as a key concern among young people who struggled in the classroom and in finding satisfactory work. In both places, I began to recognize the similar ways in which youth are problematized and the low-income urban areas they inhabit are pathologized. There are, of course, profound differences that informed youth experiences in the urban settlement of Blacksands near Port Vila, Vanuatu, and Borough, the low-income housing project on the outskirts of Charlottetown, Prince Edward Island. At the same time, there are remarkable resonances in the experiences of these young people who inhabited marginal urban spaces in Vanuatu and Prince Edward Island but who, at the same time, articulated, accommodated, and resisted their dilemmas in complex ways. By looking at these disparate places, I hope to trouble the easy reliance on the categories of North and South, traditional and modern, and centre and margin. The educational experiences of youth in marginalized places are productive sites to think through difference and the historical and contemporary connections and disconnections among people who are invariably separated by the spatial and political legacies of "worlding" encompassed in the hierarchy of first and third worlds or developed and developing worlds (Spivak, 1985). Gupta and Ferguson (1997, p. 8) have argued that if one begins with "the premise that spaces have always been hierarchically interconnected instead of naturally disconnected then cultural and social change becomes not a matter of cultural contact and articulation, but one of rethinking difference through connection."

Exploring the spatial practices of young people from the widely disparate places of Blacksands and Borough within a single frame of "growing up global" reveals connections as well as differences (Katz, 2004). Katz (2004, p. 156) argues that young people in various places throughout the world, "suffer, endure, cope with, and are tantalized by the efforts of capitalist-driven globalization in startling similar, albeit predictably different ways." By focusing on these two different and specific marginalized urban places where young people have struggled with school and work, I offer ethnographic insights of the particular (Abu-Lughod, 1991) in order to avoid the generalizations that undermine the heterogeneity and complexity of the lives of young people. Uneven development that is evident within nations and between nations, colonial legacies, and global process produce "common effects in local disparate settings" (Katz, 2004, p. 159).

Spatial metaphors abound in discussions of education and, more generally, in knowledge production. Haraway's (1988) idea of "situated knowledge" suggests that all knowledge claims are views from somewhere and, as such, are partial and infused with power dynamics. Such a perspective demands that researchers and educators be accountable, for we do not simply describe but, rather, inscribe margins and centres. Marginality, shaped by power and perspective, rests on the articulation of a normative centre that is authoritatively mapped. In this chapter, I shall consider how marginality is produced and normalized through the educational experiences of youth in Blacksands and Borough and, at the same time, suggest how both margins and centres are reconfigured through the everyday practices of young people. This chapter tacks between urban settlements and schools and between young people and educators, all of whom draw attention to how ideas of margin and centres are reinforced and resisted.

Place Making in a Global World

Globalization defines how the political, economic, social, and cultural processes are becoming increasingly worldwide in scope and are affecting individual lives and local communities. According to Appadurai (1996, p. 228), global-ization refers to a series of shifts in the global political economy that have intensified since the 1970s when "transnational, flexible and irregular forms of organization, labor, finance, technology, and technological capital began to be assembled in ways that treated national boundaries as mere constraints or fictions." Globalization in Vanuatu is characterized by deepening global economic processes including offshore banking, tourism, development aid, neo-liberal agendas of economic restructuring, labour migration, and growing foreign investment. The real estate market is now driving the urban economy where gated communities of foreigners and crowded urban settlements of those born in Vanuatu increasingly define the physical and social landscape around the capital of Port Vila where unemployed youth "kill time." Evangelical churches with headquarters in far-off places field foreign missionaries, recruit new members, and build new churches. All of these developments are part of the hypermodern landscape of globalization in Vanuatu. With a population of about 235,000 and more than a hundred languages, Vanuatu is characterized by an extraordinary linguistic and cultural diversity.[2]

Metaphors of connections and networks are central to our descriptions of the contemporary processes of globalization where interconnections are fabri-cated through new temporal and spatial regimes characterized by the intense circulation of commodities, people, technologies, and ideas that define the "new globalism" (Tsing, 2004, p. 336). Tsing (2004, p. 336), however, cautions against "over valorizing connection and circulation" for the market model that undergirds globalization and is lauded for promoting the equalities of circula-tion that may also justify "policies of domination and discrimination." Massey (1991, p. 27) has argued this point:

> Different groups and different individuals are placed in very distinct ways
> in relation to these flows and interconnections ... some people are more in
> charge of it than others; some initiate flows and movement, others don't:
> some are more on the receiving end of it than others; some are effectively
> imprisoned by it.

Massey's comments are particularly useful in understanding the marginalized places of the young people that I am concerned with in this chapter. The task at hand is how to capture the constraints imposed on youth without overlooking or exaggerating their agency and resistance.

The participation of young people in global youth culture is encoded in various kinds of communication, aesthetic expressions, and the consumption of images and products that relentlessly circulate. In Vanuatu, for example, the practice of "eye-shopping" was a staple activity of young people, suggesting how their gaze apprehended the commodities that they wanted, but could not afford, to buy (Mitchell, 2003). I also saw how young people were fascinated by the use of video cameras in the Vanuatu Young Peoples' Project, where they used videos as a means to speak about themselves and their experiences to new audiences in new ways. While aspects of global youth culture are widely shared, the singular notion of global youth culture obscures the ways in which differences and inequities are produced, maintained, and enforced at local levels. Authors of a recent review of youth, equity, and education have argued that emphases on youth agency and resistance in global youth studies may fail to confront the material limitations that constrain young people who live in difficult daily circumstances and who are exacerbated by their lack of access to education and employment (Hull, Zacher, & Hibbert, 2009). Based on her research in rural Sudan and urban United States, Katz (1998, p. 142) contends:

> For some young people the best that they can hope for themselves is rather narrow, and this is more punishing now than ever before because of how much more they have learned to want thanks to the reach of globalised cultural production. These issues, which are environmental in the broadest sense, have deep, and largely unexplored, effects upon young people's constructions of identity, in how they see their "place" in the world, and ultimately, in how they produce the world to come.

Education as an institution and as a long-standing instrument of modernity in both colonial and post-colonial contexts shapes the lives of youth in particular ways to fit the shifting contours of global economies and government agendas. The everyday experiences of young people in places as different as Vanuatu and Prince Edward Island are connected through experiences of schooling. Young people in dispersed places are linked through the transnational educational flows as "the global spread of a corporate curricular ethos is dispersed via the World Bank and other international agencies" (Kincheloe, 1997, p. 21, as cited in Hull et al., 2009). The circulation of educational ideologies and processes and the pursuit of education across and within borders are, as noted, integral to globalization. Pacific educators are now questioning the value assumptions underpinning education and globalization and their claims of cultural neutrality. Thaman (2007, p. 9), for example, explains: "We know that the cultural neutrality of education, as well as globalization, is neither possible nor desirable, and that partisan beliefs and values like other beliefs and values, are embedded in their own cultural curriculum and agenda."

Place Making in Blacksands

Many observers of globalization have cautioned that an emphasis on the global dimensions of space should not deflect our attention from the intense experience of the local practices of place making. According to Escobar (2001, p. 140), place is as much an agent as a fixed location:

> Place continues to be important in the lives of many people, perhaps most, if we understand by place the experience of a particular location, with some measure of groundedness (however unstable), sense of boundaries (however permeable), and connection to everyday life, even if its identity is constructed, traversed by power, and never fixed.

Maira and Soep (2004, p. 263) have also complicated the relationship between the local and global by arguing that young people "strategically, draw on the meanings of multiple 'locals' in their lives. Youth culture helps shift, sometimes even distort an easy mapping of local/national/global." The importance of place making at the local level and its capacity to defy marginality is evident in the practices of youth in Blacksands and Borough. In Vanuatu, it is widely believed that "places make people" for they are both "the mediators and the vectors of identity" (Bonnemaison, 1985, p. 37). This approach to place resonates with de Certeau's (1984, p. 117) idea of space as a relational concept or, as he says, a "practiced place," "composed of intersections of mobile elements." This idea captures the intensity and movement that attends youth practices of place and the links between space and subjectivity.

In Vanuatu, the idea of the gift economy is used to frame cultural ideas and practices of sociality and subjectivity. Ideas of place and personhood are integral to the gift economy where reciprocity and relationality are privileged. Personhood is believed to be composite and contingent on relationships rather than on the bounded and autonomous subject upon which Western education is based. In Bislama, the *lingua franca* in Vanuatu, *kastom,* encompasses the cultural knowledge, sociality, and social processes that are unique to Vanuatu-born people (Bolton, 1999). Such practices were shaped by colonial encounters and continue to be articulated against the post-colonial contingencies and processes of global capitalism. Place making materializes specific linguistic and cultural practices that are central to identity in Vanuatu. In this context, new urban settlements such as Blacksands represent a radical departure from the ways in which relationships were previously created through place. The squatter settlements that emerged with independence in 1980 represent for many both the failure of modernity and the failure of *kastomary* knowledge. Young people living in settlements such as Blacksands are constantly pressed "to go back" to their villages, but, for many, however, going back is not an option. Many who have grown up in town do not have the skills, knowledge, and connections to live in their ancestral places for reasons that I shall discuss later in this chapter. Living in an urban settlement, I was struck not only by the large numbers of young people living there but also by the relentless tirades against them, which came from all quarters. Youth were ostensibly blamed for urbanization, modernization, Westernization, moral decline, and the loss of tradition. Such depictions are a bitter departure from Mead's (1928, reprinted 1992) gentle and playful descriptions of youth that informed the earliest anthropological work in Pacific societies. There is in Blacksands and Borough, it seems to me, an extraordinary capacity to blame the young for systemic changes and constraints that they have not authored but to which they respond through various acts of resistance. Places such as Blacksands are stigmatized and pathologized. Youth in urban settlements who do not have a place in school—or in the work place or village—are represented as being unruly, signifying the dangers and desires of modernity. However, many young men whom I met also embrace the *kastom* or customary practices. Through this identification with *kastomary* knowledge and practices, they craft and secure their own sense of place in their urban slums. As part of the research on youth undertaken by the Vanuatu Young People's Project, young people were asked about their interest in customary knowledge and its relationship to education. Rueben, for example, simply stated *kastom* "*is our way of life and our identity*," while Johnston pointed to its moral code "*When you learn* kastom *you walk straight.*" For many of these young people, their school experience was a source of anxiety, alienation and disappointment. As Johnny from Vanuatu explained:

> *When I was in school and didn't pass I felt no hope. I thought I was no good.*
> *I felt no good because everything I had learned from class six to form four*
> *didn't result in any gain for me.* (Quoted in Mitchell, 1999, p. 10)

In contrast to the alienation produced within school, *kastomary* practices underline the cultural value of respect that underpins the reciprocal and rela-tional aspects of personhood that are not privileged in Western-inspired educa-tion. Some of the young people who took part in the research project felt there was a conflict between *kastomary* practices and formal education. Jimmy, who was a student at the time explained, "*[e]ducation is good because you learn what is happening around the world and in your country. On the other hand when you are more educated you can lose your* kastom *and culture.*" By retrieving *kastom* as a source of identity and a strategy for place making in their settle-ment, young people counter their marginal status and formulate an alternative view of modernity that is not contingent on success in formal education.

Place Making in Borough

Young people living in the low-income area of Borough in Prince Edward Island also deployed place-making strategies to counter the stigma of poverty and marginality. One of the defining aspects of Borough is the perception that people from outside do not go there because of its reputation. Young people such as Jacy described how the Borough was referred to as "the ghetto" by those who live there and by those who do not. When I asked young people from Borough to tell me why they think people call their place a ghetto, their answers converged around the issues of violence, poverty, and drug use. In response to this representation of their place, young people began to refer to their community as "the Bronx" because, as Henry told me, "it is hard core." The Bronx may seem a long way from Prince Edward Island, but in the spatial imaginary of the young people their marginality is both confirmed and celebrated with ideas of the Bronx. The identification with the Bronx lends a cosmopolitanism and "street cred" to their places. It also shows how local places are constituted through other global localities real and imagined. The identification with the Bronx suggests how marginalized young people devise counter-tactics for resisting images imposed on them and how they in turn construct their own images. Place making always involves a construction "rather than merely a discovery of difference" (Gupta & Ferguson, 1997, p. 13). It is not surprising that the young people in Borough had to embellish their low-income housing area for not only is it stigmatized, but it is also largely empty of the social and economic facilities that were originally planned for it. There is a fast food outlet at the edge of the community and a convenience store. When we started the project with youth, they had been barred from the community hall, and the municipality had hired security guards to prevent youth from acts of vandalism and graffiti, which had become routine occurrences. Given the intensely local nature of the lives of children and young people, the lack of public funding for programs for youth, housing, and neighbourhoods hit them harder than other urban dwellers (Katz, 2004, p. 163). Young people from low-income housing areas often spend more time in their local areas and adjacent public spaces. They are more visible.

Questions of visibility and invisibility are "material" (Katz, 2004, p. 163), and, as Hebidge (1988) notes, youth are invisible until they become a problem. Young people become problematic simply by living in low-income areas such as Borough and Blacksands. Their problematic status is accentuated when these young people drop out, or fail at, school. They are subject to far more surveillance than their "prep" counterparts in better-off neighbourhoods. Marginalized spaces are subject to more policing, which becomes a normalized part of day-to-day life. Xavier from Borough explained how he is routinely summoned by the police to sit in their car to report who is doing the graffiti, the vandalism, the stealing, and the drugs. Xavier, Benson, and other young men who have dropped out of school all receive unwanted police attention. Such encounters with police produce antagonistic relationships with yet another institution. Young people in the settlement of Blacksands are also routinely questioned by the police whenever there is a problem, and they have been routinely subjected to police violence (Mitchell, 2011). The disciplinary practices of the state are brought to bear on the young who are struggling with the effects of poverty and class differences in their everyday lives. Problematizing youth subjectivities and pathologizing the spaces they occupy are two strategies that define marginalization. The preceding examples from Blacksands and Borough suggest that the social and political processes of place making are "embodied practices that shape identities and enable resistance" (Gupta & Ferguson, 1997, p. 6). These youth practices are also essential to offset the marginality encoded in school experiences and the everyday unpredictability of living in marginal places that are themselves seen as failures.

Marginality and the Classroom in Borough

The recent report on "Education for All" by the UN Educational, Social, and Cultural Organization (2010, p. 9) maintains:

> Most governments are systematically failing to address the extreme and persistent education disadvantages that leave large sections of their population marginalized. These disadvantages are rooted in deeply ingrained social, economic and political processes and unequal power relationships—and they are sustained by practices within the classroom.

Discourses and practices about youth and education intersect in pedagogy. As Lesko (1996, p. 453) suggests, classroom practices are informed by teachers' views and definitions of youth and childhood, and these views determine the forms and levels of their involvement in the classroom. In both Blacksands and Borough, young people I know "ran away" from school because they found the classroom unbearably alienating. Truancy is often a response to an intolerable situation and represents an act of agency (Tilleczek, 2011). In Borough, some young people purposefully leave school to avoid further marginalization. This is evident when they leave school rather than be placed in the general class or non-academic stream when they fail exams. As Dawna explained, "*if you are in general (class) then people will think you are stupid and then it's all over.*" Many young people leave school rather than be regarded as "stupid" or rather than reveal their learning or their personal difficulties. All such revelations would only confirm other people's ideas that they are troubled and troubling. School, according to Norton, "*screws us over.*" Leaving school is easily done. Generally, students will not be allowed to return after 20 days of absence. This tactic is the easiest way to ease out of a tight situation and far more acceptable than conceding defeat by being placed in the general class. Henry, a young man from the Borough, explained that many of these young people believe "*[t]hey can go back to school next year or they can get their General Education Diploma (GED) or high school equivalency later on.*" Formal education is deferred rather than ended. However, Henry also observed: "*[m]any of them don't get their GEDs for it is way harder than school.*" While removing themselves from school and deferring their education are acts of agency, such actions may deepen their marginality in a number of ways. As explained, it brings them into closer contact with the police, and it ensures that their jobs will be menial and their pay minimal.

Marginality is not simply "located in a certain place" but "is set apart from and opposed to other places" (Gupta & Ferguson, 1997, p. 13). Young people from Borough have created a place for themselves at their high school as other student groups do. They habitually meet during breaks from class at a place they call "the corner," which is located at the edge of the parking lot of their school. While this meeting place at the edge of the school property marks the marginality they feel, it also provides a protective place for the Borough youth. Their "corner" distinguishes them from students belonging to other social and economic classes known as "preps" or "geeks" who occupy other places inside the school such as the stairs and the cafeteria. At their high school, young people from the Borough are referred to as "dirts" by the other students. As Gilbert told me, "*[k]ids from Borough are called "dirts" and I don't know why.*" The term encapsulates the marginality imposed on the youth from Borough at their school, setting them apart from others.

Not surprisingly, young people from Borough learn that schooling reinforces their class positions, which is evident in the assignment of categories such as dirts, geeks, preps, and so on. Teachers are not always aware or reflexive about their own class biases or those of the school. Jenna insists: "*The teachers hate us because we are not preps not good at school and not good at sports and they know we are from the Borough.*" Regarding teachers, Marian asks: "*Aren't they there to make things better?*" When young people routinely tell me that they want "*more encouragement from teachers,*" they are asking for a relational context in which to learn. Students from Borough also "*want more fun*" and "*to do more things outside the classroom.*" Such requests reveal their desire to learn, however subdued it is by their sense of failure in the school setting, and, at the same time, offer a critique of the existing programs. My experience in working with out-of-school youth on research projects in both Blacksands and Borough confirmed their capacity and interest in learning.

Inside and Outside: Spaces of Expertise

Spatial strategies and metaphors are salient to understanding educational experiences at various levels. I have been discussing young people and their settlements and schools, but I shall now turn to the formulation of educational programs where insiders and outsiders and local and global processes converge and increasingly conflict. In contemporary Vanuatu, one of the core problems in the ongoing development of the formal education system is the reliance on outside experts who do not understand the local culture and do not question their own biases (Niroa, 2004; Thaman, 2007). There is a tension between the local insider and the outside experts who invariably fail to consult with local people about what they know about learning and teaching. John Niroa (2004, p. 26) argues that "[t]he schooling system has been successful in marginalizing our local forms of education ignoring all the knowledge we have about ourselves." Thaman (2007, p. 8) confirms that in most of the donor-supported educational reforms and restructuring, consultation with people at the local levels is sidelined:

> Instead what happens is the wholesale importation of practices and values under the guise of human resource development, enlightenment, cash employment, good governance, human rights, freedom and democracy, etc. in the hope that at the end of the reform period, people will change.

Contemporary education in Vanuatu is shaped by its colonial past, global flows, and local factors, including a rapidly growing population, geographical distances, and extraordinary linguistic diversity that place enormous demands on the under-resourced government. Since independence in 1980, Vanuatu has invested in education, however, access to, and the quality of, education in rural areas remains problematic as it is in some urban settlements. Many young people have discontinued school because their families cannot afford the fees or, as earlier explained, students were "pushed out" at secondary level due to a shortage of spaces. Niroa (2004) argues that the system as it now stands benefits only a minority of students and "operates on the law of the survival of the fittest." He further argues that "[w]hen you systematically marginalize ... what is the majority of the students then you breed inequality, injustice and poverty that will threaten the security of all" (p. 28). The inequities of the education system that Vanuatu has inherited and maintained are particularly poignant in a place where egalitarianism is an important cultural value. Underlining its power, Niroa writes: "If we accept that schooling, as we know, is the greatest agent of change, we need to rethink its processes" (p. 27).

Corbett (2007, p. 63), in his insightful research on education in rural Nova Scotia, also draws attention to the effects of urban-centric education policies shaped by the expert knowledge of outsiders. There is, he argues, a conflict between the "institutional discourse of formal education" with its standardized curricula and the practices of place and personhood enacted by youth in their local communities. This tension, Corbett argues, shapes the identities, educational levels, and migration patterns of young rural people of maritime Canada. Corbett's analysis may be applied to understanding the structural changes that were undertaken in the late 1960s in Prince Edward Island when an expert-driven province-wide development plan was launched. This comprehensive development plan was designed to modernize the island and, not surprisingly, education was central to this plan. One of the aims of the plan was to widen access to secondary education by building regional rural high schools. This meant that young people from small communities did have better access to high school when they were bused from their farming and fishing communities into larger centres for high school. At the same time, new discourses of authority divorced from rural areas displaced rural knowledge and introduced marginality through social and spatial dislocation. Corbett (2007, p. 251) has suggested that "schooling is a quintessential institution of disembedding" and increasingly extracting social relationships from their local contexts and inflecting new spatial and temporal dimensions that link distant locations to local places. From his perspective in Vanuatu, Niroa (2004, p. 26) would agree with Corbett's contention that education invariably offers an urban-centric generalizing view of the world, which displaces local institutions and practices:

> The schooling process has ignored our local knowledge as legitimate parts of the education systems. This has led to the majority of school leavers to become failures, moreover the failures find fitting into their local settings hard, thereby making them double failures in two worlds.

While living in Vanuatu, I had time to think about Niroa's contention that these young people, in fact, had been set up to fail twice—in the competitive education system and in their inability to find places in their own society that is largely rural and agrarian. As noted, work for many in the new global order is narrow and punitive. While many of the urban migrants whom I knew in the settlement had come to town with the hopes of improving their children's opportunities in education, such efforts have often resulted in the displacement and deskilling of children. Katz (2004, p. 159) argues that in places as different as rural Sudan and the inner city of New York, young people are being "displaced from futures that have been reasonably secure just a generation earlier." She also argues that "it seemed ... that in both places, large segments of the generation currently coming of age were being derailed to a marginalized zone in which there were few guarantees for sustained—let alone meaningful—work as adults" (p. 1232).

Young people in Blacksands and Borough are constantly preoccupied with the problem of finding work and express disappointment in the failure of education to secure work. Today, in many places around the globe, the possibility for employment is constrained by capital's mobility, which tends "to produce more homogenized and narrow work landscapes locally" (Katz, 2004, p. 158). This scenario sums up the experience of many of the young people looking for work whom I met in Blacksands and Borough. As Philip from Port Vila put it, "*[g]ood work such as office work is only possible for you if have degrees and diplomas. So those who of us are only school leavers, if we're offered jobs we might just have to take them, even if we don't like them. This is because of the level of our education.*" As I have suggested in this chapter, many young people such as Philip have internalized the instrumental and urban-centric idea of education and of what constitutes "good work."

The links between the education of young people and migration, as noted at the outset of this chapter, are salient in understanding how education and globalization are linked. The search for educational opportunities fuels the global demographic shift from rural to urban areas. Internal migration to towns and immigration to other countries that have superior educational facilities are part of the contemporary global movements. Migration is propelled by people who believe that education will provide a means to improve the prospects of their children and their families by providing opportunities for wage- or government-sector employment. Many of the young people whom I met in the urban settlement in Vanuatu have the added burden of knowing that their parents have migrated and spent scarce money on educating them, hoping that their education would enhance wage earning in the family. Many youth have been unable to overcome the marginality they hoped to rewrite through migration for education.

Reconfiguring Marginality

The educational experiences of young people from Blacksands and Borough reveal the fault lines embedded in the universalizing and linear narratives of progressive development at the individual, institutional, and national levels. Attending to the structural constraints and complex practices of young people in two very different places suggest that the situation of young people and their imagined transitions to adulthood have been affected by the past, the current restructuring of the world economy and changing national agendas that resonate locally. In this chapter, I have made a case for considering the marginal spaces that young people experience in education in two very different places, for it unsettles the tendency to obscure uneven development here at home and to assume the inevitable underdevelopment of places such as Vanuatu.

The exercise allows us to rethink differences through connection. I have also pointed to the various tactics of place making through which young people have undermined their enforced marginality. For example, young people's interest in *kastomary* knowledge and practices in their urban settlements, which are far from their ancestral places, is a way of negotiating their everyday lives and displacing their "failure" in school and in the wage economy. There is a recognition that young people can lose their place or become displaced through their formal education—*kastomary* knowledge helps restore this sense of place. Their tactics are not a rejection of modernity but, rather, an alternative definition of what it means to be modern. Practices of modernity, like the everyday negotiations of the local, are better understood as being multiple rather than singular. Young people in Blacksands reclaim *kastomary* knowledge that privileges different kinds of subject formations and moral landscapes, while young people I knew in Borough rewrite marginality through various spatial strategies. Ideas of centre and margins continue to map youth experiences in both Blacksands and Borough, but people are actively resisting these spatial hierarchies.

If we track marginalized places, Vanuatu would certainly qualify by standard international measurements with its low per capita income and high levels of international aid. And, yet, when one moves away from such indicators and looks more closely at social institutions and cultural practices, Vanuatu is by no means marginal. This is the point Pacific educators Thaman and Niroa underline in their critique of the educational priorities and practices enforced by outside experts in the name of globalization and governance. Vanuatu, as noted earlier, has been described in cultural terms as a gift economy in which social relationships are privileged and a socio-centric view of self is cultivated. This way of becoming human has been contrasted with the individualism of the wage economy of capitalist societies where social relations are largely commodified and personhood is bounded. The core ideas of reciprocity and relationality ideally constitute human action and sociality in Vanuatu. With the gift economy, there is recognition that humans incur, accept, and repay social debts, and it is through these practices that places and persons are "made."

Mead (1928) put South Pacific youth on the map by drawing attention to the different cultural content and contexts of adolescence in Samoa and the United States. She travelled to the Island of Samoa in the 1920s to investigate if, in fact, adolescence was universally experienced as a time of "storm and stress," as leading American psychologist Stanley Hall had suggested. Mead's research showed the importance of understanding the specificity of local cultural practices rather than relying on universal and essentializing explanations to understand youth. Almost a hundred years later, we continue to have pressing questions to ask and hegemonic ideas to challenge about youth and their education.

While the West has long drawn on cultural differences to explicate or validate Western ideas, non-Western actors are often not recognized as equal partners in cultural and knowledge production (Ong, 1999, 1). What if we did recognize other partners and started to rethink education by drawing on the Pacific model of sociality encompassed in the gift economy? After all, we in the West have not just shared, but often imposed, our models of education and economy on Pacific islanders. Borrowing ideas from the gift economy suggests that education would not be confined to the dictates of shifting wage economies and commodified human relations. It would, instead, privilege relationality and reciprocity, which the young people whom I met want in their classrooms and in their communities. This would require imagining the education process in new ways and in new kinds of spaces. Recognizing youth as sites of agency and spaces of knowledge production, rather than as a problematic stage of linear development that consigns some youth to the margins, is important. Such a move would recognize, as Dawna says, that youth *"have things going on too."*

Notes

1 I conducted research in Vanuatu from January 1996 until June 1999. I have since returned four times for further research. The gender dimensions of marginality and education need far greater analysis than can be offered in this chapter.

2 These population figures are from the 2009 National Household Survey conducted by Vanuatu's national statistics office. Currently 40% of the population is under 15 years of age suggesting that education will remain an important issue.

References

Abu-Lughod, L. (1991). Writing against culture. In R. Fox (Ed.), *Recapturing anthropology* (pp. 137-162). Santa Fe, NM: School of American Research Press.

Appadurai, A. (1996). *Modernity at large: Cultural dimensions of globalization.* Minneapolis: University of Minnesota Press.

Bolton, L. (1999). Women, place and practice in Vanuatu: A view from Ambae. *Oceania 70*(1), 43-55.

Bonnemaison, J. (1985). The tree and the canoe: Roots and mobility in Vanuatu societies. *Pacific Viewpoint 26*(1), 30-62.

Bucholtz, M. (2002). Youth and cultural practice. *Annual Review of Anthropology, 31,* 5-52.

Corbett, M. (2007). *Learning to leave: The irony of schooling in a coastal community.* Halifax, NS: Fernwood.

De Certeau, M. (1984). *The practice of everyday life.* Berkeley, CA: University of California Press.

Escobar, A. (2001). Culture sits in places: Reflections on globalism and subaltern strategies of localization. *Political Geography, 20,* 139-174.

Gupta, A., & Ferguson, J. (1997). Culture beyond "culture": Space, identity and the politics of difference. In A. Gupta & J. Ferguson (Eds.), *Power and place: Explorations in critical anthropology* (pp. 33-51). Durham, NC: Duke University Press.

Haraway, D. J. (1988). Situated knowledges: The science question in feminism as a site of discourse on the privilege of partial perspective. *Feminist Studies, 14*(3), 575-599.

Hebidge, D. (1988). *Hiding in the light: On images and things.* London: Routledge.

Hull, G., Zacher, J., & Hibbert, L. (2009). Youth, risk and equity in a global world. *Review of Research in Education, 33*(1), 117-159.

Katz, C. (1998). Disintegrating developments: Global economic restructuring and the eroding ecologies of youth. In T. Skelton & G. Valentinen (Eds.), *Cool places: Geographies of youth cultures* (pp. 130-44). London: Routledge.

Jeffery, C., & McDowell, L. (2004). Youth in comparative perspective: Global changes, local lives. *Youth and Society, 36*(2), 131-142.

Lesko, N. (1996). Past, present, and future conceptions of adolescence. *Educational Theory, 46*(4), 238-262.

Lloyd, C. B. Behrman, J. R., Stromquist, N. P., & Cohen, B. (Eds.). (2005). *The changing transitions to adulthood in developing countries.* Washington, DC: National Academies Press.

Maira, S., & Soep, E. (2004). United states of adolescence?: Reconsidering US youth studies. *Nordic Journal of Youth Research 12(3)*, 245-269.

Massey, D. (1991). A global sense of place. *Marxism Today, 38,* 24-29.

Mead, M. (1928, reprinted 1992). *Coming of age in Samoa: A psychological study of primitive youth for Western civilization.* New York: Morrow.

Mitchell, J. (2003). "Killing time" in a postcolonial town: Young people and settlements in Port Vila, Vanuatu. In V. Lockwood (Ed.), *Globalization and culture change in the Pacific Islands* (pp. 358-376). Upper Saddle River, NJ: Prentice-Hall.

Mitchell, J. (2011). "Operation restore public hope": Youth and the magic of modernity in Vanuatu. *Oceania 81*(1), 36-50.

Mitchell, J., Vanuatu Young People's Project (1999). *Young people speak: A report on the Vanuatu young people's project, Vanuatu Cultural Centre, April 1997 to June 1998.* Port Vila, Vanuatu: Vanuatu Young People's Project.

Niroa, J. (2004). Why we need to rethink education in Vanuatu. In K. Sanga, J. Niroa, K. Matai, & L. Crowl (Eds.), *Re-thinking Vanuatu education together* (pp. 25-31). Vanuatu: Institute of Pacific Studies.

Ong, A. (1999). *Flexible citizenship: The cultural logics of transnationality.* Durham, NC: Duke University Press.

Spivak, G. (1985). Three women's texts and a critique of imperialism. *Critical Inquiry, 12*(1), 243-261.

Thaman, K. H. (2007). Education and globalization in Oceania. In L. Hufford & T. Pedrajas (Eds.), *Educating for a world view: Focus on globalizing curriculum and instruction* (pp. 1-14). Washington, DC: University of America Press.

Tilleczek, Kate. (2011). *Approaching youth studies: Being, becoming, and belonging.* Toronto: Oxford University Press.

Tsing, A. (2004). *Friction: An ethnography of global connections.* Princeton, NJ: Princeton University Press.

UN Educational, Social, and Cultural Organization. (2010). *Reaching the marginalized: EFA Global monitoring report.* Online: http://unesdoc.unesco.org/images/0018/001865/186525e.pdf.

On the Coast 2, photograph by Elliott Tilleczek

A Time for Dreams: The Right to Education for First Nations Children and Youth Living On-Reserve

Jennifer King, Chelsea Edwards, and Cindy Blackstock

First Nations schools in Canada receive approximately $2,000-3,000 less per student, per year for elementary and secondary education on-reserve (Council of Education Ministers [CMEC], 2010). Many First Nations schools are in deplorable condition, infested with mould, rats, snakes, or, as in the case of Attawapiskat First Nation, sitting atop a toxic site contaminated by thousands of gallons of diesel fuel (Office of the Parliamentary Budget Officer [PBO], 2009). Too often, First Nations families are forced to send their children to schools hundreds of miles away from home, either because there is no school in the community or because the existing school is so underfunded that youth do not have an equitable opportunity to succeed in post-secondary training or education. Being so far away from family at such a young age and with few supports puts youth at considerable risk, and it has resulted in a pattern of tragic death among First Nations students living in urban centres (Garrick, 2011).

These are not new or unknown issues (Auditor General of Canada 2000, 2004, 2011; PBO, 2009; Royal Commission on Aboriginal Peoples, 1996). The nature and impact of this discrimination is well documented, yet Canada continues to deny First Nations children and youth living on-reserve the right to equitable funding, "safe and comfy schools," and culturally based education. Canada's position seems to be that some children deserve less, simply because they are First Nations and simply because they live on-reserve (Blackstock, 2011a).

This chapter begins with the story of Shannen Koostachin, a 13-year-old Cree leader who challenged Canada to ensure "safe and comfy schools and equitable education" for all First Nations children and youth. We go on to describe the campaign named in her memory, highlighting a recent submission to the United Nations Committee on the Rights of the Child entitled *Our Dreams Matter Too* (First Nations Child and Family Caring Society of Canada [Caring Society] & Office of the Provincial Advocate for Children and Youth [Provincial Advocate], 2011). Grounded in this context, we go on to document the funding inequities experienced by First Nations children and youth living on-reserve, contrasting this picture against the international norms set out in the *United Nations Convention on the Rights of the Child* (*UNCRC*).[1] We argue that the inequities in education and other services for children and youth on-reserve amounts to racial discrimination by the government of Canada and that there is absolutely no excuse for this ongoing rights violation. Drawing on letters written by Aboriginal and non-Aboriginal children and youth, we discuss the impacts experienced by First Nations students on-reserve and close by offering a path forward rooted in collective action and meaningful reconciliation.

While the focus of this chapter is education, inequities in services for children and youth exist within the broader context of socio-economic conditions experienced by many First Nations living on-reserve. This injustice includes poverty arising from the economic development restrictions in the *Indian Act*, the lack of meaningful engagement by Canada with First Nations as distinct and self-determining peoples, the poor state of many homes on-reserve, and a lack of clean water, sanitation, and affordable healthy foods in some communities (First Nations Child and Family Caring Society, 2011).[2] These conditions are further compounded by the systemic, deliberate underfunding of education and other services (such as child welfare and health care) on-reserve, making it that much more difficult for children and youth to realize their dreams (Blackstock, 2011a).

Shannen's Story

Shannen Koostachin was a youth leader from Attawapiskat First Nation. Attawapiskat is a northern community on the James Bay coast in Ontario, 1,200 kilometres north of Toronto. The nearest road is 400 kilometres away. The first language in the community is Cree and the second language is English. Like most children and youth in the community, Shannen never went to a "proper" school. The elementary school in Attawapiskat, J.R. Nakogee Elementary, was closed the year Shannen started kindergarten due to a massive diesel fuel leak. The pipes beneath the school had been leaking for several decades, causing children and teachers to experience severe headaches, nausea, and nosebleeds. By the time the J.R. Nakogee Elementary was finally closed in the year 2000, the school grounds were contaminated by nearly 30,000 gallons of fuel (*Education is a right*, n.d.).

As a result of the closure, the children and youth of Attawapiskat have been going to elementary school in portables for more than ten years. The portables sit on the playground of the contaminated school and are so run-down that the windows do not close properly, the heat fails on a regular basis, and mice have infested the buildings. The portables were supposed to be a temporary solution, but, despite a decade of promises by three consecutive ministers representing the Department of Indian and Northern Affairs (INAC), Shannen finished her elementary school years without ever setting foot in a real school.

Shannen and her peers endured the portables for eight long years, and they wanted better for the next generation of children in Attawapiskat. They saw children in the community losing hope and dropping out by Grade 5 (Blackstock, 2011a). Shannen knew that the school conditions and inequities in education were not something non-Aboriginal children and youth were forced to endure, and it was simply not right that First Nations students had to suffer. She worked with other young people in Attawapiskat to launch the Attawapiskat School Campaign, inviting non-Aboriginal children and youth to join with First Nations students to demand a proper education. The campaign employed YouTube, Facebook, and the Web as communication media to ask children and youth to write to the government of Canada and demand a new school for Attawapiskat and other First Nations in need. Thousands answered the call (*Education is a right*, n.d.).

Halfway through Shannen's Grade 8 year, Attawapiskat received a letter from Chuck Strahl, then minister of the INAC, saying there would be no new school for the community. Shannen's class decided to cancel their graduation trip and use the funds to send three students, including Shannen, to Ottawa to personally ask the government of Canada for a new school. INAC Minister Chuck Strahl did meet with the youth but refused to give them a new school, saying his government could not afford it. Shannen told him that she did not believe him. She told the government that she would not give up the fight for a proper education because "school is a time for dreams and every kid deserves this."

Shannen was true to her word. She co-wrote a letter to the Canadian government saying that students from Attawapiskat would submit a report to the United Nations Committee on the Rights of the Child when Canada came up for review in 2011, to tell the world about the terrible schools and discrimination experienced by First Nations children and youth (Caring Society & Provincial Advocate, 2011). She spoke to union leaders, community groups, children, and youth, encouraging them to stand up for what is right. Shannen and her Attawapiskat peers co-hosted a human rights conference for 500 non-Aboriginal students in Toronto to inspire them to stand up for their rights and help ensure every child in Canada gets a proper education (foby101, 2008).

In 2008, Shannen was one of 45 children in the world to be nominated for the International Children's Peace Prize in recognition of her efforts to promote the cultural and education rights of First Nations children and youth in Canada. In the face of growing public pressure, Canada announced in December 2009 that it would begin negotiations for a new school in Attawapiskat. Tragically, Shannen Koostachin passed away six months after the announcement in a car accident, hundreds of miles away from her loving family. Like many First Nations youth, she was forced to leave her family at the age of 13 to attend an urban high school. Shannen loved her community but knew the secondary school in Attawapiskat was too under-resourced to offer the sort of education she needed to realize her dream of becoming a lawyer. Construction began on the new school in Attawapiskat in 2012 and is expected to be ready for the 2013-14 school year (Aboriginal Affairs and Northern Development Canada, 2012). However, there are more than 40 other First Nations communities needing new schools and another 29 awaiting urgent renovations (AFN, 2010).

Shannen's Dream

Shannen's legacy is one of unity, hope, and action.[3] Within hours of her passing, youth in Attawapiskat created a Facebook page called Shannen's Dream. They decided the best way to honour their hero was to ensure that Shannen's dream of "safe and comfy schools" and culturally based education would become a reality for all First Nations children and youth. The Shannen's Dream campaign calls on Canada to provide safe and comfy schools and culturally based, equitable education for all First Nations children and youth on-reserve. The campaign engages Aboriginal and non-Aboriginal children and caring adults to support Shannen's Dream via a Web-based petition, letter writing, rallies, marches, and other education and awareness-raising activities. Chelsea Edwards, a youth leader from Attawapiskat First Nation and spokesperson for Shannen's Dream, describes the campaign this way:

> Eleven years of broken promises, eleven years of negotiations. Yet, here we still stand waiting for our dreams to come true, waiting for what every child deserves. It's not just about my community Attawapiskat any more, it's about ALL children in Canada who have the right to a "safe and comfy school." Just like Rosa Parks as she started the civil rights movement, we have been sitting at the back of the school bus our entire lives. It was Shannen who rose and walked to the front of the bus, with the company of many children. The back was not a place where we wanted to be, where NO ONE should be. Shannen's Dream is now the biggest movement for children by children in Canadian history. To ensure that equitable funding, proper resources and facilities are accessible to children, right where

they are. Then please join hands with us in solidarity, as we make sure that every child has equal rights as any other Canadian citizen. Be sure to sign the online petition at http://www.shannensdream.ca. Meegwetch!

Shannen's Dream is now supported by over 5,450 children, organizations, and adults (Shannen's Dream, 2011). They carry her dream forward.

Our Dreams Matter Too

In 2011, First Nations youth fulfilled Shannen's promise by submitting an alternate report to the United Nations Committee on the Rights of the Child on the occasion of Canada's third- and fourth-period review. Entitled *Our Dreams Matter Too*, the report presents a series of letters from children describing the impacts of discrimination in education and calls on the committee to investigate Canada's ongoing and systemic breaches of children's rights, as experienced by First Nations children and youth living on-reserve (Caring Society & Provincial Advocate, 2011).

Throughout this chapter, we share excerpts from letters written by Aboriginal and non-Aboriginal children and youth in support of Shannen's Dream. Letters from First Nations children and youth, many of which also appear in *Our Dreams Matter Too*, emphasize the importance of culturally based education, especially the desire to learn and preserve their Indigenous languages. They also share feelings of disappointment and frustration. First Nations children and youth know that their schools are very different from those off-reserve. Such questions of fairness and equality are echoed in letters written by non-Aboriginal children and youth. Together, these letters point to several key themes—a two-tiered education system, children's rights, Canada's priorities, impacts of educational apartheid, and the true meaning of reconciliation—which inform the organization of this chapter. Their words ground us as we explore the sometimes abstract world of funding models, human rights regimes, and government double-speak. Indeed, their letters draw attention to truths that adult eyes may prefer not to see.

Canada's Two-Tiered Education System

> Most people think that if you live in Canada you automatically have an education, but that's not true. (Jasmine, Ontario)

The story of children and youth in Attawapiskat First Nation is not unique. Conditions in some First Nations schools rival that of the world's most desperate countries. Why does this injustice continue to happen? The answer lies with Canada's federal government. While provincial legislation and standards apply on-reserve, the federal government is responsible for funding services in First Nations communities, including education. When the federal government chooses to fund services at a lesser level (or, in some cases, not at all), the provinces/territories typically do not "top up" the difference, resulting in a two-tiered system where First Nations kids living on-reserve receive less than other children and youth in Canada (Blackstock, 2011a). Less funding means fewer services and, therefore, less benefit and opportunity for First Nations kids.

> A long time ago our ancestors made a "treaty" with the white people that included education. Now, the government doesn't give us the same amount of money as the others, they give us less. To me, I think this is Racism, It's not fair that we get less money. So it's about time someone stood up and brought up the past about the treaty. We are going to fight for this. We need our education. (Christa, Kitigan Zibi Anishinabeg)

The inequities experienced by First Nations students on-reserve are well documented by a variety of sources (AFN, 2010, 2011; Auditor General of Canada, 2000, 2004, 2011; Blackstock, 2011a; Caring Society & Provincial Advocate, 2011; First Nations Education Council [FNEC], 2009; PBO, 2009). Indeed, this chapter relies heavily on Canada's own reports to demonstrate that the federal government not only knows about the discrimination experienced by First Nations children and youth but also has made a conscious and deliberate decision not to address it. First Nation communities must meet provincial/territorial standards, but they must do so with less money and in the face of greater need. There are two factors that drive the inequality: the child/youth must be First Nations and must live on-reserve (Blackstock, 2011a). Let us be clear, this is a form of inequality not experienced by other children or youth in Canada. It is discrimination based on identity and place and is specific to First Nations living on-reserve.

> For grade 7, I had went to a city school and they had lots of resources. Science labs, better gym equipment, more library books and better, bigger lockers. It is unfair that we do not have these resources in our school, and as children of Canada we deserve good resources too. Children are the future, but we cannot succeed in the future if we don't have the same learning resources as other children. And because of that, some children have to change schools and go off-reserve. (Braxton, Enoch Cree Nation)

In contrast to provincial/territorial funding for education, which has undergone major reforms in the last 20 years, funding for First Nations education is based on a national formula developed in 1987 and last updated for population and living costs in 1996 (FNEC, 2009). Estimates suggest that First Nations schools receive $2,000-3,000 less per student, per year, for education on-reserve (AFN, 2009, as cited in CMEC, 2010; AFN, 2010, 2011). This amount means less money for books, supplies, equipment, and teacher salaries. Unlike schools funded by the provinces/territories, First Nations schools receive no funding for basic resources such as libraries, computers, and software, extracurricular activities, teacher training, or principles. First Nations students receive no core funding for special education or school boards and no funding to support the preservation and revitalization of First Nations languages or for the development of culturally appropriate curriculum (AFN, 2010; Blackstock, 2011a).

> The lack of funding is a concern, the lack of resources is a concern, but the lack of cultural content in our school is the biggest concern for me. If we had more funding, there would be more possibilities to include cultural activities. If we had a better sense of culture, we would be more confident, which would lead to success in life ... I've been in Algonquin immersion up to grade 6 for the afternoons every day at school, earnestly trying to learn my language and culture and then, there was suddenly nothing. There was no more option for me to take classes that offered me teachings of my culture and language because the school didn't have the money to pay for another teacher. (Wesley, Kitigan Zibi Anishinabeg)

These shortfalls are compounded by a lack of funding for school infrastructure, called capital expenditure. Capital expenditure refers to money set aside for new schools as well as replacing and rebuilding existing infrastructure. In 2009, the Office of the Parliamentary Budget Officer (PBO) reported significant underfunding in the INAC's capital expenditure for First Nations schools on-reserve. As stated in the PBO's report, "[the] INAC's plans for capital expenditure are underfunded to the tune of between $169 million in the best case, and $189 million in the worst-case scenario, annually" (PBO, 2009, p. 12). The PBO also reported shortfalls in funding for the operation and maintenance of First Nations schools, to the tune of $11 million per year.

> If I was an adult, and I was a builder, I would build a school for them.
> (Griffin, Timiskaming First Nation)

It is important to note that although First Nations schools are obligated to meet provincial/territorial standards, students on-reserve are not protected by the same legislative guarantees that regulate other schools in Canada. In provincial/territorial schools, students are protected by legislation governing everything from classroom size to the quality of school buildings, from teacher-student ratios to special education (Caring Society & Provincial Advocate, 2011). These protections do not exist for First Nations students living on-reserve.

> I have a great school, it has a computer lab, a gym, a yard, and pencils. Why do we have great schools, but people in Aboriginal communities hardly have any schools? I think it is unfair. Kids are the future, so if Canada keeps being racist there will be more problems. (Ari, Ontario)

Canada's response when confronted with the aforementioned discrimination and inequality is generally one of excuses and misdirection. For instance, the federal government contends that it spends about the same amount per student, per year as the provinces/territories (Goyette, 2010). In fact, a big chunk of the money allocated for "First Nations education" actually goes to provincial and federal schools, as tuition for First Nations students studying off-reserve. As a result of this and other external allocations, the amount of money "left-over" for children and youth going to school on-reserve falls well below the national average (FNEC, 2009; Goyette, 2010). As Blackstock (2011a, p. 10) observes, "Canada will often cite how much it spends on First Nations children without drawing attention to the fact that this amount falls far short of what is required."

> I am glad I have a school. Imagine that when you were a kid and you didn't have a school, you probably wouldn't be prime minister right now. The kids in Attawapiskat don't have a proper school, if you gave them one when they grow up they could take your place. They are just as good as you, but you actually have a proper education in which you probably learned about not treating others unfair, which is exactly what you are doing. Well, not just you but all the governments in Canadian history and this is your chance to fix it! (Rowan, Ontario)

Education for First Nations Children On-Reserve: A Time for Dreams?

> Shannen asked for a school. The government didn't listen. This is a hard letter for me to write. (Harry, Ontario)

What does underfunding mean for First Nations kids going to school on-reserve? For students in one Manitoba community, it means going to school in portable trailers because the school's pipes are infested with snakes. Underfunding means starting the school year in tents. It means going to school in shifts because the available school buildings are too small and overcrowded for all students to attend at the same time (Blackstock, 2011a). In the Lubicon Cree community of Little Buffalo, underfunding means checking to see if the red light above the pumphouse is flashing. A flashing red light means the pumphouse is out of water and that the school is likely closed. The only running water in Little Buffalo is in the school, and even this water is neither clean nor reliable (Amnesty International Canada, 2011).

> Our schools are so run down that they are hardly functionable. They close down at least 2 to 4 times a month! Most parents don't even want to send their kids to school here anymore ... And some years we can't even get a Cree teacher, which makes us unable to even learn that! ... Sadly I feel like half of

our kids will drop out in high school because of lack of education.
(Justice, Enoch Cree Nation)

In addition to these issues, other health concerns include extreme mould, high carbon dioxide levels, sewage fumes in the schools, frozen pipes, and unheated portables with students suffering from cold and frost bite. In some instances, conditions are so bad that communities have no choice but to simply abandon the school building entirely, despite a lack of alternative infrastructure (AFN, 2010). According to the PBO (2009), there are 803 First Nations schools across Canada, ten of which are listed as "closed." Seventy-seven of the schools are listed as "temporary structures" or "portables." Less than half (approximately 49%) of the 803 schools are in "good" condition (PBO, 2009).

> *Imagine if your kids were in the portables or you were in a portable or Canada was in portables, how would you feel? Why don't you give First Nations children appropriate schools, but you give us a school? We need to treat everyone equally.* (Henry, Ontario)

In too many cases, funding inequities force youth to leave the community to pursue a proper education—either because there is no school in their community or because underfunding makes it impossible for schools to offer the sort of education and opportunities available off-reserve. This is especially true for high school students. As a result, First Nations youth may find themselves in a new and unfamiliar environment without an adequate network of support. The consequences of this scenario can be tragic. In Ontario alone, seven First Nations students have passed away since the year 2000 while attending high school outside of their communities. All were citizens of the Nishnawbe Aski Nation (NAN), who were studying hundreds of miles away from home in Thunder Bay (Garrick, 2011).

A Rights-Based Approach to Education

> *[T]his is a children's right, therefore this should not be a problem.*
> (Jack, Ontario)

Underfunding of education on-reserve constitutes discrimination under multiple international human rights instruments, including the *International Convention on the Elimination of All Forms of Racial Discrimination* (1965), the *International Covenant on Civil and Political Rights* (1966), the *International Covenant on Economic, Social and Cultural Rights* (1966), the *UNCRC* (1989), and the *Declaration on the Rights of Indigenous Peoples* (2007).[4] As this chapter is guided by the voices of children and youth, our focus is on discrimination as it relates to the *UNCRC*. The *UNCRC* defines "children" as all persons below the age of 18 years. This definition means that the rights set out in the convention also apply to a significant portion of the youth population, including most high school students. In this context, references to children and children's rights must be understood as encompassing not just the very young but also all those under the age of 18.

Non-discrimination is a pillar of the *UNCRC*. Article 2 of the convention obligates state parties to ensure the rights of every child within its jurisdiction, without discrimination. This includes the right to education, as set out in Articles 28 and 29. While "discrimination" is not explicitly defined, the term is generally understood to imply any distinction, exclusion, restriction, or preference based on race, colour, sex, language, or any of the characteristics set out in Article 2 (Hodgkin & Newell, 2007; United Nations Human Rights Committee [HRC], 1989). States have a responsibility to ensure that Indigenous children enjoy their rights under the convention on "equal level with other children" (United Nations Committee on the Rights of the Child [CRC], 2009).[5]

That said, the principle of non-discrimination should not be taken to imply "sameness." As noted by the Committee on the Rights of the Child (CRC) (2009, para. 5 [emphasis added]), "[t]he specific references to indigenous children in the Convention are indicative of the recognition that they require *special measures* in order to fully enjoy their rights." States are obligated to ensure that the services and benefits received by Indigenous children are equal to those of other children. However, beyond this effort, states also have a responsibility to ensure the equity of Indigenous children within their borders. Equity means looking at outcomes and identifying what is needed to ensure equal opportunity and a chance for success, including additional resources as required.

> *Our language has a great affect on us. It has an effect on our Spirit, which makes us proud people and a proud nation ... We will continue our traditions and celebrate life as it goes by every day. We are unique and we are proud of who we are.* (Katina, Kitigan Zibi Anishinabeg)

> *I think learning about my culture is important. My mosom (grandfather) teaches me about sundances and talking Cree. I've been to round dances, feasts, and pow-wows. They are fun to go to. I feel good because I see my family and elders. In school, we learn these things in Cree class. We also learn Cree in a Grade 2 class. My culture is important to me.* (Owen, Saulteaux First Nation)

First Nations children should have the same opportunity to succeed as other children in Canada, but in ways that honour their distinct rights, cultures, and languages. Indeed, the right to culture, language, and identity is core to the UNCRC. Article 30, for instance, highlights the right of Indigenous children to use their own language. As stated by the CRC (2009, para. 62 [emphasis added]), "[i]n order to implement this right, *education in the child's own language is essential.*" Yet as described earlier, current federal funding models do not provide any money for the perseveration of Indigenous languages or the development of culturally appropriate curriculum.

> *Why do I need to have learned somebody else's language and not my own in order to receive my diploma while attending a native school??? Why am I expected to meet the province's expectations for high school when we're not treated like the other schools in the province? Why aren't we learning OUR LANGUAGE??? In order to be successful in life, we have to be proud of who we are. In order to be proud of who we are, we have to know and understand who we are. We need more opportunities and resources to do so.*
> (River, Kitigan Zibi Anishinabeg)

Canada has a responsibility to implement measures that ensure the right to education is realized in a manner consistent with the UNCRC. For First Nations, this responsibility includes equitable funding for students on-reserve as well as the flexibility and resources for communities to develop and implement culturally based curriculum and language programs. It also means a willingness to explore creative solutions, such as long distance education programs (CRC, 2009). Such measures are critical in light of the tragedies experienced in Ontario. No child, parent, family, or community should have to weigh the right to education against the right to community, culture, and safety.

A Question of Priorities

> *We would like you to ask the Government of Canada why there are no schools in many of our communities and why the level of funding we receive for education is less compared to communities in other parts of Ontario and Canada. We also want to know why we have to fight so hard for what our peers in other parts of Canada are able to take for granted.* (Youth Team, Shannen's Dream Campaign)

Rather than embrace its responsibilities under the *UNCRC*, Canada has made a point of asserting that human rights instruments, such as the *UNCRC*, are not directly enforceable under Canadian law. Canada's response to the multiple rights violations experienced by First Nations children and youth on-reserve has been to hide behind legal technicalities (Blackstock, 2011a), while citing supposed budget constraints and other barriers to implementation. When youth from Attawapiskat met with the INAC's minster in 2008, they were told that Canada "didn't have the money" for a new school (foby101, 2008). The youth of Attawapiskat "didn't believe that a country as rich as Canada couldn't afford to build a school for children who had gone 8 years on a poisoned school ground" (Caring Society & Provincial Advocate, 2011). We do not believe it either.

> *Please don't build diamond mines, build schools because people are more important than diamonds.* (Serena, Ontario)

Canada has said that it cannot afford equity for First Nations children and youth on-reserve. We argue that it is not a question of money but, rather, a question of priorities. In truth, Canada is one of the wealthiest countries in the world, fully capable of implementing the *UNCRC* in a real and meaningful way. At the time when Shannen Koostachin and her peers visited then-Minister Chuck Strahl, Canada had a budget surplus of $20 billion (Caring Society & Provincial Advocate, 2011). This fact raises questions about how Canada chooses to allocate its resources as well as the transparency in government spending. The PBO's report (2009) on First Nations schools found the INAC's past spending on both capital expenditures and operating and maintenance to be much lower than budgeted. Between 2002 and 2008, about $121 million earmarked for capital expenditure and operating and maintenance was "diverted" or "reallocated" to other programs, amounting to a shortfall of about $20 million per year (PBO, 2009).

> *How am I supposed to appreciate these luxuries like gym, computers, and field trips when aboriginal children don't even have schools to go to? ... The charter of rights clearly states that every Canadian has the right to a proper education. They're citizens too, aren't they? ... Some of these kids could grow up to become lawyers or doctors, but we are depriving them of the chance to be the people who they really could be.* (Zoë, Ontario)

The PBO's report (2009) highlights a lack of visibility in the INAC's financial reporting. Canada's Parliament allocates a certain amount of money for First Nations education, but there are no set guidelines or requirements around how much of this money should go towards school infrastructure. It is left to the INAC to estimate the necessary expenditures and allocate monies accordingly (PBO, 2009). This lack of transparency enables the department to shuffle monies away from school infrastructure in favour of other "priorities," as defined by the INAC. First Nations generally have no control or influence over this process. In the words of the children and youth of Attawapiskat, "our community has to live at the whims of the Department of Indian Affairs" (Caring Society & Provincial Advocate, 2011, p. 15).

> *It's not fair that we don't have the same amount of money like the other schools near our community. We want to learn as much as them. Why should it be different? We have dreams and we want to realize them.*

Without this funding, some of us won't make it to college or university.
We need an education to succeed in life. (Jeremy, Kitigan Zibi Anishinabeg)

So how does Canada choose to spend departmental money? Research appears to be a popular option. Aboriginal peoples are the most researched people on earth, and issues of education are no exception (Ormiston, 2010). While research is necessary to inform good policy and decision making, especially with regard to children and youth, it can also be used as an excuse to avoid taking action. Policy-makers will often call for more research even when there is sufficient evidence to take meaningful steps (Blackstock, 2011c). According to the Auditor General of Canada (2000), at least 22 studies concerning First Nations education were carried out between 1991 and 1999 with the INAC's knowledge or involvement—in one department region alone. In 2004, the Auditor General of Canada noted what while the INAC had carried out more studies, little substantive progress had been made. In fact, the time estimated to close the education gap between First Nations living on-reserve and the Canadian population had actually increased slightly, from about 27 to 28 years (Auditor General of Canada, 2004).

All kids need good, fun, safe schools please. The Aboriginal kids need every-
thing we need. All kids are the same. Why don't you give nice schools to all
kids? (Zoe, Ontario)

At the core, equity for First Nations children and youth on-reserve is not an issue of money or budget surpluses. It is about how Canada chooses to allocate its resources. Canada has money for tax breaks and prisons. It has money for military spending and overseas development projects, including millions of dollars for schools in Afghanistan (Goyette, 2010). While we recognize that education is a right of every child, in every country, it seems incongruous that Canada would commit to spending millions of dollars to build schools in another country, while children and youth within its own borders are languishing in portables, without heat or clean water, and dealing with contaminated land and extreme mould.

The Impact of Educational Apartheid

It's hard to feel you can have the chance to grow up somebody important
when you don't have proper resources like libraries and science labs. That's
why some of our students begin to give up in grade four and five. They just
stop going to school. (Shannen Koostashin, speaking at a youth conference
in Toronto, Ontario, in 2008)

In 2008, the Ontario Secondary School Teachers Federation published an article in its newsletter entitled "Education is a right not a privilege unless you are a

First Nations child." The article went on to say that "two standards of education exist in Canada and that a situation of Educational apartheid exists in Canada" (Caring Society & Provincial Advocate, 2011, p. 16). Indeed, as the word apartheid suggests, Canada's treatment of First Nations kids sends a certain message. Canada continues to deny equitable funding, "safe and comfy schools," and culturally based education for First Nations children and youth living on-reserve. Over time, justifications such as "we don't have the money" or "just wait a little longer" begin to sound like "you are not as important as other kids" or "you are not as valued." It creates feelings of hopelessness, frustration, and disappointment.

> To me a good education means a promise to a better future, a life to call my own instead of constantly having to struggle to keep my head above the waters of doubt, insecurities and the pressure of drugs closing in on our community. When I see the state of some of our community members, it hurts a lot knowing that they had that right to a good education that they didn't receive ... Without proper education, what is there to look forward to in life? (Jasmin, Timiskaming First Nation)

According to the Auditor General of Canada (2011), only 41% of First Nations youth, ages 15 and older living on-reserve, graduate from high school, compared to 77% of Canadians as a whole. There are also differences in educational attainment between First Nations living on- and off-reserve. The 2006 Census found that First Nations living off-reserve were more likely to graduate from high school and obtain a college diploma or university degree than those living on-reserve (Statistics Canada, 2008). We argue that the lower graduation rate among First Nations youth is directly related to the underfunding of education on-reserve. It is difficult, not to mention demoralizing, to learn in overcrowded schools, which are located on contaminated land and infested with black mould, mice, and snakes, without books, computers, or equipment.

> We work hard to try and make sure our education is at the level of the white boys and girls. What you give us will affect the rest of our lives and indicate the direction of our futures. As an individual, I am scared for my own education and how my life that's ahead of me is going to be like, if I don't qualify to get into college. Life for us will gradually get worse, as yours gets easier, and that's not fair. We deserve better, much, much better. (Vicky, Kitigan Zibi Anishinabeg)

Moving Forward: Reconciliation Means Not Saying Sorry Twice

> They apologized to us once for doing wrong, and they're putting themselves in the same position to come right back and apologize to us again. (Jordan, Kitigan Zibi Anishinabeg)

The ongoing discrimination against First Nations children and youth is particularly troubling in light of Canada's recent (2008) apology for harms experienced by Aboriginal peoples during the residential school era. As Blackstock
(2009; 2011b) has written, reconciliation means not saying sorry twice. Yet
First Nations children and youth continue to experience inequitable treatment, policies of discrimination, fewer services, and fewer benefits. Inequities
in education undermine the potential of thousands of First Nations kids living
on-reserve, violating not only their right to a proper education but also their
right to grow up proud of who they are and strong in their language and culture.
Indeed, Canada's treatment of First Nations children and youth constitutes so
many rights violations that it may seem difficult to know where, or how, to
move forward. In fact, the answers are quite clear.

Simply put, discrimination against First Nations children and youth is not
a legitimate fiscal restraint measure. For too long, the federal government has
said "no" to First Nations kids or "you get less" or "you'll have to wait"—not
because Canada lacks the necessary resources but, rather, because discrimination is an effective way to save money. Measures to protect culture and language
in education are not unprecedented in Canada—a similar system exists in
Quebec to protect the rights of francophone children. The right to education
is enshrined in treaties between First Nations and the Crown, the Canadian
Constitution, and numerous international human rights instruments. First
Nations people on-reserve seek only that which is available to all other child
and youth in Canada: proper schools and equitable services.

> To me a good education means having a good school, keeping children's
> dreams help up high, letting them know they need a good education to go
> where they want to go in life and making them proud in what they do!
> (Victoria, Timiskaming First Nation)

Moving forward, we must remember our power as individuals and as collec-
tives, as children, youth, and adults, as Aboriginal peoples, and as allied
Canadians. Former Auditor General of Canada Sheila Fraser tabled numerous
reports detailing the inequities and discrimination experienced by Aboriginal
peoples, and First Nations children in particular (Auditor General of Canada,
2000, 2004, 2008, 2011). Yet when faced with the question of "what can be
done," Fraser pointed not to further studies or investigation but, rather, to
awareness and political pressure (Canada, 2009). As Fraser described, political
pressure means calling on Canada to answer for the inequities experienced by
First Nations children and youth. It means asking what the government is planning to do about the situation and holding Canada responsible for its obliga-
tions and commitments. We encourage teachers to raise these issues in their

classrooms and to provide opportunity for children and youth to respond to the discrimination experienced by First Nations in Canada. Readers are also asked to join the Shannen's Dream movement at http://www.shannensdream .ca. Reports and promises are not enough. Canada must be held accountable.[6]

> *I am writing to tell you we shouldn't have to fight for our rights. So give us equal money please! You are pretty mean if you're supposed to help children but if you don't help children, you're just going to make them bug, bug, and bug you! So you better!!! Thank you for reading my letter. I'm anxious to see some changes VERY SOON!* (Connor, Timiskaming First Nation)

Making Shannen's Dream a Reality

Shannen Koostachin wanted you to know that First Nations children and youth across Canada have dreams. They dream of becoming doctors, teachers, grass dancers, engineers, cooks, producers, and other things. She wanted you to know that First Nations children and youth want to be successful people who help make their communities stronger (Caring Society & Provincial Advocate, 2011). We write this chapter in an effort to share Shannen's story—now we ask you to help make her dream a reality. Aboriginal pedagogies hold that stories have power; they will change you if you let them. Stories also come with a certain responsibility. As storyteller Thomas King (2003, p. 60) has said, "Don't say in the years to come that you would have lived your life differently if you only you had heard this story. You've heard it now." But, this is not the end of the story. Aboriginal and non-Aboriginal children and youth are fighting to tell a new story about First Nations education in Canada. What story will their story say about you?

Notes

1 *United Nations Convention on the Rights of the Child*, signed at New York, 20 November 1989, UNTS 1577 (1990), pp. 3-178, online: http://treaties.un.org/Pages/ViewDetails .aspx?src=TREATY&mtdsg_no=IV-11&chapter=4&lang=en, which defines "children" as all persons below the age of 18 years. Under this definition, the rights set out in the convention also apply to a significant portion of the youth population, including most secondary school students.

2 *Indian Act*, R.S.C., 1985, c. I-5, online: http://laws-lois.justice.gc.ca/eng/acts/I-5/ FullText.html.

3 Shannen's Dream, online: http://www.shannensdream.ca.

4 *International Convention on the Elimination of All Forms of Racial Discrimination*, 7 March 1966, UNTS 660 (1969), pp. 195-318, online: http://treaties.un.org/pages/ ViewDetails.aspx?src=TREATY&mtdsg_no=IV-2&chapter=4&lang=en; *International Covenant on Civil and Political Rights*, 16 December 1966, UNTS 999 (1976) pp. 171-348, online: http://treaties.un.org/Pages/ViewDetails.aspx?src=TREATY

&mtdsg_no=IV-4&chapter=4&lang=en; *International Covenant on Economic, Social and Cultural Rights*, 16 December 1966, UNTS 993 (1976), pp. 3-106, online: http://treaties.un.org/Pages/ViewDetails.aspx?src=TREATY&mtdsg_no=IV -3&chapter=4&lang=en; and *Declaration on the Rights of Indigenous Peoples*, Doc A/RES/61/295 (13 September2007), online: http://www.un-documents.net/a61r295 .htm.

5 Canada uses the term "Aboriginal" to refer to the distinct First Nations, Métis, and Inuit peoples within its borders. The international community, however, refers to Aboriginal and other First Nations peoples as "Indigenous peoples."

6 On 27 February 2012, a private member's motion supporting Shannen's Dream was unanimously adopted by the House of Commons. The motion declares that "all First Nation children have an equal right to high-quality, culturally-relevant education" (*House of Commons Debates*, 2012). It remains to be seen whether this motion will lead to meaningful change for First Nations children.

References

Aboriginal Affairs and Northern Development Canada. (2012). Minister Duncan and Attawapiskat First Nation announce awarding of construction contract for Attawapiskat First Nation's new school (News release). 6 March. Online: http://www.aadnc-aandc.gc.ca/eng/1331042853001.

Amnesty International Canada. (2011). A new video by Lubicon youth shows what it is like to live without clean running water (News release). 22 March. Online: http://www.amnesty.ca/media2010.php?DocID=416.

Assembly of First Nations (AFN). (2010). *Some children in Canada are receiving a lower standard of education than others. Why?* (Brochure). Ottawa: AFN.

Assembly of First Nations (AFN). (2011). *It's our time: A call to action on education. A year in review 2010-2011*. Ottawa: AFN.

Auditor General of Canada. (2000). *Indian and Northern Affairs Canada: Elementary and secondary education* (2000). Online: http://www.oag-bvg.gc.ca/internet/English/parl_oag_200004_04_e_11191.html.

Auditor General of Canada. (2004). *Indian and Northern Affairs Canada: Education program and post-secondary student support*. Online: http://www.oag-bvg.gc.ca/internet/English/parl_oag_200411_05_e_14909.html.

Auditor General of Canada. (2008). *First Nations child and family services program: Indian and Northern Affairs Canada*. Online: http://www.oag-bvg.gc.ca/internet/English/parl_oag_200805_04_e_30700.html.

Auditor General of Canada. (2011). *Programs for First Nations on reserves*. Online: http://www.oag-bvg.gc.ca/internet/English/parl_oag_201106_04_e_35372.html.

Blackstock, C. (2009). The occasional evil of angels: Learning from the experiences of Aboriginal peoples and social work. *First Peoples Child and Family Review, 4*(1), 28-37.

Blackstock, C. (2011a). *Jordan & Shannen: First Nations children demand that the Canadian government stop racially discriminating against them* (Shadow report: Canada third and fourth periodic report to the UNCRC). Ottawa: First Nations Child and Family Caring Society of Canada.

Blackstock, C. (2011b). The Canadian Human Rights Tribunal on First Nations child welfare: Why if Canada wins, equality and justice lose. *Children and Youth Services Review, 33*(1), 187-194.

Blackstock, C. (2011c). Wanted: Moral courage in Canadian child welfare. *First Peoples Child and Family Review 6*(2), 35-46.

Canada. (2009). *Proceedings of the Standing Senate Committee on Aboriginal Peoples* (Issue Brief no. 20). Online: http://www.parl.gc.ca/Content/SEN/Committee/402/abor/20evb-e.htm?Language=E&Parl=40&Ses=2&comm_id=1.

Council of Ministers of Education, Canada (CMEC). (2010). *Strengthening Aboriginal success: Summary report* (CMEC summit on Aboriginal education, 24-25 February 2009). Online: http://www.cmec.ca/Publications/Lists/Publications/Attachments/221/aboriginal_summit_report.pdf.

Education is a right: Fighting for Attawapiskat (n.d.). Online: http://www.attawapiskat-school.com/Home.html.

First Nations Child and Family Caring Society of Canada. (2011). Letter demanding equity for First Nations children in an open letter to all political party leaders. Online: http://www.fncaringsociety.com/sites/default/files/docs/OpenLettertoGovernment-April1-2011.pdf.

First Nations Child and Family Caring Society of Canada (Caring Society) & Office of the Provincial Advocate for Children and Youth (Provincial Advocate). (2011). *Our dreams matter too: First Nations children's rights, lives, and education* (An alternate report from the Shannen's Dream Campaign to the United Nations Committee on the Rights of the Child on the occasion of Canada's third and fourth periodic reviews). Toronto: Office of the Provincial Advocate for Children and Youth.

First Nations Education Council (FNEC). (2009). *Paper on First Nations education funding*. Ottawa: FNEC.

foby101. (2008). *Shannen Koostachin: Attawapiskat youth forum* (Video file). 8 November. Online: http://www.youtube.com/watch?v=shXKTTKsZt0.

Garrick, R. (2011). Family can find closure after Wabasse laid to rest. *Wawatay News.* Online: http://www.wawataynews.ca/archive/all/2011/5/26/family-can-find-closure-after-wabasse-laid-rest_21471.

Goyette, L. (2010). Still waiting. *Canadian Geographic, 130*(6), 48-64.

Hodgkin, R., & Newell, P. (2007). *Implementation handbook for the Convention on the Rights of the Child* (fully revised, 3rd edition). New York: UN Children's Fund.

House of Commons Debates. 41st Parl., 1st Sess. No 84 (27 February 2012). Online: http://www.parl.gc.ca/HousePublications/Publication.aspx?Language=E&Mode=1&Parl=41&Se%20s=1&DocId=5401022.

King, T. (2003). *The truth about stories: A Native narrative.* Toronto: House of Anansi Press.

Office of the Parliamentary Budget Officer (PBO). (2009). *The funding requirement for First Nations schools in Canada.* Ottawa: PBO.

Ormiston, T. (2010). Re-conceptualizing research: An Indigenous perspective. *First Peoples Child and Family Review, 5*(1), 50-56.

Royal Commission on Aboriginal Peoples. (1996). *Report of the Royal Commission on Aboriginal Peoples.* Ottawa: Indian and Northern Affairs Canada.

Shannen's Dream. (2011). Online: http://www.shannensdream.ca.

Statistics Canada. (2008). *Educational portrait of Canada, 2006 census.* Catalogue no. 97-560-X. Ottawa: Minister of Industry.

United Nations Committee on the Rights of the Child (CRC). (2009). *Indigenous children and their rights under the convention* (50th Session, General Comment no. 11). Online: http://www2.ohchr.org/english/bodies/crc/docs/GC.11_indigenous_New .pdf.

United Nations Human Rights Committee (HRC). (1989). *Non-discrimination* (37th Session, General Comment no. 18). Online: http://www.unhchr.ch/tbs/doc.nsf/0/ 3888b0541f8501c9c12563ed004b8d0e?Opendocument.

The Blue Bliss, a painting by Angel Ho

chapter 6

Marginalization Inside Education: Racialized, Immigrant, and Aboriginal Youth

Joanna Anneke Rummens and George J. Sefa Dei

Youth Marginalization and Its Discontents

> *It means to me that they're kids whom the system has failed and it has turned them off of school ... because ... when you look at the kids who are dropouts and they turn around and do something and then succeed at it, it means that they had the capability but it was not tapped ... If the system had provided the necessary nurturing for those kids, they would have made it.* (Marilyn, Afro-Canadian mother)[1]

We cannot discuss youth marginalization in all of its complexities without connecting it to processes of exclusion/inclusion and the concomitant devaluation of bodies, experiences, cultures, and histories that take place within our communities. Some of these exclusionary practices are structural and systemic in nature. Many have deep historical roots. Most of us would agree in principle that a truly democratic society is one that is fully inclusive of all. This is, however, easier said than done due to entrenched practices of entitlements to power, privilege, and resources that serve to defend parochial interests.

Marginalization is a social devaluing of others that functions to ensure, and simultaneously justify, disproportionate access to scarce societal resources including material wealth, political power, and social prestige. These social exclusions then serve to relegate individuals from certain social groupings towards the boundary edges of the societal sphere, well away from the core of central import (Rummens and Dei, 2010). Marginalization is a social process, not a label. It is an action that yields a desired end result.

Simply understanding the contemporary dislocations brought about by various forms and degrees of social exclusion avoids serious attempts to address the existing chasms and inequities within our communities along lines of race, ethnicity, gender, class, sexuality, language dis/ability, age, and religion. Understanding is not doing—it is but a starting point. Truly addressing marginalization must also be about subverting the seductive dominant talk of "inclusion" that merely signals and barely addresses questions of power, privilege, accountability, and transparency. In rethinking and working with prevailing conceptual models and existing notions of inclusion, an important question to ask is how do we hope to achieve change by adding to what already exists when that which already exists is the source of the problem in the first place? (see Dei, 2008).

To ensure truly equitable, meaningfully substantive integration of our diverse youth in all aspects of social, economic, and political life, we must work together to remove any semblance of marginalization within our communities. Dealing with multiple social dislocations requires shedding the chains of past exclusions that continue to manifest themselves today in the non-recognition of histories and contributions, the devaluation of experiences and knowledge, and the challenged senses of self and collective worth experienced by some individuals and population groups among us. When certain bodies, knowledge systems, and lived experiences are selectively excluded from social sites and spaces, they effectively become the "disappearing act." This is the first thing that needs to be acknowledged and made visible.

Marginalization is a systemic social problem that has become deeply embedded in many of our social institutions, including our education system. This fact also needs to be acknowledged. Learning, itself, occurs within distinct socio-political contexts—the same is therefore also true of teaching. This is why exclusionary practices in the very schools entrusted with the responsibility of not only educating but also socializing our children must be dealt with directly and forcefully. It is why the structures, processes, and experiences of educational delivery need to be carefully re-examined. Educators' attitudes, behaviours, knowledge, training, and practices are equally key to the creation and maintenance of learning communities that are truly welcoming and supportive of all youth.

Young learners today (both inside and out of the school context) are not disembodied—our diverse youth are instead disembodied. Marginalization and exclusion is something that is done to them, something that we do. It is, moreover, something that is done to some while not to others. These points are critical, especially as they suggest the way forward towards possible solutions. The attendant sorting, categorizing, labelling, valuating, stereotyping, and discriminating processes have profound consequences not only for the well-being of youth but also for many of their life outcomes. Both the short- and long-term impacts of such marginalization and exclusion on our youth are significant. Race, class, sex, gender, and sexual orientation have all been shown to be critically consequential for engaging in schooling and education (see Dei et al., 2010), and they are linked to both academic performance and educational outcomes and successful subsequent transition into the labour market (Rummens, 2009).

If we want to ensure better outcomes for all of Canada's children, it is not enough to understand what marginalization is and know what it does to our youth. Something also needs to be *done*. There are limits to merely acknowledging differences as strengths without responding concretely to the difference as a key site of power relations that advantage some while disadvantaging others. We must instead define and situate real equity broadly within a radical inclusive educational practice, which not only pays attention to sites of marginality in schools for different bodies but also seeks to address these processes of exclusion effectively. This action may require an honest acknowledgement that even our collective quest for solidarity in anti-oppression work can sometimes mask underlying tensions, ambivalences, and ambiguities if differential power and privilege is not carefully considered and substantively addressed.

How might we best understand marginalization from the vantage point of those who have been systematically and structurally marginalized within our society? How do our marginalized young learners perceive and experience it and how does it affect them? Who exactly is being excluded or pushed to the margins? By whom? How exactly is this done through everyday schooling?

What would real inclusion and integration actually look like? As fellow citizens, how do we ensure that our social institutions are truly responsive to the multiple needs and concerns, resources, and contributions of an increasingly diverse body politic? How do we as educators ensure that all of today's learners develop a sense of shared entitlement and mutual responsibility and are truly nurtured through a deep sense of belonging and connectedness to their schools and thus to their society? How do we collectively move beyond the bland, seductive politics and discourse of the inclusion of "difference" or "otherness" to a practice of transparency and accountability that is able to place the very real issue of continued youth marginalization squarely at the centre of critical educational practice?

Towards a Deeper Understanding of Youth Marginalization through Education

> *I can tell you the reason why I dropped out! ... The school that I went to, they made me feel like I wasn't smart enough to do the stuff. They told my parents to send me to a technical school. They treated Blacks like we had no brains...*

and that the Chinese were smarter, the Whites were better, so I just said,
"Forget it!" (Victoria, former "dropout")[2]

Experiencing Marginalization at School

It is incumbent upon us to seek to learn and come to know how our diverse youth see themselves and make sense of their marginalization experiences as well as to understand how such multiple, repeated social exclusions actually impact young learners. Marginalization is, at its very essence, a feeling of not being valued, coupled with the knowledge that one's presence is not respected nor is one's absence missed. It is an action—and becomes a practice—that does not allow certain bodies and collectivities to become full participants in society and members of its citizenry. Many of these experiences of exclusion accurately reflect and reveal historic social inequities that continue to exist within our educational system.

Marginalization is very real in the lives of youth who are targeted in this way. It is often deeply felt by youth who experience it, especially by those who feel additionally silenced and thus unable to express their concerns. Regardless of whether the exclusionary attitude, practice, or outcome is intentional, acci-dental, or simply perceived—or why it even occurred—the impact on youth's well-being is often the same. Simply put, youth marginalization is painful, harmful, and detrimental both to individual lives and to society as a whole. It results in a waste of knowledge, a squandering of skills and inherent poten-tial, as well as missed opportunities. Youth marginalization affects individuals directly, communities differentially, and society more broadly. In the area of education, marginalization and exclusion can lead to youth being actively pushed out of school. It can also lead to young learners becoming so disaffected and disillusioned with the prevailing educational system that they leave of their own accord. We all lose when any one of us develops a sense of disconnection, alienation, or even hopelessness within our social system.

Marginalization must be understood as including physical, psychological, and emotional violence—such as bullying, racism, and sexism—among its various expressions. While marginalization is, in and of itself, a form of violence, it can in turn also engender subsequent alienation and disruption as disenfran-chised youth develop a sense of hopelessness and act out on their marginality and exclusions, causing further harm both to themselves and to others. In effect, marginalization undermines social cohesion and, along with it, the cherished goal of peaceful co-existence of different bodies within a truly equitable society.

Youth marginalization and "exclusion" through schooling and educa-tion needs to be understood as something more than mere omission—delib-erate or otherwise—of life ways, knowledge systems, and every-day lived experiences. Social exclusion is instead a political, material, psychological, and spiritual mindset, action, and practice that favours some and disadvantages others. Conversely, inclusion is not simply a "seeing," nor an "adding" or "bringing in." One can, after all, be included while continuing to exist on the margins of social life. Rather, true inclusion is about "centring." Real social inclusion and integration is about ensuring equitable outcomes for all of our diverse youth, by directly addressing and compensating for existing differentials in power, prestige, privilege, status, and resources, and simultaneously challenging any unexamined sense of entitlement devoid of matching mutual responsibility to others.

The Marginalized, the Marginalizer, and the Bystander

Who gets marginalized? In theory, anyone may be pushed to the margins of social interactions and societal import. In practice, it is those who are "most different" from those who wield societal power who tend to be most affected. In this process, the very markers of this difference or otherness are made socially salient though social interaction at the expense of shared commonalities (Rummens, 2003). Any discussion of youth marginalization must therefore necessarily recognize the diverse subpopulations that are so affected as well as the commonalities and differences both across and within them. Canada's racialized youth may be of either immigrant or non-immigrant backgrounds. At the same time, our first- and second-generation immigrant and refugee youth are, in turn, ethnoculturally diverse as members of minority status cultures and language groupings. They also often have religious practices and beliefs that differ from those of other Canadians. Many newcomers, particularly those from more recent migration cohorts, are from these racialized populations. This reality means that many immigrant and refugee youth may be seen to differ from their school peers on more than one identity criteria—in this case, in terms of newcomer status, culture, language, religion, as well as visibility. Our indigenous Aboriginal youth in turn reflect multiple culturally distinct ways of life, linguistic groupings, as well as social systems. They have been similarly racialized, socio-economically disadvantaged, and systematically disenfranchised beginning from the time of European contact. Important to note is that while marginalization trajectories may be unique both to specific individuals and different groups both within and over time, the overall processes of social exclusion are often very similar. The same is true of the attendant detrimental impacts and outcomes.

Who marginalizes? We do; we all do. It is something in which every one of us participates as a social actor, both as active participants and silent observers, whether we do so knowingly or not. Any individual who employs socially salient identity criteria—such as age, sex, gender, culture, religion, physical appearance, socio-economic status, sexual orientation, ableness, or any other identity marker—to socially disadvantage another individual based on perceived group characteristics actively engages in exclusionary practices. Anyone who sees and accepts this activity is also a knowing participant. It is we ourselves who do the marginalizing, whether through overt intent or unintended consequence, through active commission or errors of omission, by doing something as well as by doing nothing. "To marginalize" is an active verb, an action that translates all too often into a disenfranchising adjective. What it means is that social marginalization and exclusion is also something that we ourselves can do something about.

Marginalization Processes within Our Educational System

> My parents wanted to make sure I had access to many resources as possible to help me to succeed but I know at other schools students are kind of at the entry of school, they're labelled and from that point on they're relegated to this label and there's no way to move out of it and especially minority students. They don't receive the support that they really need to succeed and even those that well, might have succeeded in other environment are kinda held back because of the label placed on them because this is the path they're going to take and they don't have a choice in it ... So I think that we do need more people to be informed that, minority students, students from different backgrounds receive the support that they need. Whether it be through a guidance counsellor or some, some academic advisor, someone from their culture who understands their specific needs and can guide them throughout their academic career, rather than placing them in these streams and not allowing them the opportunity to grow up in ways that they might have grown if they were not placed under these labels that might kinda impede them. (Jumo, African-Canadian university student)[3]

How does social marginalization and exclusion happen within education as one of our key social institutions? How exactly does it take place? What forms does it take?

Youth marginalization happens through the discursive positioning of bodies, their physical and social placement within institutional settings, and dominant perceptions of the value and relevance of their ideas, knowledge, and experiences. It happens through labelling, stereotyping, and differential expectations. In the specific case of schooling, marginalization and exclusion occur via both the official and the hidden curriculum, through classroom pedagogy, and in instruction work with diverse youth.

Within the educational system, youth marginalization can take place in different ways, often simultaneously and at multiple levels. One way is through visual knowledge and physical representation (see Dei et al., 2000; Dei, James-Wilson, and Zine, 2002). Marginalization through *visual representation* occurs when the experiences of some youth—for example, racialized minorities, immigrant cultures, linguistic minorities, Indigenous populations, women, working-class youth, bodies with disabilities—are either not represented or poorly or inaccurately portrayed in the visual culture and landscape of schools. Similarly, marginalization through *knowledge representation* occurs when there is no active learning of the multiple and diverse cultures, histories, experiences, and knowledge systems from which affected youth come both in their own and their collective schooling. Marginalization through *physical representation* occurs when some youth find it difficult or impossible to see themselves, their group, or their society physically represented in the composition of the teaching staff or student body. Many students from both advantaged and disadvantaged population groups attend and complete their schooling without ever having been taught by an indigenous, cultural, racial, or religious minority faculty member or by an instructor with physical disabilities. For many minority youth, marginalization means never having seen themselves reflected visually, physically, and/or substantively in their schooling career. For others, it also means having their group histories hidden, contributions denied, and voices silenced.

Another way by which many youth are effectively marginalized in our schools is through differential *linguistic valuation*. Language can be a site and place of youth marginalization when there is no conscious attempt made by educators and school administrators to openly acknowledge the inherent value of, or encourage, promote, and enhance the learning of, local/Indigenous, minority, and first languages of learners who are not of the dominant culture or cultures. In so doing, the English and French languages are reified as the sole mode of transmission of culture, history, identity, and ancestral knowledge of culturally diverse learners. Those students who subsequently insist on also using their cultural/Indigenous languages as a mode of communication are then seen as problematic—their resistance and attempts to question, and even subvert, the dominant official language and discourse that they feel minimizes, denigrates, and penalizes them is neither understood, accepted, nor rewarded. In such contexts, simply having a different accent can constitute all too frequently grounds for effective exclusion from the merit and reward badges of schooling.

Marginalization can also occur via the school-home interaction dynamic. The family/community and school interface is often structured in a way that favours the middle-class family experience. Wealthier parents often constitute the most powerful voices in schools as they are more able to volunteer time and provide additional resources to their children's schools. These additional educational inputs and supports are geared towards improving student—and thus school—academic performance outcomes and help ensure that these parents have a more privileged status. It is possible, particularly in inner-city/urban schools, for the needs, concerns, and experiences of youth from poor, working-class, and racial minority backgrounds to be devalued or ignored merely from a lack of similar attention by equally committed, though less well-resourced, parents. In recent years, a number of Canadian schools have embarked upon laudable approaches aimed at creating spaces of knowledge and power sharing that enable greater involvement in schools by all families from all communities, including those most disadvantaged or marginalized. These initiatives include welcoming elders into the school community, the integration of cultural knowledge systems into daily teaching, as well as the active seeking of broader parental input into pedagogy, instruction, and curricular development. Such efforts translate into a greater sense of social valuation, meaningful inclusion, and, thus, school relevance for students from these communities. Care needs, however, to be taken even within such progressive initiatives to guard against the tendency to privilege some communities' experiences over others. When some parents' voices are heard more loudly over those of others, youth from disadvantaged backgrounds whose communities are less well reflected feel all the more marginalized within the school system. All too often, the conventional colonizing practice of merely inserting parental and community representation into already existing hierarchical structures of schooling simply recreates and amplifies the social exclusion already experienced by disadvantaged youth from more marginalized communities.

The Need for Equity and Value-Based Education

> I think that they're discouraged and they feel like they can't make a difference if they go ... they feel like they're not part of it, that they're different, that they can't learn ... A lot of people were told that they were stupid in elementary school, especially a lot of my friends and ... they hear it so much it's like a self-fulfilling prophecy. You just hear it all the time and their family doesn't say anything like, "No, you're not" and so they just say, "Okay, I'm not smart, I can't do it." (Charlene, Grade 11 student)[1]

At its most fundamental, marginalization occurs through the non-visibility or denial of existing social power differentials. Given that social differences—marked by racial, linguistic, cultural, religious, sex, gender, and/or dis/ability identity criteria—have always been consequential for schooling outcomes, schools that do not actively promote, facilitate, support and sustain equity and values-based education contribute directly to the production of marginalized young learners. Bodies can be seen to matter in schooling and education precisely because social differences are used as sites and expressions of identity and relations of power. It is these very social identifications that are used as grounds for various forms of discrimination and oppression that subsequently translate into educational practices that can end up marginalizing and excluding some learners from their own schooling. Both blatant and subtle/hidden racist, sexist, classist, and homophobic labelling and stereotyping, in conjunction with teachers' low expectations of some learners, inflict huge emotional, psychological, physical, and material damage on affected students. Negative stereotyping and exclusions in the educational curriculum and in school texts have similarly been found to be a source of youth disaffection and disengagement for this very same reason. When curricular and instructional approaches fail to foreground questions of social difference and power relations, which are delineated via identity criteria that are deemed to be socially salient such as class, ethnicity, language, race, religion, age, sex, gender, sexual orientation, or dis/ability, young learners are actively and very effectively marginalized.

Marginalization also occurs through the non-recognition of different culturally based knowledge systems as well as shared group experiences. It may be noted that many learners who come from indigenous Aboriginal or racialized, immigrant, and refugee backgrounds have already been culturally socialized to appreciate and respect local cultural resource knowledge bases as well as the power of multi-centric knowing. The ideas, norms, and cultural knowledge embedded in everyday living constitute a form of indigenous philosophies possessed by many of our peoples and communities. These philosophies often emphasize the intergenerational knowledge of community elders as cultural custodians and emphasize mutual respect, social responsibility, and community building as well as the integral connection between the individual and his community. Schooling that disconnects learners form such cultural wisdom often ends up creating tensions and contradictions for many young learners. Unable to cope with a school culture that rewards the separation of community knowledge from official academic school knowledge, many of these youth end up feeling disaffected by, and disengaged from, the entire school experience itself. Such disconnect and decoupling of local/traditional/communal knowledge from the official knowledge system of schools helps to create young learners who either become compartmentalized learners or young people who are de-rooted or separated from their cultures, families, and communities.

While it is true that some learners may not be bothered by such physical, mental, cultural, and spiritual separations, for others it creates youth disillusion and disaffection with schools. It is important to realize that there are yet other students who have difficulty, or are unable to navigate or cope, with such separation given their community's historical encounters with colonization, continued lived experiences with oppression, or ongoing challenges of migration acculturation and resettlement (see Rummens et al., 2008). For refugee students with traumatic war experiences and newcomer immigrant students, the problem of engagement with, or disengagement from, school does not lie in any inherent weakness and incapability but, rather, with the failure of educators to use our youths' personal and collective histories, stories, and experiences/epiphanies as entry points into, and resources for, teaching, learning, and knowing for all learners.

It should be remembered that for many young learners, engaging teaching and learning is fundamentally an emotionally felt experience. An exclusionary education that fails to take into consideration and emphasize the affective and psychomotor domains of the learner through appreciation of love, justice, and responsibility and focuses instead solely on cognitive competencies will end up creating disengaged learners. As illustration, many Indigenous learners are socialized in their homes and cultures to engage with revealed knowledge acquired through intuition, revelations, dreams, and visions. Their cultural systems actively promote social values that enhance the spiritual, emotional, psychological, and moral character development of the learner. These learners are thus embodied spiritually, something that is in turn understood relationally and not as a hegemonic or fundamentalist belief or practice. Home-based teachings and learnings focus on the concepts of self, personhood, and connections of the inner/outer space and environments. There is an idea of embodied knowing and an embodiment of the learning process that speaks directly to significant political and social relations that are established and sustained via bodies, minds, and senses. In brief, many Indigenous students are traditionally socialized into learning that emphasizes the society-culture and nature nexus, a form of learning that speaks to inter-relationships and connectedness, to love, respect, and generosity for humanity, to an understanding of the inter-relationship between rights and responsibilities, to the dynamics of power relations, as well as to the connections of the individual/self to the community/group. What both research and other culturally based knowledge systems clearly point to is that unless our educational system finds a way to also recognize, harness the power of, and work productively with emotions, spiritual essence, and intuition, as a significant way of learning and knowing, some students will continue to feel marginalized and excluded from the schooling process.

The Need for Co-operative Education

I think the best [experience] was being able to study and work and spend
most of my time with the students at X and the staff because I learned a lot …
just sharing a lot of experiences and seeing things that are similar to most
of us … I came here in 2001 and some are here for 20 years, another come

from somewhere else and, yet, there are things that connect us ... Dealing
with people and the staff and also just being taught about African writers,
Native writers, and seeing that they contribute in this society too, as well as
being able to see other points of view, not only Eurocentric, you know, but
seeing the bigger picture; not only one model. Those were the best. (Nashia,
African-Canadian "continental" university student)[5]

Sometimes it is not so much what is done as what is not done to achieve greater equity in learning experiences. Another factor that both creates and recreates youth marginalization through schooling is the absence of co-operative education. Youth who do not perform to already established rigid guidelines of school success defined strictly in terms of "academic performance" may feel further marginalized by actions of schools that create and recreate this particular measure of "educational success." Co-operative education seeks to counteract this result by establishing individual success in learning as a collective responsibility. Theoretically, co-operative education is about creating a "community of learners." It views schooling as a shared community activity in which each participant has a responsibility to each and every other and seeks to ensure the educational success of each for the benefit of all. Co-operative education is built upon the assumption that every single learner has something valuable to contribute to the learning process, both her own and that of her classmates. This approach to education thrives upon collective learning experiences in which every learner implements their responsibility to help another succeed in their respective learning journey as well.

Co-operative education helps mitigate unexamined perceptions of youth from disadvantaged communities as being neither smart nor high achieving. When experienced difficulties are attributed to the individual or family without critically examining the structures for educational delivery that may be creating the educational failures in the first place, such preconceived views serve to marginalize these learners even further. Such pathologizing and blame of certain youth, families, and communities contributes directly to their feelings of exclusion and effective marginalization in classrooms and schools as well as within the educational system itself. In sharp contrast, co-operative education involves pedagogic and instructional practices that explicitly promote collective responsibility for individual learning by redefining "educational success" itself much more broadly to include both academic and social success. It views success in schooling and in education in a much more holistic way. "Success" is not simply deemed the flip side of failure, nor is the success of some students "served up" for consumption to help explain away the "failure" of yet other students.

Instructional and pedagogic practices geared towards collective learning promote mixed ability classes that ensure that so-called "high achieving" or "performing" students develop a sense of responsibility to assist those facing learning challenges or social disadvantages. From this perspective, true success is seen as something beyond and much larger than individual accomplishments and achievements as measured solely by test scores. Instead, success is about social responsibility, and it is this goal that creates, engenders, nurtures, and sustains both a sense of accomplishment and a feeling of self and collective worth among all concerned. Such a broader definition of success recognizes and embeds both individual and community contributions directly within the learning process itself and effectively holds systems, structures, and institutions accountable for making individual and collective success possible for everyone.

Responding to the Challenge of Youth Marginalization in Schooling and Education

Given the multiple levels and mechanisms of youth marginalization, how can we as educators, school administrators, and policy officials work together to remove sites of youth marginality and empower all learners from all racial, cultural, linguistic, religious, and class backgrounds, while still being fully inclusive of sex, gender, sexual orientation, and dis/ability?

Talking a Critical Inclusive Approach to Education

> You couldn't express it … because you have to assimilate and you have to be like everyone else. So, you had to be like they be. If you didn't, then you're a troublemaker or you're the strange kid that's got this, you know, psychological problem. But even nowadays when you say it's more expressed, even still, you're looked upon as a troublemaker because you want to learn your identity and something other than [in a] class[room] where you feel … wrong. You don't feel it. And, you bring it up and … you're a troublemaker now because you're going against the school. So even though they say you can express yourself … it's not the same still. To me, it's all a big puff of smoke.
> (Richard, "at risk" student)[6]

What is very much needed in rethinking our education system is careful attention to the systemic and structural inequalities of schooling itself so that more effective educational perspectives and strategic responses that facilitate and enhance the learning process for all of our youth can be formulated (Dei, 2010). There needs to be a clear recognition that students come from diverse backgrounds and that they experience "different educational realities" that cannot easily be understood when viewed as "challenges" and "problems." Educators can then begin by working with pedagogic and instructional ideas that help reconceptualize schooling for a diverse learning community. We need to be trained to place learners, their histories, experiences, cultures, and knowledges at the very centre of their own educational journey. This goal enables each learner to experience a profound sense of inherent self-worth as well as collective responsibility towards, and ownership of, his own learning process. Schooling must highlight the centrality of culture to knowledge production (pedagogy) and emphasize the importance of reaffirming and reinforcing the myriad identities of our increasingly diverse youth.

Critical inclusive education is primarily aimed at developing the learner's agency, self-actualization, and social responsibility (Asante, 1991). By working with the ideas of community, solidarity, mutual interdependence, and collective histories, young learners and their educators begin to value, recognize, and appreciate each other as contributing to the learning of each and to the joint education of all. The idea of "schooling as community" can help to ensure that every learner develops a stake in their education; that no one is marginal to their own educational process; and that the contributions of each learner affirms the sense of the collective well-being of all learners. Similarly, the idea of "community education" may be engaged to ensure close relationships, mutual understanding, and social bonding between school personnel, parents, families, elders, and communities who share a common interest in, and commitment to, ensuring successful educational outcomes for our youth. This notion helps to build co-operation among learners, teachers, and caregivers that counters a sense of individualness that sees the learner as being but one within a sea of individuals. Educators working directly with knowledges about and from within the different cultures, histories, heritages, and intellectual agencies of their students' communities, and who centre these experiences directly in the learning process itself, provide a much needed sense of youth ownership, control, and agency over their own learning, schooling, and education.

This is particularly true for Indigenous, immigrant, and other racialized minority students from communities with colonizing histories. These histories must be told—not just from the perspective of the colonizer but also of the colonized—and subsequently engaged as a necessary exercise in their emancipation. Such history establishes the contexts for producing knowledge and affirms their positive resistances and contributions to decolonization. Teaching history in a way that stresses the resilience, sacrifice, survival, and richness of accumulated knowledge within their respective communities effectively grounds the specific concerns, aspirations, and interests of these youth and enables them to become learners with the ability to tap into their own creativities and resourcefulness. Such grounding, creativity, and resourcefulness become sources of youth empowerment. Locally generated or produced knowledge that reflects cultural histories and social interactions is critically important to all students, yet it has been selectively denied to so many of our young learners for so long. When such knowledge is instead considered socially valuable and politically relevant to schooling, it maintains the learner's fit and connection with their group's, or people's, aspirations, lived experiences, and educational practices. It tells the learner that such goals matter, that she or he matters, that he or she belongs. Under such inclusive contexts, schooling can no longer be a site for reproducing marginality and exclusion (see also King, 2005; Ladson-Billings, 1994; and Willie, Garibaldi, and Reed, 1991).

We need a holistic approach to revisioning schooling and education—one that focuses on meaningful strategies and interventions through visual, knowledge, physical, and linguistic representation, an inclusive family/community and school interface, co-operative education, equity and value-based education, and critical inclusive education. We need also to promote Indigenous/community/local cultural knowledges in schools and recognize personal experience as well as spirituality as important sites of learning for many of our youth (see Dei et al., 2000; Dei et al., 2002). Schooling and education that addresses youth marginalization and fosters a sense of empowerment from within the education system will require that our schools ensure that the representation of the experiences, histories, knowledges, and contributions of all groups are placed at the very centre of youth learning. Contrary to concerns that this goal might balkanize the curriculum as well as the student body, this approach is intended to let learners engage in school from their respective vantage points and allow them to connect their unique and particular experiences with the larger society. These histories, cultures, and experiences are interconnected—no one can truly understand their own group histories, experiences, and cultural knowledge in isolation except as it is linked to those of others within the wider society. Such a holistic form of education educates all learners in the complete history of ideas, events, and practices that have shaped, and continue to shape, human growth and development.

The educational approach to addressing youth marginalization that is being suggested goes beyond an "add-and-stir" approach to a truly inclusive approach, which highlights the centrality of multiple knowledge systems, the strength of shared experiences, and the physical representation of all bodies within the school, including in positions of power and influence. The critical inclusive approach affirms the local and Indigenous cultures and languages of our students. It also seeks to ensure that we have institutional processes and procedures in place within schools to directly address students/youth concerns, including any sense of marginality, as they arise. Working with a broader critical view of inclusion helps highlight the question of power and social difference. In fact, a more critical and holistic understanding of inclusion is about ensuring that schools are welcoming for all and particularly responsive to the

needs and concerns of a diverse school population by addressing head-on questions of difference, diversity, and power as articulated through the lens of race,
ethnicity, language, religion, gender, class, disability, or sexual orientation. This
approach calls for acknowledging the valuable contributions that all parents and
local communities can bring into the educational system—resources that may be
effectively tapped to educate all learners. It calls for breaking the false separation
of schools and communities and for opening up schools as community spaces
for all, so that no group has a sense of entitlement to their schools at the expense
and exclusion of others. It ensures that the school is and remains a public space
belonging to a community comprised of the collective citizenry of the nation.

A critical inclusive approach to schooling and education calls for developing in all learners a sense of pride in their unique contribution to knowledge
production and to defining educational success as something that stretches
beyond academic success to social success. This achievement can only be
accomplished when schooling and education is seen as the collective shared
responsibility of all students, educators, school administrators, parents, local
communities, and policy-makers and when their respective contributions to
the learning process are fully acknowledged by all. A critical inclusive approach
to education also requires schools to have in place effective enforceable strategies to deal with racist, sexist, classist, homophobic, and other oppressions
structured along the lines of visibility, culture, language, religion, and disability
when and where these occur. All forms of violence, including physical, psychological, and emotional violence resulting from bullying, stereotyping, and
labelling of students, need to be addressed as systemic problems rather than
as the individual actions of a few. At the same time, school administrators and
educators should also be charged and held accountable to actively make social
inclusion happen for their learners.

Given that marginalization and exclusion results in physical, emotional,
and spiritual damage to learners, educators need to furthermore find ways for
schools to strengthen the spiritual sense of self of young learners as a way of
additional empowerment. We must face head-on our discomfort with spirituality (not to be conflated with religion) by working with spiritual knowings
that are solution oriented and affirm the complex identities of our learners.
Engaging spirituality in a critical way calls for dismantling what Shahjahan
(2007) calls the "spiritual-proof fence" by encouraging educators to be courageous in speaking about our different spiritualities and how they impact both
teaching and student learning. The notion of spirituality engages the existen-
tial self and connections both to the group and broader community as well
as to the meaning and purpose of life. A discussion about spirituality cannot
evade issues and questions of power. Classroom pedagogy must challenge the

spurious dichotomy between material and non-material. Critical educators should not be afraid and must shift the discourse on spirituality to action-oriented spirituality and spiritual praxis that allows us to transform our circumstances. This task can be accomplished more easily if we create a space in our schools for local cultural and Indigenous knowledge and teachings that emphasize community, social responsibility, mutual interdependence, love of self and others, self-awareness, and self-discipline, together with respect for our elders and the natural world that sustains us.

Transformational Mechanisms

The school curriculum itself is a vital entry point and effective tool for such trans-forming education. It offers a clear path to follow through which we might bring about educational change. As we, as educators, search for ways to deal with youth marginality and exclusions in our schools, it is important that we evaluate the appropriateness of curriculum materials and resources by asking certain critical questions. These include the "who," "what," "how," and "when" questions that surround the making of curriculum texts. What is included in these teaching and learning aides? Equally important, what is missing? There needs to be a critical analysis of official school texts and educational materials for omissions, bias, and exclusions of experiences around race, culture, language, religion, sex, gender, disability, sexual orientation, and class difference. Educators need to become and remain proactive by directly questioning the existing status quo and also ensuring that there are procedures in place for centring, infusing, integrating, and synthesizing relevant inclusive materials in the school. The current lack of availability, access, and adequacy of inclusive anti-racist, Indigenous, and cultur-ally appropriate instructional materials for students, educators, parents, and community workers must be addressed directly. At the same time, we need to collectively determine ways of identifying, accessing, and effectively synthesizing relevant resources needed in the development of a more inclusive curriculum and for suggesting baseline standards and guidelines for the use of such materials.

We need to combine school, community, and local cultural knowledge resources in the search for educational spaces that respond more immediately and directly to youth marginality and exclusion in the school system. Guest speakers might be drawn from the wider community and invited to share their diverse experiences with our young learners. Parents and community elders might also be welcomed into schools, and members from diverse communities invited to contribute feedback and input into the production, validation, and dissemination of school knowledge through meetings, workshops, seminars, and conferences. Educators must draw on such a school-community interface for solution-oriented ends.

Finally, educators must seek to always engage their students directly in their own learning. This aim means empowering students to work with various print and electronic media. The use of visual aids, popular culture, and electronic media have all been found to be effective modes of communicating and educating young learners, provided care is taken to address issues of history and context. Wherever such resources are lacking, schools and educators might assist their learners in accessing relevant media and resources via bookstores and libraries.

In identifying strategies for implementing critical inclusive, equity and equity-based collective teaching and learning, we need also to suggest, develop, and evaluate baseline standards for assessing the quality of such educational practices. The instructional effectiveness of a critically inclusive curriculum might, for example, be determined by how well students are able to ask new and critical questions, raise questions of community building and social responsibility, see themselves reflected, and feel their life aspirations supported. There must also be an inclusive range of students' voices about their own learning experiences in school assessments. Most of all, there needs to be a true "listening."

In engaging these educational forums and strategies, the question of how we centre the young learner in her or his learning is absolutely critical. Educators' use of personal experiences, teachable moments, classroom and society scenarios, media outlets, and alternative texts is essential. Acknowledging the authenticity of local/students' voice and fostering critical thinking among learners helps to ensure that every learner can "come to voice." Such strategy calls for the engagement of different types of learners as well as for the creation of a decolonized space for learning to happen within a community of learners. Such centring also calls for the integration of students, parent, and community knowledges in the development of relevant and practical inclusive curriculum and instruction for all youth through the open engagement of all local communities as a starting point for conversations that may sometimes trouble our often strongly held assumptions and discursive positions.

Moving Forward Together

Proposed educational initiatives for change must begin by helping to move us away from situating the intertwined problem of marginalization and disengagement with the child or youth to an honest examination of the structures and processes of educational delivery that may in fact be playing an integral role in the difficulties perceived and experienced. Many of us are already all too aware of the existing limitations within the current school system, and, in fact, some favour the establishment of pilot schemes outside the school system to address immediately and directly some of the challenges faced by our racialized youth (see Dei & Kempf, 2012, on the Afrocentric school model). However, the needed solution is not an "either/or" but, rather, an "and/with" approach. We very much need multiple strategies of response. The strategies and interventions offered in this chapter are intended to address the problem of youth marginalization in schools working with the existing school system itself. Much needs to be done.

How are we going to work with more socially inclusive, integrative visions of schooling that help move us "outside the box" in our current educational delivery? Already there are strong voices that have already demanded Afrocentric education and other specialized schools for young learners. Efforts at educational change must necessarily engage the concerns raised by community-involved academics, education experts, and parents who have developed a compelling body of evidence and advocated strongly for their children's needs and rights for alternative/counter education. Revisioning schooling in order to address youth marginalization and exclusion means engaging local communities and parents as equal partners in the education of our youth. We cannot, and should not, dismiss concerns voiced that some schools are unwelcoming to parents and local communities. It is unwise to build up and out upon a foundation that may be cracked. All communities need to be present at the table, and it must be recognized that real involvement means much more than mere representation. Instead, the concept of "community of differences" needs not only to be taken into account but also to be enacted upon in the planning, execution, and assessment of all educational initiatives.

The staffing and professional training of our young learners' educators is absolutely critical. We are still struggling through some hard questions about whether our teachers have the training to teach youth of culturally and racially diverse populations. Are the teachers we currently have now in our schools fully representative of, and responsive to, diverse populations? Have they received the necessary professional development, and are they fully supported in its implementation? Notwithstanding good intentions, the lack of anti-racism, anti-homophobia, and anti-ablist training demonstrated by a number of educators all too readily translates into an important skill deficit that has resulted in schools being unsafe sites for many students. Concerned parents have responded with demands for a more appropriately inclusive curriculum for their kids. Such curricular and pedagogic challenges must be dealt with directly rather than being pushed "under the carpet." Schools need a holistic curriculum and inclusive pedagogic approach that fully addresses the social, emotional, spiritual, cognitive, affective, and physical development of all of these diverse learners. Equally important is contextual education that incorporates teachings about our natural, physical, and social environments, including that of the educational system itself. The strengths of a more flexible curricular and instructional approach to learning, such as high-quality play-based programs, also need to be championed and implemented.

Educators and administrators need to be alerted to the dangers of what Lewin (2008) has pointed out standardization recipes that fail to respond concretely to issues of difference, diversity, and equity among young learners. Instead, new pedagogic and instructional initiatives must embrace varied teaching and assessment methods that capture the brilliance of all children, while directly addressing any fears of failing school that may exist among learners. In addition to solid knowledge and grounding in youth development and true commitment to real parental and community engagement, there must be a focus on educational knowledge and practice to achieve equity and social justice. Much more emphasis needs to be placed on the curricular and pedagogic issues around equity and social difference than is currently the case.

We cannot, and should not, continue to universalize our learners in terms of who they are and what their experiences have been. The resulting "universal learning experience" is then presented as reasonable, natural, and neutral when in fact it does not reflect, and, thus, does not meet the needs of, all students in the same way. This is what we have been doing for much too long, and it is our diverse learners who have paid the steepest price. If we are truly serious about addressing youth marginalization through educational change, we must acknowledge this simple truth and collectively move forward to implement policies and practices designed to bring disadvantaged youth and their communities squarely inside the centre.

Notes

1   All of the names used throughout this chapter are pseudonyms to protect the privacy of the individuals. Marilyn is an African-Canadian mother responding to the question of what the term "dropout" means (Dei et al., 1995).

2   Victoria is a "dropout" who later returned to school as a mature student to complete her education (Dei et al., 1995).

3   Jumo speaks of the role of parents ensuring educational success for their children (Dei et al., 2010).

4   Charlene reflects on being disengaged at school (Dei et al., 1995).

5   Nashia gained entry into university by attending an access program at the university and describes her experience at school (Dei et al., 2010).

6   Richard is a student considered to be "'at risk' of dropping out" by the system (Dei et al., 1995).

References

Asante, M. K. (1991). The Afrocentric idea in education. *Journal of Negro Education*. *60*(2), 170-180.

Dei, G. J. S. (2008). *Racists beware: Uncovering racial politics in contemporary society.* Rotterdam, Netherlands: Sense Publishers.

Dei, G. J. S. (2010). The Possibilities of new/counter and alternative visions of schooling. *English Quarterly, 41*(3-4), 113-132.

Dei, G. J. S., Butler, A., Charamia, G., Kola-Olusanya, A., Opini, B., Thomas, R., & Wagner, A. (2010). *Learning to succeed: The challenges and possibilities of educational development for all.* New York: Teneo Press.

Dei, G. J. S., Holmes, L., Mazzuca, J., McIsaac, E., & Campbell, R. (1995). *Push out or drop out?: The dynamics of black students' disengagement from school* (Final report submitted to the Ontario Ministry of Education and Training, Ontario Institute for Studies in Education, Toronto, ON).

Dei, G. J. S., James, I. M., James-Wilson, S., Karumanchery, L., & Zine, J. (2000). *Removing the margins: The challenges and possibilities of inclusive schooling.* Toronto: Canadian Scholars' Press.

Dei, G. J. S., James-Wilson, S., & Zine, J. (2002). *Inclusive schooling: A teacher's companion to "removing the margins."* Toronto: Canadian Scholars' Press.

Dei, G. J. S., & Kempf, A. (in press). *New visions of Africentric schooling.* Toronto: Canadian Scholars' Press.

King, J. (Ed.). (2005). *Black education. A transformative research and action agenda for the new century.* Mahwah, NJ: Lawrence Erlbaum Associates Publishers.

Ladson-Billings, G. (1994). *The dreamkeepers: Successful teachers of African American children.* San Francisco, CA: Jossey-Bass.

Lewin, K. M. (2008). *Strategies for sustainable financing of secondary education in Sub-Saharan Africa* (Human Development Series, Working Paper no. 136). Washington, DC: World Bank.

Rummens, J. A. (2003). Identity and diversity: Overlaps, intersections and processes (Special Issue). *Canadian Ethnic Studies 35*(3), 10-25.

Rummens, J. A. (2009). How are we doing? Educational and linguistic integration outcomes among immigrant and refugee children and youth in Canada. *Contact: Teachers of English as a Second Language, 35*(2), 44-58.

Rummens, J. A., & Dei, G. J. S. (2010). Including the excluded: De-marginalizing immigrant/refugee and racialized students (Special Issue). *Education Canada, 50*(5), 48-53.

Rummens, J. A., Tilleczek, K., Boydell, K., and Ferguson, B. (2008). Understanding and addressing early school leaving among immigrant and refugee youth. In K. Tilleczek (Ed.), *Why do students drop out of high school?: Narrative studies and social critiques* (pp. 75-101). New York: Edwin Mellen Press.

Shahjahan, R. A. (2007). The every day as sacred: Trailing back by the spiritual proof fence in the academy. (Unpublished doctoral dissertation). Toronto: Ontario Institute for Studies in Education of the University of Toronto.

Willie, C. V., Garibaldi, A. M., & Reed, W. L. (Eds.). (1991). *The education of African Americans.* New York: Auburn House.

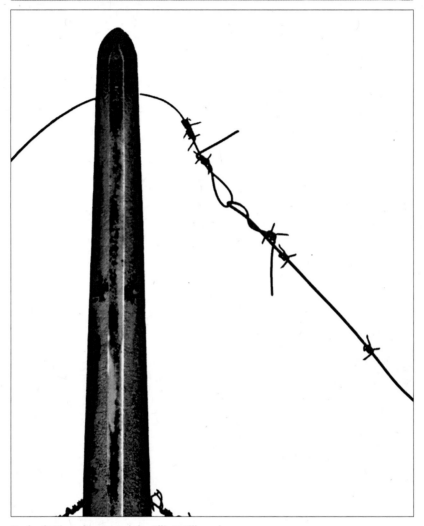

Barbed Wire, photograph by Elliott Tilleczek

Marginalized Youth in Education: Social and Cultural Dimensions of Exclusion in Canada and the United Kingdom

Andy Furlong

Introduction

The marginalization of young people in education systems is a process that occurs in all advanced societies, and, despite changes in the organization of education and in patterns of participation, inequalities remain deeply entrenched. The groups that are most prone to marginalization vary from country to country—in Canada and Australia, Aboriginal groups are vulnerable and, in Europe, the Roma have long been a concern. Immigrants who lack fluency in the national language frequently encounter difficulties, as do members of certain ethnic groups. There are also media and policy "fads" that bring specific groups to the fore. In the United Kingdom at the moment, there is concern about a group referred to as NEETs (who are defined as young people who are not in education, employment, or training), while, in Japan, there is concern about a group referred to as "freeters" (who are seen as choosing a new work-life balance in which employment is treated as secondary to leisure and social lives).

To address the question of marginalization and education, we could look at a range of vulnerable groups who are undoubtedly at risk of socio-economic exclusion, any of which deserve to be the focus of deeper analysis, but in this chapter I focus specifically on social class. There are several reasons why I privilege class analysis: first, because in all developed societies those from lower working-class families are especially vulnerable to marginalization and social class divisions are significant and tend to crosscut other divisions such as ethnicity; second, class inequalities have proven to be resistant to political manipulation and are significant in societies committed to meritocracy as well as in neo-liberal societies; third, there is a view that the mechanisms through which class inequalities become translated into marginalization have changed and that class has become less significant in late modernity (e.g., Beck, 1992). If this latter claim is true, we probably want to know how things have changed. In contexts where opportunities are framed by social class, it is important to explore the nature of the relationship between social class and marginalization since it is only through developing a full understanding of processes that we can hope to prevent class inequalities leading to marginalization and exclusion. In turn, a fuller appreciation of the mechanisms that link social class with marginalization can help us understand the processes through which other vulnerable groups become trapped in disadvantaged positions.

In terms of patterns of inequality, Canada and the United Kingdom occupy similar positions in international "league tables." Using the internationally recognized Gini index, which measures patterns of income inequality, Canada and the United Kingdom fall mid-range in a listing of the countries identified by the Organisation for Economic Co-operation and Development (OECD).[1] These two countries are much more unequal than the Scandinavian countries but much more egalitarian than countries such as Mexico and Turkey (Field, Kuczera, & Pont, 2007). A recent report by the UN Children's Fund (2010), which focuses on inequalities in 24 of the world's wealthiest countries, found that levels of child income inequality in Canada and the United Kingdom were particularly high, putting the countries towards the bottom of the league tables alongside countries such as Portugal and Greece. As the report makes clear, "the most potent fact about children who fall significantly behind their peers is that, by and large, they are children of families at the bottom end of the socio-economic scale'" (p. 18).

In the United Kingdom and Canada, the vast majority of young people now remain in full-time education until the age of 18, although those who drop out earlier are overwhelmingly drawn from less advantaged families and there is a strong association between social class and educational attainment (Furlong and Cartmel, 2007). In the context of educational attainment, there is also a strong association between low social class and a lack of basic skills in literacy and numeracy, which are essential to survival in modern labour markets. Highlighting this relationship, a recent OECD report concludes that "poor basic skills mean less chances of a job, worse health, more criminality and a shorter life" (Field et al., 2007, p. 26). With entrenched class-based inequalities being reproduced through education systems that favour those with pre-existing socio-economic advantages, it is important that we fully understand the mechanisms occurring within our systems of education.

In this chapter, I focus on the processes through which marginalization occurs within modern educational contexts. I begin by discussing the concept of marginalization and go on to examine changes in the relationship between inequality and educational outcomes before going on to examine the ways in which changing educational structures and their interface with modern transitions impacts on the process of marginalization. With a strong focus on social class, the chapter explores the ways in which cultural orientations impact on educational attainment and examine the extent to which modern educational experiences have affected patterns of engagement. Finally, I conclude by highlighting some of the policy implications that can be drawn from the research findings.

Marginalization and Exclusion

> Poverty, like gravity, affects everything we do, especially where we go to school and the type of schooling we experience. Poverty is a system, a culture, and an institution ... It predicts poor housing, violence, malnutrition, dependence on public transport, family crisis, single-parent homes, divorce, child neglect, low test scores, and school drop-outs. (Farnen, 2007, p. 290)

Before focusing on educational inequalities, we need to be clear about what we mean by marginalization and how it differs from social exclusion, which is the other concept used to describe the situation of materially disadvantaged groups. Both marginalization and exclusion are terms that are often used as part of a discourse of poverty. Through being deprived of income or material resources over an extended period of time, people can become detached from the lives that are customary in a given society. Social exclusion is the more extreme concept and can perhaps be thought of as one of the possible consequences of prolonged periods of marginalization. If marginalization is about being away from the mainstream, out on the margins of society, exclusion means being more or less cut off from society and in a situation of economic and social isolation. Social exclusion is about disenfranchisement and about being prevented, through a lack of resources, from being able to participate in the types of activities that are taken for granted by citizens in a given society. Social exclusion is a relatively new concept of European origin (Berghman, 1995), which Room defines as "multidimensional disadvantage, which is of substantial duration and which involves dissociation from the major social and occupational milieu of society" (cited in Berghman, 1995, p. 25). In educational contexts, exclusion is frequently used in a different way and can relate to prolonged or indefinite expulsion from school (often linked to behavioural issues) or to isolation linked to physical or mental impairments.

As part of a process, marginalization is hard to define because it occurs in a variety of contexts and can be cumulative. In education systems, for example, those with disabilities may be marginalized—they are not necessarily excluded from participation but, rather, through a variety of processes frequently come to occupy peripheral positions that may not reflect their qualifications or intellectual capacity. Marginalization is frequently linked to a resource deficit, but it can also be linked to culture and to subjective orientations as well as to policies that enforce the separation of those with certain characteristics, such as disabilities. In education, for example, a young person can be marginalized because they lack the resources to participate fully due to a deficit of basic skills or due to family finances and poverty. In a cultural context, some young people may not regard education as a worthwhile endeavour and may reject the goals and values of the school. If we are to prevent social exclusion, then it is necessary to ensure that children and young people are not marginalized within educational contexts, but such attention has to involve interventions that address both structural and cultural dimensions.

To prevent marginalization at every level, education has to be about equity and inclusivity, but while most people may agree that education systems need to be underpinned by social justice, there is little agreement about what a socially just system would look like in practical terms. At its core, social justice relates to the principle that every effort should be made to ensure that individuals and groups all enjoy fair access to rewards. It is about creating a "more equitable, respectful and just society for everyone" (Zaijda, Majhanovich, & Rust, 2006, p. 13). Yet social justice is not necessarily about equality—it can be about providing equal opportunities to access to an unequal reward structure. In a society committed to the ideals of social justice, it is recognized that fair treatment and equal opportunities for everyone can only be brought about by imposing restrictions on the behaviour of some individuals or groups. And this is where the problem lies—the provision of opportunities to members of less advantaged groups is uncontroversial, but restricting the opportunities of the middle and upper classes through a system of positive discrimination has proved much more controversial.

Rawls' (1971) idea of social justice involves more than the equal opportunity to access unequal labour market positions, and it has important implications for educational policy. Rawls argues that any reward system that provides advantages to those who display superior performance is likely to result in a form of distribution that is essentially arbitrary and favours those with pre-existing advantages. In other words, while some educationalists may regard talent, ability, or effort as attributes that merit reward, to provide differential privilege on the basis of something such as ability (which is randomly distributed) or effort (which is conditioned by family circumstances) is likely to result in the reproduction of inequalities and therefore runs counter to the idea of social justice.

In less idealistic terms, in a recent OECD report, equity was presented as having two dimensions: first, fairness, which means "ensuring that personal and social circumstances—for example, gender, socio-economic status, or ethnic origin—should not be an obstacle to achieving educational potential" (Field et al., 2007, p. 11). The second dimension, inclusion, "implies ensuring a basic minimum standard of education for all—for example everyone should be able to read, write and do simple arithmetic" (Field et al., 2007, p. 11). In this context, the prevention of marginalization in education involves activities targeted at groups as well as individuals. On the macro level, it will involve monitoring inequalities and taking positive action if any group is shown to be performing less well, while, on an individual level, it would involve triggering interventions targeted at pupils who are failing to thrive educationally and lacking a grounding in basic skills. Interestingly, in the United Kingdom, a new *Equality Act* has just been passed, which requires all local authorities to monitor and act on social class differences in access to all public services, including education.

Inequality in Education: Macro Perspectives

> [H]ow well children do in school and college is strongly influenced by social class background. More specifically, the more disadvantaged the social class background, the lower level of educational attainment that is likely to be achieved. Moreover, young people from less advantaged class backgrounds are less likely to take up the opportunities available to them to progress through the educational system, even where they are sufficiently qualified to make the progression. (Pring et al., 2009, p. 32)

Focusing on patterns of inequity in education, the first point to make is that, irrespective of social class, young people today remain in education longer and leave with superior qualifications to those of earlier generations. In Canada and the United Kingdom, most young people remain in school until the age of 18, and higher education is increasingly a mass experience. In the United Kingdom, for example, more than four in ten young people progress to higher education, and there is a policy commitment to raise this number that to 50% over the next few years. Yet while these changes have impacted on young people from all social classes and while in some countries the attainment gap between social classes has narrowed, it remains significant in all advanced societies, including those that have made great efforts to reduce class-based inequalities, such as the Scandinavian countries.

Despite some variation between countries, young people's educational attainment and patterns of participation are strongly affected by the class position of their parents in all OECD countries, and, in Canada, it has been argued that compared to other sources of inequality, such as gender and ethnicity, "class background seems to be the far more enduring source of educational inequality" (Guppy & Davies, 1998, p. 123). In Canada, there is also clear evidence of an association between poverty, family income, and levels of parental education and patterns of educational participation and attainment (O'Reilly & Yau, 2009; Wotherspoon, 2004). In Toronto, a recent school census highlighted a strong relationship between family income, parental education, and ethnic origin and performance in reading, writing, and math. The performance gap was particularly wide between those whose parents had a college education and those whose parents had no post-secondary education (O'Reilly & Yau, 2009). In the United Kingdom, the National Equity Panel discovered that in the most deprived neighbourhoods, around three in ten young men achieve examination results that place them in the top half of the attainment range, while, in the least deprived neighbourhoods, the corresponding figure is seven in ten. For young women, 50% of those in the least deprived neighbourhoods could be placed in the top quartile of the attainment range, compared to a fifth of those from the most deprived areas (Hills et al., 2010).

In terms of basic skills, the Programme for International Student Assessment surveys also show that, internationally, patterns of literacy and numeracy are affected by social class. In Canada, for example, young people from the lowest socio-economic status quartile were two and a half times more likely to fall into the bottom quartile for attainment in math than their more advantaged peers, while, in the United Kingdom, they were more than three times as likely to show poor levels of attainment in math (Field et al., 2007). Less advantaged young people are also more likely to drop out of high school and less likely to participate in post-secondary education or to attend university. Across the OECD countries, young people with educated parents are "between two and six times more likely to complete tertiary education themselves" (Field et al., 2007, p. 39).

In a review of trends in participation in higher education in the European Union countries, it has been argued that "a constant factor in all member states for which data are available, is that while absolute participation rates have increased for all socio-economic levels, the relative rates have rarely changed" (Green, Wolf, and Leney, 1999, p. 204). Drawing on data from several countries, Raftery and Hout (1993) propose a theory of "maximally maintained advantage." Essentially their argument is that educational expansion tends to occur in a way that results in little change in class-based differentials until a "saturation point" is reached. In other words, working class gains only tend to occur once middle-class participation has reached the point when virtually all young people from middle-class families are benefiting. We see evidence to support this theory in the expansion of higher education in the United Kingdom where the first beneficiaries of change were middle-class females.

The persistence of class-based inequalities in education is perhaps not surprising given that, despite some changes—particularly in the ways in which modern transitions impact on education—there are a lot of basic inequalities that remain unchanged. Children's early experiences within the family still provide them with an essential preparation for formal processes of education and lay the foundations for patterns of inequality and marginality (Lareau, 1993). Some children begin school able to read simple words, identify colours, count, and do simple arithmetic. Others have to acquire these skills within the school environment and may be seen as being less bright from the outset. Some children may be used to sitting quietly and paying attention to an adult who is providing instructions, while others may not. Throughout their time in education, those from more advantaged families often have access to educational resources in the home environment and support from family members who have some knowledge of the curriculum and who can help with homework (Farnen, 2007). In addition, middle-class families frequently stress the importance of education, highlight potential benefits, and are able to use their knowledge to secure advantages in an educational marketplace. By contrast, working-class families may have narrow occupational horizons, less direct knowledge of educational benefits, and may be unable to support their child beyond the end of compulsory education (Social Exclusion Task Force, 2008).

The school may also help reinforce family disadvantage (Lareau, 1993). Teachers may have lower expectations regarding the ability of working-class children and may fail to offer adequate levels of encouragement. In turn, working-class pupils are more likely to be placed in lower ability streams where they may mix with pupils who share their class background, reinforcing pre-existing perspectives and limiting their opportunities to familiarize themselves with the assumptive worlds of their middle-class peers (Dickar, 2008). There is also an extent to which schools themselves are stratified—most obviously into public and private sectors but also in terms of the neighbourhoods that they serve. Some schools have a poor social mix, contain large numbers of disruptive students, have high dropout rates, and lack a tradition of progression to higher education (Devine, 1996; Social Exclusion Task Force, 2008). In this context, research shows that social background has a greater impact on educational outcomes in cases where levels of social stratification between schools are significant (Field et al., 2007). Similarly, patterns of inequality are reinforced where pupils are placed into ability streams at an early stage (Field et al., 2007; Spina, 2000).

The separation of young people into vocational and academic tracks has a similar effect, but the issues here are slightly more complex. Some young people show no aptitude or interest in the academic curriculum, and there are clearly benefits in providing high quality vocational alternatives. If we look at countries that have a strong separation between vocational educational routes and academic pathways, such as Germany, there is strong evidence that the vocational alternative reduces unemployment among young people and smoothes the transition to employment. In other words, a strong vocational track helps reduce marginalization (Heinz, 1999). However, there is also evidence that these same processes limit the opportunities for upward social mobility (Shavit & Müller, 2000). Where vocational tracks are established, it is important to ensure that the lines of movement between different pathways remain open and that vocational qualifications are regarded as being equivalent to academic qualifications for the purposes of admission to college or university. This is an easy idea to subscribe to, but a tougher one to put into practice.

While there are strong continuities over time and many similarities between countries in the ways in which social class impacts on educational experiences, it is important to reflect on the ways in which changes in patterns of educational participation impact on outcomes. Undoubtedly, education has become more important to young people. The labour market has changed and opportunities for poorly qualified young people are severely limited. In the new knowledge economy, it is not just the lack of basic skills, but even the lack of advanced skills that can lead to marginalization within labour market contexts. In these circumstances, young people are participating in education for much longer, and the vast majority have a strong awareness of the link between educational attainment and subsequent life chances (Biggart and Furlong, 1999).

Increased participation comes at a price and can lead to the emergence of fresh inequalities. We increasingly need to focus on educational pathways that are followed at the post-compulsory stage. Not all families can afford to support their offspring through long periods of post-compulsory education or training, and even if state support is available there are still important lines of stratification. Evidence from the United Kingdom shows that young people from less affluent families are frequently debt adverse and reluctant to take out student loans to finance their studies (Callender, 2003). Young people from poorer families frequently select courses on the basis of cost, not simply in terms of fees but also in terms of overall costs, which may include the need to move away from home, travel costs, the length of the course, and the perceived linkages between their course and future employment (Furlong and Cartmel, 2009). This finding can result in young people from less affluent families selecting courses in less prestigious institutions, choosing shorter courses, and considering courses with strong vocational orientations. In addition, less affluent students frequently work long hours to survive in education, which can interfere with their studies and prevent cross-class social interaction (Farnen, 2007).

These changes also require young people to develop an ability to manage the complexity of educational structures, make informed choices, and manage educational careers. For those with inside knowledge who have direct experience of the ways in which education is delivered and the implications of various choices, the process can be relatively straightforward, but for those from families with little experience of post-compulsory education it can be difficult to navigate effectively, and marginalization can occur through poor choices (Ball, Maguire, & Macrae, 2000). Education has been subject to a process of marketization in which knowledgeable consumers with spending power are advantaged, while others can be marginalized (Ball, 2003).

Cultural Marginalization

> [M]uch of what our interviewees said about school can be understood in terms of the competition, played out day to day in the classroom, between a generally alienated but instrumental orientation to school and a complete disengagement from its formal processes and strictures. The choice to pursue a more instrumental approach ... was balanced against strong informal sanctions in the opposite direction. Those who worked hard in class, completed homework or revised for exams risked "getting tortured" (at worst, severe bullying and exclusion from friendship groups). (MacDonald & Marsh, 2005, p. 54)

Marginalization is clearly a highly structured process in which groups of young people who lack various resources can struggle to compete on equal terms with their more advantaged peers. However, class cultures can also impact on educational orientations and are regarded as playing an important role in the reproduction of inequalities and in the processes of marginalization. Many researchers have highlighted the ways in which lower working-class cultures can be at odds with the middle-class culture of the school. The classic work in this case is the study carried out by Willis in the United Kingdom in the 1970s. Willis (1977) argued that boys from lower working-class families frequently resisted the authority of the school and rejected school-based values that were based on deferred gratification, placed a premium on academic success, and valued mental labour over manual labour. According to Willis (1977), the "lads" that he studied had no desire to enter middle-class jobs. They wanted to be able to prove their masculinity through manual labour and full engagement in working-class culture and lifestyles without any unnecessary delay. In other words, through immersion in working-class culture, they were active participants in the reproduction of inequalities, and, where marginalization occurred, it was triggered through their own actions.

In recent years, the idea that class-based resistance is central to the reproduction of inequalities has increasingly been challenged, partly because education has become much more central to the lives of all young people who participate for longer periods of time and come to understand the restricted range of job opportunities available to those without qualifications. In many Western countries, today's youth grew up in a period in which the occupational structure changed significantly, and many of their parents experienced upward social mobility as a consequence. As a result, expectations changed, and there was a degree of convergence in class cultures. With a serious decline in unskilled manual jobs in factories and building sites and with education becoming more crucial to labour market outcomes, resistance is no longer such a central part of working-class orientations towards school, although it still exists, and instrumentalism becomes more common (Biggart & Furlong, 1999; MacDonald & Marsh, 2005). As Côté and Allahar (2007) suggest, even in higher education, many students can be described as "reluctant intellectuals."

However, if instrumentalism is the glue that holds young people in the school system, then they have to have a degree of confidence that their efforts will pay off. Young people living in poor communities who lack role models that can demonstrate the link between educational attainment and lifestyles are not going to have any confidence in this "academic bargain" and may continue to reject the idea of academic conformity. And there is also a tension here. In lower working-class peer groups, it is often not seen as "cool to be clever" (MacDonald & Marsh, 2005; Williamson, 2004), and therefore the rewards for breaking with peer values, which may result in bullying or shunning, have to be obvious.

The idea that class cultures are reference points that shape young people's assumptive worlds is a theme developed most coherently in the work of Bourdieu. For Bourdieu (1977), these class-based assumptions (what he referred to as a *habitus*) represent a form of cultural capital that is used in education and the labour market to secure advantages. Those who lack cultural capital run the risk of marginalization, while those who possess cultural capital have a valuable asset that can be used to secure favourable outcomes and that will offer a degree of protection in educational and labour market careers. In fact, Bourdieu (1977) thought that as educational policies were introduced to reduce the impact of structural resources on patterns of participation, cultural capital would become increasingly central to the reproduction of advantage. This idea is supported by a lot of school-based research that highlights the ways in which cultural capital is regarded by teachers as a proxy for intelligence, while those who lack this capital are seen as being stupid or disinterested. The work of Lareau (1993) provides rich illustrations of the ways in which middle-class parents mobilize their cultural capital to secure educational advantage for their children.

If class cultures serve as a reference point through which educational opportunities are evaluated, then it is clear that active and prolonged engagement in education requires some sort of accommodation of an identity as a learner. Young people have to be comfortable to describe themselves as students and have to work out what that means to themselves in terms of involvement in their communities, in the here and now, and in the context of future lives and careers. In relation to this line of thinking, Reay (2005) talks about class-based "authenticity." For Reay, the effective participation of working-class students is not about casting aside a working class identity but, rather, about being driven by a desire to accommodate their new experiences within a framework that respects their working-class roots. As Reay (2005, p. 7) puts it, "for the working class student authenticity most often meant being able to hold onto a self rooted in a working class past."

Recent work on youth transitions has highlighted the importance of these subjective accommodations through the concept of biography. Essentially biographical approaches have been used as a way of understanding how individuals make sense of their lives within the dynamic processes of transition and change. As individuals, we reflect on past experiences as a way of framing future plans and try to make sense of our lives through putting together a coherent story. In a sense, part of the biographical project of youth relates to the construction of a sense of selfhood in which there is a reasonable degree of congruence between objective and subjective experiences. In the past, young people were, to an extent, able to use the experiences of significant others (especially family members or peers from the same class positions or with similar educational attainments) to help them construct road maps. In the modern world, it is argued that rapid processes of social change and the fragmentation of experiences make it extremely difficult to plan for the future or manage lives (subjectively or objectively) in a meaningful sense. Indeed, I have suggested that there is often a mismatch between objective experiences and subjective interpretations that can lead young people to blame themselves when things do not turn out as they had expected (Furlong & Cartmel, 2007).

In this context, meaningful engagement with education must involve the incorporation of education into the biography in a way that links positive outcomes in the future to participation and attainment. The concept can also be thought of as a way of coming to terms with the ways in which outcomes are linked not simply to the material resources of class but also to a set of subjective capacities through which individuals are differentially equipped to manage their lives. Here, Ball, Maguire, and Macrae (2003) have tried not only to highlight the advantages derived by those who are able to act as biographical engineers but also to recognize that some young people have limited coping resources. In this context, it can be argued that schools have an important role to play in teaching life management skills and helping build young people's capacity for reflexive action and helping them to become aware of the very real structural barriers that must be negotiated. Similarly, Wyn (2009) has argued that in late modernity educationalists have an important role to play in helping young people to become effective self-navigators.

Conclusion: Lessons for Policy

In conclusion, I want to pull out some of the main implications of research on youth for educational policy. Briefly, what can be done to reduce the chances of marginalization and minimize the impact of socio-economic origins on educational outcomes? First of all, we should not try to fool ourselves that education systems are able to fully compensate for deeply entrenched socio-economic divisions. As Bernstein (1970) puts it, "education cannot compensate for society." We are currently living through the aftermath of a world recession and may come to witness a greater polarization rather than a trend towards greater equality. In the short to medium term, social mobility is not going to be brought about by a sudden growth of opportunities at the top end of the labour market. Commentators such as Beck (2000) would argue that in the Western worlds we are far more likely to witness a reduction in professional and managerial positions and the expansion of precarious job opportunities. The impact of social class has proven to be extremely resistant to change, and, while economic conditions may be against us at the moment, I still believe that education can make a difference.

Inequality and marginalization is not simply part of the context in which we, as educationalists, operate. It is a core responsibility of education at all levels to actively strive to reduce the impact of one's social background on educational experiences and outcomes. Some groups will inevitably come into the educational system being much better equipped to learn, and this advantage is not necessarily about ability or resilience but, rather, about resources and initial advantage. To tackle these inequalities so as to prevent marginalization, it may be necessary to focus on the less advantaged rather than on the more vocal and demanding middle classes. It is certainly necessary to monitor performance at the group, as well as at the individual, level with a view to triggering appropriate interventions where we become aware of underperformance.

Another issue that we need to address is the question of whether education is fit for its purpose in contemporary society. If we look closely at schools today in either the United Kingdom or Canada, we might want to conclude that, in essence, they are more similar than they are different to those that existed in the heyday of industrialism. Young people are still expected to sit down and listen to formal lessons in traditional subjects. While progress has been made, on the whole the teacher is in control and the pupil is the subject rather than an active and empowered participant. It is the teacher—or often the state—that decides what the young person needs to know and how best to impart that knowledge. In this context, the Australian educationalist, Wyn (2009), has argued that if we are to equip young people with the skills they need in the modern world we need to abandon what she calls the "industrial model," which prioritizes narrow outcomes such as qualifications and focuses on "socially orientated outcomes" such as capacity building, independence, and decision making. In the modern world, young people are going to have to be proactive, are going to need to be able to take decisions in unfamiliar situations, and are going to need to determine how and when to use education and training to further their goals.

Underpinning these issues is the question of how we help working class kids to fit into, and even thrive within, a middle-class world. Research shows us that the way to do it is not to try and get them to turn their backs on their own culture or to work in ways that constantly values middle-class culture over working-class culture—such effort simply leads to alienation. Working-class students have to be able to accommodate new ideas within an existing framework to maintain an authenticity. Certainly more working-class teachers could help provide effective role models—the sort of changes we have seen in recent years mean that parents may be less able to provide their children with an adequate knowledge of the occupational world or offer suitable guidance. We also need to ensure that schools and classrooms contain a broad social mix to provide a context in which young people can broaden their social horizons.

Finally, we can learn some lessons from research on youth transitions. Young people's transitions from school to work are less likely to be linear movements. The greater complexity and protraction of transitions mean that backtracking has become much more common, and people need to be able to return to education as the need arises or as their interests shift. As such, a "one-size-fits-all" model of education no longer meets the needs of young people. There are signs that education is becoming more flexible and imaginative—there is a greater concern to try and engage young people of all ages, including those who have left early with few qualifications. Despite these positive moves, young people are still being marginalized in the United Kingdom and Canada, and we have to continue to develop innovative ways of engaging those most vulnerable.

Notes

1   Gini index, online: http://data.worldbank.org/indicator/SI.POV.GINI/.

References

Ball, S. J. (2003). *Class strategies in the educational market: The middle classes and social advantage*. London: Routledge-Falmer.

Ball, S. J., Maguire, M., & Macrae, S. (2003). *Choice, pathways and transitions post-16*. London: Routledge-Falmer.

Beck, U. (1992). *The risk society: Towards a new modernity*. London: Sage.

Beck, U. (2000). *The brave new world of work*. Cambridge: Polity Press.

Berghman, J. (1995). Social exclusion in Europe: Policy context and analytical framework. In G. Room (Ed.), *Beyond the threshold: The measurement and analysis of social exclusion* (pp. 10-28). Bristol, UK: Policy Press.

Bernstein, B. (1970). Education cannot compensate for society. *New Society, 15*, 344-347.

Biggart, A., & Furlong, A. (1999). Educating "discouraged workers": Cultural diversity in the upper secondary school. *British Journal of Sociology of Education, 17*, 253-266.

Bourdieu, P. (1977) Cultural reproduction and social reproduction. In J. Karabel and A. H. Halsey (Eds.), *Power and ideology in education*. New York: Oxford University Press.

Callender, C. (2003). *Attitudes to debt: School leavers and further education students' attitudes to debt and their impact on participation in higher education*. London: Universities UK.

Côté, J. E., & Allahar, A. L. (2007). *Ivory tower blues: A university system in crisis*. Toronto: University of Toronto Press.

Devine, J. (1996). *Maximum security: The culture of violence in inner-city schools*. Chicago: University of Chicago Press.

Dickar, M. (2008). *Corridor cultures: Mapping student resistance at an urban high school*. New York: New York University Press.

Farnen, R. F. (2007). Class matters: Inequality, SES, education and childhood in the USA and Canada today. *Policy Futures in Education, 5*, 278-302.

Field, S., Kuczera, M., & Pont, B. (2007). *No more failures: Ten steps to equity in education*. Paris, France: Organisation for Economic Co-operation and Development.

Furlong, A., & Cartmel, F. (2007). *Young people and social change: New perspectives*. Maidenhead, UK: Open University Press.

Furlong, A., & Cartmel, F. (2009). *Higher education and social justice*. Maidenhead, UK: Open University Press.

Green, A., Wolf, A., & Leney, T. (1999). *Convergence and divergence in European education and training systems* (Bedford Way Papers no. 7). London: Institute of Education.

Guppy, N., & Davies, S. (1998). *Education in Canada: Recent trends and future challenges*. Ottawa: Statistics Canada.

Hills, J., Brewer, M., Jenkins, S., Lister, R., Lupton, R., Machin, S., ... Riddell, S. (2010). *An anatomy of economic inequality in the UK: Report of the National Equity Panel*. London: Government Equalities Office.

Heinz, W. R. (1999). Job entry patterns in a life-course perspective. In W. R. Heinz (Ed.), *From education to work: Cross-national perspectives* (pp. 214-231). Cambridge: Cambridge University Press.

Lareau, A. (1993). *Home advantage: Social class and parental intervention in elementary education*. London: Falmer Press.

MacDonald, R., & Marsh, J. (2005). *Disconnected youth? Growing up in Britain's poor neighbourhoods.* London: Palgrave.

O'Reilly, J., & Yau, M. (2009). *2008 Parent Census, Kindergarten to Grade 6.* Etobicoke, ON: Toronto District School Board.

Pring, R., Hayward, G., Hodgon, A., Johnson, J., Keep, E., Oancea, A., ... Wilde, S. (2009). *Education for all: The future of education and training for 14-19 year olds.* London: Routledge.

Raftery, A. E., & Hout, M. (1993). Maximally maintained inequality: Expansion, reform and opportunity in Irish education 1921-1975, *Sociology of Education, 66,* 41-62.

Rawls, J. (1971). *A theory of social justice.* Oxford: Oxford University Press.

Reay, D. (2005). *Who goes where in higher education: An issue of class, ethnicity and increasing concern.* London: Institute for Policy Studies in Education, Metropolitan University.

Shavit, Y., & Müller, W. (2000). Vocational secondary education: Where diversion and where safety net? *European Societies, 2,* 29-50.

Social Exclusion Task Force (2008). *Aspirations and attainment amongst young people in deprived communities.* London: Department for Children, Schools and Families.

Spina, S. U. (2000). Introduction: Violence in schools. In S. U. Spina (Ed.), *Smoke and mirrors: The hidden context of violence in school and society* (pp. 1-40). Lanham, MD: Rowman and Littlefield.

UN Children's Fund. (2010). *Report Card 9: The children left behind.* New York: UN Children's Fund.

Williamson, H. (2004). *The Milltown boys revisited.* London: Berg.

Willis, P. (1977). *Learning to labour.* Farnborough, UK: Saxon House.

Wotherspoon, T. (2004). *The sociology of education in Canada: Critical perspectives* (2nd edition). Don Mills, ON: Oxford University Press.

Wyn, J. (2009). *Touching the future: Building skills for life and work.* Camberwell, Australia: Australian Council for Educational Research.

Zaijda, J., Majhanovich, S., & Rust, V. (2006). Introduction: Education and social justice. *International Review of Education, 52,* 9-22.

Tears and Fears, drawing and poem by Anwesha Sen

chapter 8

On Being Poor in School

Kate Tilleczek

Introduction

> I want to tell you what it is like to never have had the chance of feeling
> excited about being educated. It is hard to feel pride when your classrooms
> are cold and mice run over our lunches. It is hard to feel you can have a
> chance to grow up as somebody important when you don't have proper
> resources like libraries and science labs. That's why some of our students
> begin to give up in Grade 4 and 5, they just stop going to school. (Shannon
> Koostachin at Attawapiskat Children's Rights Forum, Toronto, 2008)

We must no longer speak of a hidden curriculum in schools. This is not because it no longer exists but, rather, because the problem is no longer hidden. We are witnessing a rabid staying power of inequity, new forms of marginalization, growing income inequality, and the breakdown of public education. We are left instead to consider the cryptic curriculum of public education that is curious, enigmatic, and embedded in the human relationships and structures that marginalize young people already "in-risk" (Tilleczek, 2011) and "put at disadvantage" (Smyth, Down and McInerey, 2010; Smyth, 2010). This chapter discusses stayed and emerging forms of disadvantage. It invokes the idea of a cryptic curriculum, which persists despite the efforts of committed educators, parents, young people, and critical social scientists.

Canada continues to harbour many divisions that marginalize youth even though we have been naming the problem of the hidden curriculum of schooling for decades. This chapter examines how these divisions have remained entrenched and illustrates, through three narratives, the ways in which *being poor* at school is experienced by some of Canada's young people. Examining experiences, intersections, and social processes of marginalization across regional, social class, identity, and cultural divisions illustrates the culminations of severely flawed educational and youth policies. While Canada is often viewed as a civil and well-adjusted society relative to others, these divisive processes undermine the lives of youth and continue to incite marginalization in the face of some courageous attempts to build equitable public education.

Three new R's of schooling have congealed through two decades of teaching, research, parenting, and in conversation with thousands of young people and those closest to them. These three R's reverberate into the current critique of public education: *reflection, reproduction,* and *resistance.* They continue to be of use in the analysis of the experience of being poor at school. Young people from impoverished families are poor in social and economic terms relative to their classmates, and too many enter a spiral of decline based on the human relationship and structures they encounter in school. They therefore become poor in supports and academic outcomes. We all have stories to tell about the double jeopardy of being poor at/in school, and invoking reflection and narrative and biography is an important way to see social class and its reproductive and resistence process at school. The stories speak to what is unique but similar for youth as they negotiate positions of marginality at school (VanGalen, 2004). In this chapter, I present three stories against the backdrop of growing income inequality. By way of introduction, meet Ryan, Emily, and Kristen; each shares experiences of being poor at school as the chapter unfolds.

Ryan's experience in school was disheartening. Harsh economic conditions, substance abuse, and an overwhelmed, uncaring school counsellor reinforced his depression and lack of hope for the future. When many of Ryan's friends left school, he did as well. However, despite his discouragement and the challenges that still lay ahead, he hopes to return to school. He feels that education is the only way that he can escape poverty. Unfortunately, finding the financial and emotional support to return seems unlikely in the present system.

Kristen now lives on her own with her 2-year-old son. Her life has involved a series of moves and instabilities related to living in poverty. She finally has her own little apartment and receives slightly more assistance than she would on welfare, due to the fact that she has been a ward of the state for the majority of her life. Kristen has never known any semblance of financial security, nor any other type of security, for that matter. In the past 12 years, Kristen has moved over 50 times, which gives her an average of 2.8 months at each address. If she remains where she is now for another two weeks, the duration of three months will already have exceeded her average length of time at one residence. Furthermore, this is the first time in the last 12 years that she has not lived in a foster or group home. Yet this desperate situation is the best one she has been in since early childhood.

Emily dealt with a multitude of challenges each day that forced her out of school. Poverty was an integral part of her life and a main feature of these many challenges she faced. Other students were classist and created a violent and vicious ethos for Emily at school due to her "poorness" and her difference in appearance. She found it difficult to get a job to ease the financial strain, and there was no one inside or outside of the school available to help her. The principal was unsupportive and critical, and requests for tutorial help were not readily available. Constant familial moves added to the lack of stability and chaos of Emily's life. Each of these strains culminated in pushing Emily from school before she had a chance to attain a diploma.

Growing Divisions

Recently, the Organisation for Economic Co-operation and Development (OECD, 2009) published its first report on the well-being of children in *Doing Better for Children: Country Highlights.* The country-by-country analyses detail the trouble spots for policy consideration. They demonstrate that incomes at every level have risen over the past two decades, while the income gap between the richest 10% and the poorest 10% of the population has also grown. The country note for Canada shows that "both inequality and poverty rates have increased rapidly in the past 10 years, now reaching levels above the OECD average" (OECD, 2009, p. 1). Canadian highlights suggest that governments should increase spending on early childhood while, at the same time, equally ensuring that spending on youth is more appropriately channelled into meeting the needs of the most disenfranchised "teenagers."

The past 20 years has seen a significant increase in income inequality affecting more than three-quarters of OECD countries, with Canada, Finland, Germany, Italy, and the United States showing growing gaps between the rich and the middle class as well. Children and young adults are experiencing the change most profoundly since they are now more likely to be poor than people reaching retirement (OECD, 2009).

In addition, poverty is not distributed equally across all social groups in Canada. The 2001 Census in Canada demonstrated that 18.4% of all Canadian children were living in poverty. However, of those who had recently immigrated to Canada, the poverty rate is 49.0%, all immigrants to Canada had a rate of 40.4%, Aboriginal children a rate of 40.0%, and visible minority children had a rate of 33.6%. The daily lives of Aboriginal children and youth in Canada continue to be predominated by poverty, social exclusion, discrimination, and determination as these two Aboriginal youth from our Early School Leavers Study (Tilleczek, 2008) describe:

> It all depends on where you are. When you are on reserve back home it's fine because everybody is getting along but as soon as you leave the reserve you get funny looks ... or certain comments toward Native people and I don't think it's right.

> Out of my family, nobody has graduated from high school yet. So, I wanted to be the first to graduate, and I WILL be the first ... I think my mind is more set on what I want to do than I did before I left. I have been taking all the courses that I need and I want to get into college.

Blackstock (2009) and others continue to revisit and review growing bodies of evidence regarding the disproportionate oppression faced by indigenous children, their families, and communities (e.g., Assembly of First Nations, 2002; Chandler, 2010; Tilleczek, 2008a). Many forms of "epistemic violence" against Canada's First Nations and Indigenous people have been demonstrated by Chandler (2010) and others (see Chapter 5 in this volume). Most pressing is the disregard and undermining of various ways of living and knowing that have been eradicated from social and educational policies and practices. Traditional knowledge in education and health concerns is critical in restoring the confidence and respect necessary for the development of strong senses of identity and confidence in a future. For Aboriginal and impoverished children and youth, the most notable and ongoing forms of division show up in ill health and education.

Health status as measured by the United Nations shows that Canada has been the top country on the United Nations' Human Development Index ten times (a measure of life expectancy, literacy, education, and standard of living). However, in 2009, Canada was ranked fourth, and, within Canada, Aboriginal communities ranked sixty-third in 1990 and sixty-second in 2006. The Canadian Institute for Wellbeing (CIW) has also shown a decline of 11.9% in the share of the population that considers itself in excellent or very good health, a decline most marked among Canadian youth (cited in Arundel and Associates, 2009). This decline is matched by a steadily increasing share of youth who report problems with "everyday functions." Visible minority youth on average, have poorer health, lower incomes, and higher rates of poverty (CIW, 2009).

However, economic growth and increases in average incomes have not necessarily contributed to better health in wealthy countries of late. And ill health and poor educational outcomes are not produced by material poverty alone, even though health and social problems are strongly associated with income. As Wilkinson and Picket (2009) have shown in detail, it is the distribution of incomes in society or the levels of relative income inequality that have the greatest influence on health and social outcomes. Income inequality is measured in the proportion of income going to the richest and poorest members of society. The greater the income gap and disparity, the greater the income inequality (among the wealthiest nations, those with high levels of inequality include Singapore, the United States, Portugal, and the United Kingdom). In Wilkinson and Pickett's calculations, Canada is about midway in inequality of the "wealthiest" nations. However, the OECD has shown that this gap in income has been growing for Canada in the last ten years.

Societies with the greatest levels of income inequality are also those that have a large number of impoverished citizens and also perform least well on any number of social measures according to Wilkinson and Pickett's (2009) global analysis. They list a number of the health and social problems that are found wanting in societies with high-income inequality. These include levels of trust, mental illness and addiction, life expectancy and infant mortality, obesity, educational performance, teenage births, homicides, imprisonment, and social mobility. They show the strong tendency for these health and social problems (taken alone or as a composite) to occur less frequently in more equal societies. Therefore, it is necessary to analyze income inequality as well as the experiences of living in these divides.

Being Poor in School

Emily

Emily has just left her mother's home and has spent her first night at a group home. She is 18 years old and is five months pregnant. Emily has changed schools three times during high school and, in a total of four years, has only completed Grade 10. She left school several months ago, shortly after the word spread among the students that she was expecting. Throughout her life, Emily has moved many times, especially during the periods when she lived with her mom. They would often move every month, and the Children's Aid Society removed her twice from her home.

The only stable residence was when she stayed with her father and stepmother from age 12 to 16. When she returned to her mom's house in Eastern Canada, Emily had a lot more freedom than she had at her dad's, but she found the home to be even more stressful. Her mother

*struggled with addictions. Whether her mother was working or
partying, Emily was often left to care for her two younger sisters.
She regularly cleaned the house, cooked supper, washed the floors,
did the dishes, and made sure her sisters cleaned their rooms.*

*At school, Emily often felt uncomfortable regarding her family income
level, family composition, hand-me-down clothes, Eastern provincial
accent, and physical traits. Many days, Emily came home from school
crying because other girls were picking on her. On these nights, she
often stayed at her boyfriend's house instead of at home as she was not
getting along well with her mother. After the episodes at school, her
mother would tell her to "just get over it" and go back to school. Her
mom wanted her to complete her high school education but offered no
practical support. The fights with girls escalated as more people began
picking on Emily. Eventually, Emily was skipping school nearly every
day, whether by herself or with her boyfriend. Her grades dropped.*

*Emily is frustrated that her only work experience was a Saturday job
she got through the high school that only lasted for two months and
earned her $50 each day. Now that she is pregnant, MacDonald's will
not hire her. Her boyfriend, who still lives in Eastern Canada, is working to save money to get an apartment. She has some clothes ready for
the baby when it arrives.*

*Throughout school, Emily had tutors to help her, and she managed
to have marks that ranged from 60 to 70%. Grammar was always a
problem, and Emily found it frustrating that the computer could not
catch all of her errors. School seemed too hard! In the new school she
started attending in September, she placed requests for tutors, but they
did not come through fast enough. The due dates and exams seemed to
be coming up rather quickly, and Emily grew more distressed. In order
to make social connection in the new school, Emily volunteered to work
on the school yearbook. However, she did not easily understand the
way they were used to doing things, and the other students were not
very nice to her. This seemed to be because she was a newcomer, was
quiet, and wore different clothes. They often talked behind her back
and challenged her to fight. Emily cried a lot and recalls the stress she
experienced at school one particular day. She and another student were
about to give a presentation, and Emily just could not do it. She asked
for permission to use the washroom and simply left school for the day.*

The principal was not helpful in Emily's opinion. Since the principal had known Emily's boyfriend when he was younger, one day she told Emily that physical and emotional abuse were likely to occur if she stayed in that relationship. The principal told her at least once to leave school. In addition, once the pregnancy was public information the principal pressed Emily to consider having an abortion. This suggestion was the breaking point for Emily. It was something she could not consider and would not be pressured into. After that conversation, she never returned to school.

Young people like Emily live the effects of social inequalities in their daily lives in the community, in the street, and in the work place. However, much of the rubber of social inequality hits the road for young people in school. Inequality in society gets "under the skin" and into the daily lives of people via processes of social comparison and the resultant experiences of vulnerability, anxiety, discrimination, and threat (Wilkinson & Pickett, 2009). Research with young people transitioning into secondary school demonstrates that a perceived relative social status was experienced as a more pressing problem than actual familial income (Tilleczek et al., 2010). If students feel "poorer" in relation to their friends, their transition to high school was made more problematic via social exclusion. Large-scale social and economic trends arrive in the already complex lives of many youth and are too often mistaken simply for latent "personal" or psychological problems. The entrenched epistemological fallacy of modern societies as detailed by Furlong and Cartmel (2007) is therefore fed by policy-makers and educators who insist on localizing and addressing problems as being embedded in the individual rather than in complex social inequalities. Two decades of sociological study of youth and education has done little to impact this policy situation.

For instance, a recent review of all high school-leaving programs in the United States reported that only 50 programs had ever been evaluated and were considered to be "exemplary." A majority (64%) of the exemplary programs addressed more than one risk factor, about one-quarter of them (26%) identified programs addressing three factors, and 18% addressed four or more factors. Yet still over one-third of the identified programs (36%) addressed a single risk factor (National Dropout Prevention Centre, 2007). The majority of these programs continued to address risk factors only in the individual and psychological realm of student social attitudes, values, and behaviours. Only 14 programs acknowledged family background, poverty, or ethnicity, although these were considered to be "unalterable factors" and therefore not addressed in school practices.

Ryan

Ryan is 21 years old and has changed schools twice during high school and does not know how many courses he has taken or if he is actually earned any credits beyond Grade 7. In the interview, Ryan avoided eye contact and spoke softly. He was hesitant at first, but by the end of the interview he even joked around a little.

Ryan's parents have been unemployed for a long time. When drunk, Ryan's father was abusive towards the children and towards Ryan's mother. More recently, his parents have become more civil. When enrolled in school, just getting up in the morning was difficult for Ryan. He did not want to get up, and his parents seldom woke him up or told him to go to classes. On the one day they did wake him up, he left the house but hid in town to avoid going to school. Although he officially left high school after four years, he "pretty much stopped going" to classes after the first two years.

He wishes that the school had provided a way for him to study at home. He requested this sort of home study, but it was not given to him. He did receive help from a special education teacher and has special test accommodations. While in school, Ryan was suspended about 15 times for "not listening."

In addition, alcohol and drugs were a big part of his life around the time he left school. All of Ryan's friends had also left school, so he did the same. There did not seem to be much to do in his town except get high or drunk. Any community activities that were started failed because they were so poorly attended. With his sister's boyfriend being a dealer, drugs were quite accessible. Sometimes he argued with his parents over his intoxication. Occasionally, his parents would report his behaviour to the police, and he would be taken into custody. At times like these, he promised not to drink any more.

He has a counsellor helping him work on goals and on ending his addictions to drugs and drinking. She encourages him to go back to school. At one time, Ryan had plans to go to college, but the drug use often seemed to make those plans appear unrealistic. There is now a new school near his home that he feels he should try to go to, so that he is "not on welfare programs for the rest of his life."

Canada has a patchwork of youth social policies with hit-or-miss programs and practices. For instance, Paul Martin, the former prime minister of Canada has recently launched a program to facilitate the entry of Aboriginal youth (only 50% of whom possess high school diplomas) into university by setting up a dual-credit system, whereby students simultaneously gain high school and university credits. A removal of roadblocks to educational access is on the right track, yet these allowances underestimate social reproduction and political complexities. Levin (2008) examined political and social forces that affect Canadian school systems by studying changes in institutional and cultural power in two school boards over 30 years. The ability of local school boards to attend to, and "manage," the ongoing problems and reproductions inherent in poverty in schools was deeply affected by factors beyond the control of school boards. Three such factors were the changing relationship between local boards and provincial governments (education is politically governed provincially in Canada); the "accidents" of local political events as they play out in community contexts; and the impact of growing population diversity in urban areas.

The ongoing and complex relationship between schooling and poverty in Canada must be acknowledged and understood. For youth who are captives of contemporary compulsory schooling, it could be argued that social reproduction in schools is one of the most critical processes by which they remain marginal. For Anyon (1980; 2006, p. 361), social class "is perceived as a complex of social relations that one develops as one grows up—as one acquires and develops certain bodies of knowledge, skills, abilities, and traits, and as one has contact and opportunity in the world." For students in school, their placement in distinct programs and/or treatment as "poor" often dictates continued class placements. And we know how often school experiences have differed qualitatively according to socio-economic status: "These differences may not only contribute to the development in the children in each social class of certain types of economically significant relationships and not others, but would thereby help to reproduce this system of relations in society" (Anyon, 2006, p. 380). This is the hidden curriculum that Anyon and others made visible to us so long ago. However, parents and community members expect schools to provide fair quality education for all. In Canada, this is far from what happens. Too many young people are disengaging from school and leaving school prior to graduation, and so end up remaining at a social disadvantage. Their wages are on average consistently lower than those with a high school diploma, and their unemployment rate has been five to six percentage points higher than both the national average and the rate for high school graduates since the 1990s (Statistics Canada, 2005).

Aboriginal, immigrant, visible minority, and impoverished young people from rural/remote or inner-city communities remain the most likely to leave school (Tilleczek, 2008b). Not all people, or only poor young people, struggle in school, but poverty and cultural status exacerbate the process of getting an education in Canada. Both the HRSDC (2001) and Willms (2002, p. 12) have demonstrated in the Canadian context that, while it is known that low family income affects youth, "we know relatively little about the form of the relationship between family income and children's behavioural and cognitive outcomes" in school. Indeed, the mechanisms by which poverty and low income influences young people are not well understood. In addition, these mechanisms are not being discussed in national or provincial policy, forcing to the margins any true discussion of equity in public education. We must continue to make visible the experiences and biographies of those young people who are striving to negotiate, resist, and "speak back" (Smyth, this volume) from the public education system that they inherit.

The processes by which income inequality and poverty continue to rise and affect health and schooling are well examined descriptively. Those who have done so show that school troubles are long term and multi-dimensional processes influenced by a variety of in-school and out-of-school experiences.[1] Being poor has long been understood to be a critical risk condition, and the pervasiveness of the socio-economic gradient effect in multiple health, learning, and behavioural outcomes has been documented in detail across countries (Brooks-Gunn & Duncan, 1996; Duncan et al., 1997; Keating and Hetzman, 1999). Students from lower income backgrounds are much more likely to experience trouble in school and to leave high school than are those from higher income backgrounds. Young people from impoverished homes, communities, and schools experience these "interactive troubles" (Hattam & Smyth, 2003) and/or multiple "daily hassles" (Seidman et al., 1994) that require proactive and coordinated understandings and responses.

Kristen

Kristen's parents "gave her away" at the age of 8, and Kristen feels that that this early life experience has contributed to her depleted feelings about herself. At the age of 8, Kristen became involved with the Children's Aid Society, moving among group homes, foster homes, and juvenile facilities. Many of the areas that Kristen had lived during her life were poor neighbourhoods where many people subsisted on social assistance. It was typical for Kristen to live in neighbourhoods with a lot of garbage and rats and with a high prevalence of street drugs. She recalls that one particular city she lived in had only one shelter that could hold 7 women, which is not nearly enough space to hold all of the homeless people who needed to be there. The welfare cheques seemed devastatingly low in these areas and were not easy to access in the first place. Employment was even harder to come by, and there was little help for funding bus transportation.

As Kristen aged, any contact maintained between mother and daughter was characterized by further instability since they fought "like cats and dogs." Her resentment was intensified by the disallowance of any relationship with her now 15-year-old brother and 17-year-old sister. While Kristen felt her mother was proud of her good marks in Grades 1–4, her support did not go much further than that, even while Kristen lived at home. Kristen lost all touch with her father and was able to maintain only an extremely unstable relationship with her mom.

Although Kristen liked school and felt like she was smart when she was young, she never felt she "was worth anything." Even now, Kristen feels others are always more confident than she is. In the school hallways, Kristen always looked at her feet. Even in the interview, Kristen often apologized for her answers, which she thought may have been somehow "wrong." In addition to economic status, there were many interacting factors identified that made Kristen feel marginalized and out of place at school. These factors included her speech impediment, physical traits, physical abilities, learning disabilities, mental health, family composition, and sexual orientation. She was often treated unfairly by other students. Kristen typically sat on the floor of the cafeteria, hiding in the corner of the cafeteria to eat her lunch. She tried to keep to herself, while everyone else seemed to congregate in little groups, doing all sorts of unproductive things such as smoking pot or bullying people. Kristen was hard pressed to find any other students who focused on learning in school.

Finding peers that got along with Kristen was difficult in high school. She drifted between groups, with few people to even hang out with casually. Occasionally, others would let her stand to smoke with them, but their conversations seemed incessantly focused on drugs, fighting, and sex. In the schoolyard and the cafeteria, Kristen experienced violence. It seemed to arise from her differences from other students and often appeared to simply be something for students to do. Kristen was suspended five or six times and expelled once for fighting. When people made fun of her, Kristen had trouble remaining calm and was pushed to the point of assault at times. Then, in the principal's office, Kristen was made to feel like everything was her fault since she had lost her temper. Little validation was given to the fact that she was the one being picked on initially.

In Kristen's classes, nobody wanted to be there or to pay attention to the teachers. As early as Grade 8, things were regularly being thrown around, students were stealing, and a couple of windows were broken every year. Harassing the teacher and general rowdiness seemed to be the order of each day. Seemingly contrary to the majority of other students, Kristen wanted to learn and liked to learn. She felt great pride in conquering things such as math and doing well on tests. However, she often did not learn as quickly as she thought she should. This opinion of herself, coupled with teachers who did not have enough time to help students adequately, exacerbated Kristen's disappointment when she did poorly at school. In the two and a half years of enrolment at school, Kristen only successfully completed Grade 9.

Along with these disappointments, teachers, guidance counsellors, principals, and other staff treated her unfairly at school for mental health issues. In classes, teachers did not communicate well. They allowed Kristen to see that they thought that there was something wrong with her, despite her efforts to always be on the good side of her teachers and to show them respect. She had what she calls "her own way" of doing things but generally just felt like a "really weird kid," who was "hardheaded" and emotional. Classes were "distracting," with a lot of things going on outside and very few others paying attention. In many ways, she felt like a target and, not surprisingly, skipped the equivalent of one full day of classes in high school each week.

Multiple diagnoses were given to Kristen, including bipolar disorder, borderline personality disorder, and obsessive-compulsive disorder. She felt like a "medication guinea pig" for the Children's Aid Society, always high on medication before she was even old enough to know what "high" was. Support from and through her placements with foster parents offered her some self-esteem and anger management courses. Occasionally, tutoring, after-school programs, or test rewrites were provided, but it took her two and a half years to complete her Grade 9. She failed approximately half of her academic classes and passed all of her six applied courses. Many times, Kristen missed school due to problems at home, pregnancy, and illness/disability.

A little work experience was provided through a special education co-operative course through her school. She did co-operative courses at grocery, bakery, and drug stores for a total of one year, five mornings per week. Unfortunately, she was not paid for these positions. The few paid jobs were for short periods of time working at a gas station, a pawn shop, and a department store. Somehow, Kristen had the stamina to volunteer at animal shelters, and she enjoyed extracurricular activities such as using the gym and going to dances.

At the age of 16, Kristen left school. She was living at a group home with varying qualities of staff. She felt there were no supports to stay in school. The school staff seemed to be saying: "If you wanted to go, I guess go." In retrospect, Kristen did not feel that choosing differently would have helped at the time. She actually felt pushed out by the staff and the students. She believed that even if she had delayed her decision to leave, she could not have stayed in this difficult school environment until the end of Grade 12.

At first, her plan was simply to get out of foster homes. When she became pregnant, however, she began to realize how much she wanted to return to education. She hoped her child would finish high school, and, thus, so should she. She also found that it was difficult to find employment without a Grade 12 diploma. Soon after discovering her pregnancy, she became motivated to enrol in adult learning. Things felt quite different at this school, where she was placed in a class of eight student ranging in age from 14 to 50 years. Here, she felt much more accepted and finished her schooling within six months of enrolment.

Kristen feels that since leaving high school her self-esteem has improved and that it has been easier to think with clarity. Now she can focus on herself instead of on what others think of her. She has been able to attain her own apartment. In all of the years that Kristen was in the public school system, there was only one teacher—in special education—who seemed to accept her. This teacher stood out as an exception to the rule, and she is remembered by Kristen as someone who once had students over to her house for a pool party and a barbeque. In addition, Kristen made brief mention of a maternal aunt and another adult mentor, the latter having worked at a group home that she had lived in at one time. He was especially dedicated to other's problems and helping kids work things out. Kristen has been in contact with him since the time she was 8 years old, calling him every second day and writing him letters. She was well aware of his belief that staying in school was important and felt that he was disappointed by her departure from school.

In general, Kristen feels that the school culture, parents, guardians, teachers, and other adults hold pervasive negative attitudes and expectations about young people. Surprisingly, however, she does not feel any such animosity coming from the community, media, or society. Kristen's plans for the future are to help other people change their negative situations into positive behaviour opportunities. Kristen ideally sees herself as one who can help others avoid some of the sadness she had faced. Kristen's hopes for schools are that they would address bullying more assertively and increase self-help programs.

Analyses and Directions

These young people live and breathe the cryptic curriculum of public education. An inability for schools to mediate, and more often to exacerbate, the pain of lives in chaos. Conceptually, these fragments of biography and experiences tell us about the processes of marginalization, social exclusion, and the complexities of modern social, political, and economic forces that young people negotiate. This concept of marginalization moves away from "youth-at-risk" labels, which localize problems in individuals to an appreciation for the ways in which young people attempt to negotiate, resist, and alter some of the most looming problems. This chapter is concerned with the scope and reasons for continued negative outcomes for young people who are marginalized by socio-economic and cultural status and yet live in a "wealthy" country such as Canada. As young people have so aptly told me, schools and societies must become more flexible, proactive, and caring if they are to take seriously the complex lives of contemporary youth and offer them a rightful quality of education and life.

Vital to bettering the lives of socially and economically marginalized youth is a corresponding admission of responsibility from society and public education.

Youth require supports that are politically grounded, responsive, and multi-dimensional. On the one hand, we have an enduring finding that social inequality and poverty relate negatively to many health and educational outcomes. Apparent in the daily experiences of young people at school, this effect is organized socially in the structures, practices, and treatment of poor students relative to their more privileged peers. On the other hand, the situation is complex, and possibilities for resistance and resilience occur with responsive schools, engaged communities and families, and supportive social justice-oriented policies.[2] We have known for decades that income inequality (which is now growing) and poverty have negative consequences for young people and society, and many are pushing to examine definitively what works and for whom. Scholarly work relating to the grievous effects of poverty and socio-economic inequality on children and youth has been circulating for over 40 years in Canada. The early work by the Canadian Institute for Advanced Research in the Human Development Program of the 1990s provided a comprehensive window into ailing outcomes (Keating and Hertzman, 1999). Whether the measurements were to do with health status or educational outcomes, the gaps between the wealthy and poor families in Canada have demonstrated stability. We know clearly that there is a range of systemic reasons for health and educational problems and that poverty interacts with other risk factors (Dei et al., 1997; Tilleczek, 2008b).

In order to move forward in addressing these divides in Canada, a strategic focus is required that attends to intersections between schools, families, and communities rather than to individual or community traits. We can best examine and improve the daily lives of young people by recognizing how income inequality, poverty, ethnicity, identity, and age are played out as marginalizing processes. Many have addressed these "variables," but more youth-attuned research on the mechanisms and processes is needed. Effective schools and programs are responsive to a wide range of student needs made possible through the integration of community services that address relationships between risk and protective factors (National Dropout Prevention Centre, 2007) as they are lived and enacted by youth.

To get there, we must collectively

> make loud the legislation, values, regulations, systems, and actions that perpetuate colonization and its concordant impacts on Aboriginal children and their families including those harmful and colonial philosophies and practices that are embedded ... It means understanding the harm from those who experienced it, it means setting aside the instinct to rationalize it or to turn away from it because it is too difficult to hear—or we feel blamed. It means having conversations about some of the basic values and beliefs that shape our concepts of what social work is. It means working with, versus working for, Aboriginal peoples. (Blackstock, 2009, 36)

I have divided the range of programs to prevent or intervene into three categories for simplicity; (1) early prevention programs; (2) core school strategies; and (3) those that engage integrated communities. Across each category, two consistencies emerge. The first is the need for an ethic of caring responses from educators, parents, friends, and others in the community such that a need

to engage an ongoing "community of helpers" emerges across the research literature (Tilleczek, 2008a, 2008b). For example, the "teachers-as-parents" approach
to addressing care and affectivity between teachers, students, and peers shows
promise in reinforcing well-being and school attendance for the poorest inner-
city youth who themselves decide whether or not to attend school. Schools
have become a tenable extension to home and work rather than an alienating
and irrelevant place (Blasco, 2004; see also Somers and Piliawaski, 2004). The
second consistency is some form of full service school such as schools in New
York's New Century High Schools. These schools attend to the complexity and
heterogeneity of the lives of contemporary young people and provide alternate pathways to student success (including apprenticeships programs and
vocational streams) while teaching in smaller, emotionally supportive schools
(Foley et al., 2007; Volpe & Tillecek, 1999). Low-performing high schools with
low overall grade point averages and low graduation rates cannot be fundamentally improved by attempts simply to enhance early childhood education or
by supporting high school teachers and students in working harder at existing
practices. Secondary schools with high rates of early school leaving must
be fundamentally reinvented with help from the community in order to see
significant improvement (Balfanz, 2007; Balfanz et al., 2007; Balfanz & Legters,
2004). The current Ontario Ministry of Education Student Success Initiatives is
an example of such crosscutting strategies.[3]

Early prevention programs have included parental skills training and family
outreach, better early childhood education, and literacy/numeracy programs
in elementary schools.[4] For example, the Parents as Teachers Program in the
United States melds home visits, screening, group discussions, and community
referrals to work with low-income parents of children at risk. A multi-site
experimental evaluation demonstrated rather small effect sizes. However,
increases in parental knowledge and positive child behaviour outcomes for very
low-income families were notable. Core school strategies include a range of
programs that build on the idea that schools can make a difference. These include
guidance interventions, mentoring/tutoring, peer-based programs, linking
community service experiences with academic learning, openness to diverse
identities, and better (more relevant and youth-attuned) curriculum/peda-
gogy. For example, a multi-faceted mentoring/tutoring program (ninth grade
program (NGP)) was implemented at six high schools. Each school designed its
own intervention program based on results from individual needs assessments,
with the result that a standardized, replicable intervention was not consistently
implemented at each school. However, a number of common elements existed
among the programs including tutoring, ninth grade buddy systems, freshman
class orientation, study skills, ability grouping, and teacher-as-advisor meetings.

Of the Grade 9 students, 25% were randomly selected from each school for three consecutive years. A baseline control group was randomly selected from the year prior to implementation. Results indicate that the proportion of treatment group students who left school prior to completion decreased over the three years of the program from 10% in the first year down to 4% in the third year. In addition, school attendance rates for the NGP groups for all three years were significantly higher than for the control groups (Pearson & Banerji, 1993).[5]

Engaging integrated communities includes programs that address the concern that schools cannot make and sustain these changes alone. These programs include educational system renewal such as professional development for educators, community collaboration, and integration across agencies, career education, and workforce readiness, including apprenticeship programs; out-of-school enhancements (after school and summer scholastic, recreation, and social programs); and conflict resolution/violence prevention (Canadian Council on Learning, 2005; Hammond et al., 2007). These programs also include those that attempt to re-engage the early youth in alternative schools or re-entry programs such as those evaluated in Australia, the United States, and Ontario (Wyn, Stokes, & Tyler, 2004).[6]

In conclusion, it seems fitting to invoke the seven good life teachings of the Ojibwe people (Toulouse, 2007). They are adapted here to include lessons from the Ontario Aboriginal Education Policy Framework and lessons from the Canadian Council on Learning as attempts to meaningfully organize responses to social policy and practice for, with, and about impoverished youth as they negotiate school (Canadian Council on Learning, 2005; Ontario Ministry of Education, 2006).

Respect: By having and maintaining high expectations for impoverished young people, we understand and honour the range of culture, language, and world views. This includes community-based education and training where students express a greater sense of ownership of programs that are visibly tied to their home communities.

Love: By demonstrating our belief that all impoverished youth can and will succeed through collective commitments. This includes a commitment to employment and learning that is focused on youth goals and world views.

Bravery: By committing to work towards positive change in schools and communities through the contributions, innovations, and inventions of impoverished people. This includes community action, advocacy, and voice.

Wisdom: By sharing our findings and good practices through research and practice that focuses on social justice.

Humility: By acknowledging that we have limited knowledge about the diversity of impoverished young people and communities. We must attempt to provide more examples of complexities that break down negative stereotypical and pathological views. This includes balancing the expectations across cultures and acknowledging and supporting impoverished young people's cultural and class heritage while providing relevant and educative experiences. It is important to maintain high expectations concerning educational goals and life outcomes.

Honesty: By accepting that we have failed impoverished youth in the past and by constantly reviewing the trends and stories that detail and/or encourage change in the system. For example, the alarmingly high student disengagement and early leaver rates must be understood as a context to current research.

Truth: By evaluating the emerging successes and failures of educational systems within which impoverished students find themselves as an indicator of how we are doing as a society by these young people.

Notes

Parts of this chapter were presented at International Child/Youth Research Network Conference: Growing Up in Divided Societies, Queen's University, Belfast, Ireland, 10-11 June 2011. The author would like to thank and acknowledge Veronica Christian for her assistance in writing the short stories from my early school leaver's study interviews.

1 See Tilleczek (2008b) and Ferguson et al. (2005) for the original study from which this data is presented.

2 Catterall's (1998) measurement of student resilience was based on the performance of Grade 8 students to achieve grades that were higher than expected by Grade 10 from both low achievement and low commitment to school. Social class held an interesting place in the findings such that it was significant in resilience for achievement and commitment. He found that there are large shares of young people within "risk groups" who are performing well and are committed to school, and another substantial number who show mobility out of performance-based risks (see also the International Resilience Project's emerging work).

3 The Ontario Ministry of Education is in process of evaluating the Student Success Initiative across Ontario, and no data have been released to date.

4 For example, the Parents as Teachers program (Wagner et al., 2002) and the Parents as Educators Program (Funkhouser, Gonzales, & Moles, 1997; Patterson, Reid, Jones, & Conger, 1975; cited in Prevatt & Kelly, 2003; Vitaro, Brendgen, & Tremblay, 1999).

5 The Check and Connect Program (Prevatt & Kelly, 2003; Sinclair et al. 1998). In Ontario, the Boomerang Project, which has similar characteristics, is being pilot tested. No evaluation evidence is available to date.

6   The National Dropout Prevention Center reviewed more than 75 alternative schools and identified characteristics common to successful programs. These include: a maximum teacher-student ratio of 1:10; a small student body of 250 students or less; a clearly stated mission and discipline code; caring staff with ongoing opportunities for professional development; high expectations for student achievement; academic programs tailored to individual student's needs and learning styles; flexibility in school scheduling and the involvement of the community; and total commitment to assisting every student in succeeding (Schargel & Smink, 2001).

References

Anyon, J. (1980). Social class and the hidden curriculum of work. *Journal of Education, 162*, 67-92.

Anyon, J. (2006). Social class, school knowledge, and the hidden curriculum revisited. In L. Weiss & G. Dimitriadis (Eds.), *The new sociology of knowledge*. New York: Routledge.

Arundel, C., and Associates, for Canadian Index of Wellbeing (2009). How are Canadians really doing? (Special report from the Canadian Institute for Wellbeing). Online: http://ciw.ca/reports/en/Reports%20and%20FAQs/SpecialReports/ACloser LookAtSelectGroups_FullReport.sflb.pdf.

Assembly of First Nations. (2002). *Investing in the future: First Nations education in Canada*. Ottawa: Assembly of First Nations.

Balfanz, R. (2007). What your community can do to end the drop-out crisis: Learnings from research and practice (Paper prepared for the National Summit on America's Silent Epidemic in Washington, DC). Baltimore, MD: Center for the Social Organization of Schools.

Balfanz, R., and Legters, N. (2004) Locating the dropout crisis: Which high schools produce the nations drop outs? Where are they located? Johns Hopkins University, Center for Social Organization of Schools.

Blackstock, C. (2009). The occasional evil of angels: Learning from the experiences of Aboriginal people and social work. *First Peoples Child and Family Review, 4*, 28-37.

Blasco, M. (2004). Teachers should be like second parents: Affectivity, schooling and poverty in Mexico. *Compare, 34*(4), 371-393.

Brooks-Gunn, J., & Duncan, G. (1996). *Growing up poor: Consequences for children and youth* (Paper of the Canadian Institute for Advanced Research). Toronto: Canadian Institute for Advanced Research.

Canadian Council on Learning. (2005). *Good news: Canada's high school drop-out rates are falling* (Lessons in learning report/data). Ottawa: Canadian Council on Learning.

Catterall, J. (1998). Risk and resilience in student transitions to high school. *American Journal of Education, 106,* 302-333.

Chandler, M. (2010). Indigenous education and epistemic violence. *Education Canada: Special Issue on Marginalized Youth in Contemporary Educational Contexts, 50*(5), 63-67.

Dei, G., Mazzuca, J., McIsaac, E., & Zine, J. (1997). *Reconstructing "drop-out": A critical ethnography of the dynamics of Black students' disengagement from school*. Toronto, ON: University of Toronto Press.

Duncan, G., Yeung, W., Brroks-Gunn, J., & Smith, J. (1997). *How much does childhood poverty affect the life chances of children?* (Paper of the Canadian Institute for Advanced Research). Toronto: Canadian Institute for Advanced Research.

Ferguson, B., Tilleczek, K., Boydell, K., Rummens, A., & Roth-Edney, D. (2005). *Early school leavers: Understanding the lived reality of disengagement from secondary school* (Report the Ontario Ministry of Education). Toronto: Hospital for Sick Children.

Foley, E., Klinge, A., & Reisner, E. (2007). Evaluation of new century high schools: Profile of an initiative to create and sustain small, successful high schools (Paper prepared for New Visions for Public Schools, New York, NY).

Funkhouser, J.E., Gonzales, M.R., and Moles, O.C. (1997). *Appendix A: Profiles of successful partnerships, in* Policy Studies Associates, in partnership with the National Institute on the Education of At-Risk Students (Ed.), *Family involvement in children's education successful local approaches: An idea book.* Office of Educational Research and Improvement US Department of Education. Online: http://www.ed.gov/pubs/FamInvolve/appa.html.

Furlong, A., & Cartmel, F. (2007). *Young people and social change.* New York: Open University Press.

Hammond, C., Linton, D., Smink, J., & Drew, S. (2007). *Drop our risk factors and exemplary programs: A technical report.* Clemson, SC. National Dropout Prevention Center.

Hattam, R., & Smyth, J. (2003). Not every body has a perfect life: Becoming somebody without school. *Pedagogy, Culture and Society, 11,* 379-398.

Human Resources and Social Development Canada (HRSDC). (2001). *Applied Research Bulletin, 7*(1), 1-23.

Keating, D., & Hertzman, C. (1999). *Developmental health and the wealth of nations: Social, biological, and educational dynamics.* New York: Guildford Press.

Levin, B. (2008). Does politics hinder or help educational change. *Journal of Educational Change, 8*(4), 69-70.

Organisation for Economic Co-operation and Development (OECD) (2009). *Growing unequal: Poverty and incomes over 20 years* (DELSA Newlsetter 7). Paris: OECD.

Ontario Ministry of Education (2006). *DRAFT Aboriginal Education Policy Framework: The foundation for improving the delivery of quality education to Aboriginal students in Ontario.* Online: http://www.curriculum.org/secretariat/files/May24PolicyDraft.pdf.

Pearson, C. L., and Banerji, M. (1993). Effects of a ninth-grade dropout prevention program on student academic achievement, school attendance, and dropout rate. *Journal of Experimental Education, 61*(3): 247-256.

Prevatt, F., and Kelly, D. (2003). Dropping out of school: A review of intervention programs. *Journal of School Psychology, 41*(5): 377-395.

Schargel, F. P., & Smink, J. (2001). *Strategies to help solve our school dropout problem.* Larchmont, NY: Eye on Education.

Seidman, E., Larue, A., Aber, J., & Feinman, J. (1994). The impact of school transitions in early adolescence on the self-system and perceived social context of poor urban youth. *Child Development, 65,* 507-522.

Smyth, J. (2010). Young people speaking back from the margins. *Education Canada, 50*(5), 23-26.

Smyth, J., & McInerney, P. (2010). *Hanging in with kids in tough times*. New York: Peter Lang Publishing.

Sommers, C., & Piliawsky, M. (2004). Drop out prevention among urban, African-American adolescents: Program evaluation and practical implications. *Preventing school failure, 48,* 17-22.

Statistics Canada. (2005). *Provincial drop-out rates: Trends and consequences* (Doc. 81-004-X1E). Ottawa: Statistics Canada.

Tilleczek, K. (2008a). The failing health of children and youth in Northern Ontario. In D. Leadbeater (Ed.), *Mining town crises: Globalization, labour and resistance in Sudbury, Canada*. Halifax: Fernwood Press.

Tilleczek, K. (Ed.) (2008b). *Why do students drop out of high school? Narrative studies and social critiques*. New York: Edwin Mellen Press.

Tilleczek, K. (2011). *Approaching youth studies: Being, becoming and belonging*. Toronto: Oxford University Press.

Toulouse, P. (2007). *Supporting Aboriginal student success: Self-esteem and identity, a living teachings approach* (Paper presented at the Ontario Educational Research Symposium). Toronto: Ontario Ministry of Education.

Van Galen, J. (2004). Seeing class: Toward a broadened research agenda for critical qualitative researchers. *International Journal of Qualitative Studies in Education, 17*(5), 663-684.

Vitaro, F., Brendgen, M., & Tremblay, R. E. (1999). Prevention of school dropout through the reduction of disruptive behaviors and school failure in elementary school. *Journal of School Psychology, 37*(2), 205-226.

Wagner, M., Spiker, D., & Linn, M. (2002). The effectiveness of parents as teachers program with low-income parents and children. *Topics in early childhood special education, 22,* 67-81.

Wyn, J., Stokes, H., & Tyler, D. (2004). Stepping stones: TAFE and ACE program development for early school leavers. Australia: National Centre for Vocational Educational Research.

Wilkinson, R., & Picket, K. (2009). *The spirit level: Why more equal societies almost always do better*. London: Allen Lane.

Willms, J.D. (Ed.) (2002). *Vulnerable children: Findings from Canada's national longitudinal survey of children and youth*. Edmonton, AB: University of Alberta Press.

chapter 9

Still Sleeping in the "Gay Tent"?: Queer Youth in Canadian Schools

Tom Hilton

This chapter takes a decidedly current and critical view of the schooling of queer youth in Canada. It is based on a number of sources, including the early political activism and ethnographic research work of George Smith (1998) in Ontario high schools in the 1980s and 1990s, in addition to my own current critical research/practice work during my temporary project position at the Prince Edward Island (PEI) Human Rights Commission (PEIHRC) and in PEI schools. The project's purpose is to facilitate ongoing, sustainable linkages, between the PEIHRC and PEI's Department of Education and Early Childhood Development. The chapter provides critical reflection on the policy and practices that frame "gayness" in education by working through comparisons of these historical voices. Both change and stagnation are shown to characterize lesbian, gay, bisexual, transgendered, and questioning youth's experiences as they negotiate their way through high school. The following two quotes provide a flavour for change and stagnation as well as the possible limits of "tolerance," "inclusion," and non-discrimination. These are some examples of the themes that have emerged from the research and that will be posited from my analysis of the experiences and treatment of lesbian and gay youth in Canadian schools.

> *At one time, I was very confused about my sexuality and I felt the need to talk to someone and I went to the school guidance counsellor and he responded with he's not allowed to talk to us about the subject because he'd get in trouble with the school board. He didn't give me a phone number, he didn't give me the stress line for LGYT [Gay Youth Hotline] or anything like that. He just sort of left it at that and closed the subject before it was really open, so that was another piss off and that made me stay in the closet a little longer than I had to.* (Unnamed gay student, quoted in Smith, 1998, p. 331)

I got a phone call from Ryan's junior high school guidance counsellor telling me Ryan was experiencing distress. Ryan wanted she and I to meet with him the next day so he could share what was up ... I realized later that she was giving me plenty of hints and tips on what was going on. When Ryan and I were together at home I asked if he wanted to talk about it, he said wait until tomorrow with the guidance counsellor. He did allow me to guess about what was going on, thinking I'd never guess, right? So I said "are you gay?" "well how did you know?" That was the first response out of his mouth! ... So I give him a big hug, told him I love him, and assure him everything will be OK ... we go meet with the guidance counsellor and Ryan discloses he wasn't worried about my acceptance, he was worried about my Catholic family rejecting both of us because of his sexuality ... after helping us deal with that the guidance counsellor provided me with information to connect us with PFLAG PEI [Parents Families and Friends of Lesbians and Gays] ... at that meeting and throughout Ryan's two years at that school, we couldn't have asked for a better support system. (Brenda, quoted in Hilton, 2010)[1]

From active denial to active acknowledgement of queer youth's existence in schools by school-based guidance counsellors, these two quotes suggest disparate pedagogical perspectives, connectedness to school, and research participant's comfort level with claiming their voice and identity. Importantly, these quotes are also separated by fifteen years as well as the Supreme Court of Canada's (SCC) 1998 judgment in Vriend v Alberta, which is considered by Harris (2008, p. 1) to be "one of the three most important decisions in the history of the court."[2] In their unanimous decision in Vriend, the justices ruled that the government of Alberta's exclusion of sexual orientation from proscribed grounds of discrimination within the Individual Rights Protection Act (renamed in 2009 as the Human Rights Act) was unconstitutional.[3] The justices of Canada's highest court dismissed legislation that effectively rendered all Albertans "equal in dignity and rights, except gay men and lesbians" and thereby compelled Alberta and PEI to enforce sexual orientation as a proscribed basis for discrimination in their respective *Human Rights Acts.*[4] Robinson (2006, p. 1) first identified these two Canadian jurisdictions as being "most resistant to the provision of equal rights for gays and lesbians," and I first specified the respective post-Vriend adoption processes employed by the governments of PEI and Alberta so as to better contextualize, identify, and connect issues of sexuality to the marginalization of youth within Canadian schools.

In June 1998, a mere two months after the SCC's landmark Vriend decision, PEI's legislators amended the Human Rights Act to include sexual orientation as a proscribed ground of discrimination. At the same time, legislators restricted another of the act's proscribed grounds—marital status—to opposite sex relationships. Given the judicial precedents then being established in the

Canadian courts, Herb Dickieson (1998, p. 5661), a member of the legislative assembly (MLA), characterized efforts to limit the Human Rights Act to an opposite sex definition of marital status as "discrimination within discrimination [that] kind of kills the whole purpose." Disregarding Dickieson's prophetic warning and notwithstanding Vriend's fundamental lesson that "the concept of democracy means more than majority rule," a majority of PEI's legislators voted to restrict the definition of family status to opposite sex relationships only.[5] Having been freed by their party leader and then premier, Pat Binns, "to vote their conscience" (Standing Committee on Social Development, 1998, p. 8), legislators agreed with MLA Deighan's (1998, p. 5662) reasoning that "on this issue the people have spoken loud and clear ... I feel compelled to represent what I judge and what I view to be the majority [view] of my constituents." Voting as they did to limit the act's definition of marital status to opposite sex relationships, PEI's elected representatives claimed their conscientiousness "strengthened marriage and enriched family life" (Deighan, 1998, p. 5663). The SCC, however, soon denounced PEI's brand of legislative reasoning. In M. v H., the SCC found that legislating opposite sex exclusions "promoted the view that individuals in same-sex relationships are less worthy of recognition and protection ... and contributes to the erasure of their existence."[6] In 2004, at the request of Parliament to produce a Reference re: Same Sex Marriage, the SCC reiterated "one of the most fundamental principles of Canadian constitutional interpretation ... our constitution is a living tree, which by way of progressive interpretation accommodates and addresses the realities of modern life."[7] This ruling cleared the way for Canada to become the world's fourth country to legalize same sex marriage in July 2005 (Bourassa & Varnell, 2008).

Once again forced into legislative action by external constitutional forces, PEI's legislators amended the Marriage Act in December 2005 to recognize same sex marriage.[8] As when pairing sexual orientation as a proscribed ground for discrimination alongside an opposite sex definition of marital status within the PEI Human Rights Act, PEI legislators directed a newfound tactic of segregation and discrimination at gay and lesbian individuals. In the Act to Amend the Marriage Act, legislators allowed persons authorized to perform civil marriages in PEI the right to "refuse to solemnize any marriage that is not in accordance with the person's religious beliefs."[9] Perhaps not surprisingly, In the Matter of Marriage Commissioners Appointed under the Marriage Act, 1995, Justice White of the Saskatchewan Court of Appeal declared Saskatchewan's similar legislative carve-out as "constitutionally offensive."[10] Given how "consistently conservative" PEI's paradoxical penchant for legislating discriminatory carve-outs was, while addressing issues of equality for lesbians and gays, (Robinson, 2006, p. 1) PEI's legislative perspective is hereby characterized as the "dying tree" approach to constitutional interpretation. Contrary to enacting legislation that "accommodates and addresses the realities of modern life," PEI's legislative record reinforces discrimination and denies the realities of modern life (SCC, 2004, p. 3).[11]

In Vriend's aftermath, the Alberta government withstood considerable "pressure from conservatives and religious groups" when refraining from invoking section 33, the notwithstanding clause, of the Canadian Charter of Rights and Freedoms (Wood, 2008, p. 1).[12] Described in 1981 by then Minister of Justice Jean Chrétien, the Charter's notwithstanding clause is "a safety valve [that] provides the flexibility that is required to ensure that legislatures rather than judges have the final say on important matters of public policy" (quoted in Johansen & Rosen, 2008, p. 8). Unlike PEI's prompt, yet paradoxical, legislative response to Vriend, the Alberta government ceded final say for over ten years to the SCC on this matter by doing nothing more than reading-in sexual orientation among the proscribed grounds of discrimination within Alberta's Human Rights Act. In June 2009, however, sexual orientation became written into the act with the passage of Alberta's Bill 44. Simultaneous to writing sexual orientation into the act, Alberta's Bill 44 created a new province-wide human right—the parental right to mandatory notification whenever public school lessons deal "primarily and explicitly with religion, human sexuality or sexual orientation" (Minister of Culture and Community Spirit, 2009, p. 4).[13] In curricular lessons, the Canadian Broadcasting Corporation News (2009, p. 1) framed these as "controversial topics"—upon receipt of written parental request school staff must permit student's exclusion from class "without academic penalty" (Minister of Culture and Community Spirit, 2009, p. 4). Suggestive of the human rights debate that occurred in PEI a decade earlier, Alberta MLA Hehr (2009, p. 1466) characterized Bill 44's paradoxical impact as "what the large print giveth, the small print taketh away." Helen Kennedy (2009a, p. 1), executive director of EGALE Canada, which has been Canada's national lesbian, gay, bisexual, and trans human rights organization since 1986, questioned the educational validity of Bill 44 when asking "how will future generations learn acceptance if they receive the message that there are things that should not be known or discussed?"

Notwithstanding the ambivalence of PEI's and Alberta's governments towards human rights for gays and lesbians, informed by the perspective of queer youth and their families, I compare Vriend's twin edicts of individual equality and justice as helping transform public schooling with Smith's "another piss off" (1998, p. 331) with Hilton's "we couldn't have asked for better support" (2010, p. 4). Trickling down from our nation's highest court of law into the PEI Human Rights Act and then into such school-based policies as the Eastern

School District of PEI's *Caring Places to Learn/Safe Schools Environment and Race Relations* (1999) *and Cross Cultural Understanding and Human Rights in Learning* (2011), inclusion of sexual orientation among proscribed grounds of discrimination now pervades federal and provincial public spheres. The latest North American school climate research, however, continues to illustrate that public school systems remain disrespectful, unequal, and unjust for many openly queer youth and/or those perceived to be queer, at the same time as law and policy appear to be shifting (Grossman et al., 2009; Kosciw, Diaz, & Greytak, 2008; Taylor & Peter, 2011).

How then might we begin investigating these discrepancies between the official written word of equality and justice and their everyday practices within public schooling? In first acknowledging the complexity of discrimination and its infinite subjective representations and actions, I centre past and present perspectives, experiences, and voices of queer youth and their families—in sum, a trickle-up approach from the margins—towards identifying and interrogating two sites that illustrate the potential limits to individual equality and justice in Canada's public schools: the business of sexualities in school and sleeping arrangements on overnight school trips. Consistent with Martin Luther King, Jr.'s (1963) statement that "injustice anywhere is a threat to justice everywhere," individual equality and justice are conceptualized as indivisible fundamentals of Canadian society, not as either/or, winner/loser, or zero-sum paradigms. From this perspective, I demonstrate the potential adverse effects on all youth in PEI's schools where stereotypes define individuals and resulting stigmas and injustices remain unquestioned.

> What sort of difference would it make for everyone in a classroom if gay and lesbian [queer] writing were set loose from confirmations of homophobia, the afterthoughts of inclusion, or the special event? (Britzman, 1995, p. 151)

Sharing Britzman's reluctance to frame difference (otherness) as an afterthought, special event, "one-off workshop" (Turnbull & Hilton, 2010, p. 21) and "problem needing to be dealt with" (Loutzenheiser & MacIntosh, 2004, p. 108) or "detour from real schooling" (Lipkin, 1999, p. 340), this chapter reintroduces the somewhat long-ago asked question. This chapter follows Britzman (1995), who submitted pedagogical practices of tolerance and inclusion "to the work of thought" and represented them as straight-minded symptoms of a "sentimental" education (Foucault & Rainbow, 1977). Similarly, Tilleczek, Furlong, and Ferguson (2010, p. 6) have exemplified "afterthought" approaches to tolerance and inclusion as "faulty contemporary educational practices that as a result lock in and lock out many young people from meaningful participation."

Whether youth remain locked out academically, socially, and/or economically, we position familiar, "already thinkable and recognizable" either/or binaries of tolerant straight/tolerated queer and included straight/excluded queer as limiting thought (Sedgwick, 1990, p. 156). Limitations are framed as providing inadequate pre-service teacher preparation for navigating the challenging "social complexities" (Tilleczek, 2010, p. 3) and countless identity intersections constituting the youth of twenty-first-century Canada (Taylor & Peter, 2011).

> Basically I hope that homosexuality can actually be talked about in school because I know that going through the sex education system it is just not talked about. So in Grade 6 I didn't realize, understand, or know what being gay meant. But that's when I should have known because I could have come out then and that's what makes me mad ... Finally in Grade 9, a year after my coming-out, our fantastic sex education teacher approached me to ask if we could talk about homosexuality in class. I was like "yeah, for sure." She asked if it would be OK for me to answer some questions from my class-mates and stuff because she was not an expert on it and, like, didn't know whenever I knew that I was gay. I basically had to tell her: Well, when did you know you were straight? She thought about it and then told me she got it that gay people having to explain themselves in ways that straight people don't is proof there's a problem. (Ryan, quoted in Hilton, 2010)

In making visible the daily experiences and educational practices encountered by queer youth, this work characterizes what is often espoused as "tolerance and inclusion" as perpetuating the status quo "of oppressive relationships within schools" (Kumashiro, 2004, p. 112). As attested to by Ryan in the earlier quotation, pedagogies of tolerance and inclusion that require added justifica-tions by/for/about/from the other in turn reproduce exclusions, marginaliza-tion, discriminatory treatment, and lock-outs. Embedded in this process of reproducing marginalization, these young people show how we negate the many significant cultural, policy, and legal developments having occurred in Canada and in Canadian schools since 1995. Already, limited tolerance and inclusion minimize both Savin-Williams' (2005, p. 17) "astonishment" at the breadth, depth, and "rapidity of the cultural makeover" regarding diverse sexualities and Cloud's (2005, p. 1) recognition of the "unprecedented regu-larity" of increasingly younger youth claiming non-heterosexual identities. Furthermore, continuing the marginalization of queer youth on the basis of actual or perceived sexual orientation undermines the Eastern School District of PEI (2011, p. 1) policies adopted to advance, support, and affirm equality for all learners through practices "applied with respect and regard to dignity and without bias or discrimination."

I knew there was something up with Katie since Grade 6 or 7 but I just couldn't nail it down. She had become so sullen and withdrawn. Her grades kept falling and she especially struggled with math ... so I pushed the school really hard for a learning assessment referral. They said that because of a three-year waiting list there was no sense in making the referral and they didn't ... the school system was so frustrating and, to my mind, let us both down. Anyways, so I struggled to come up with the money for a private psychologist, and it may have been a result of having come out to him that late in junior high school she finally came out to me. Given some family history, I was super concerned about depression so when she did open up with me I was so relieved and was like: "O thank god that's all it is!" I told her: "you're the same little girl I gave birth to and that's never gonna change no matter what so just go do your thing and know that I'm in your corner." (Arlene, quoted in Hilton, 2010)

As stated by Arlene, Katie's mother, "as far as Katie's experiences in school, which became my experiences in school, Junior High School (JHS) was hell" (Arlene, quoted in Hilton, 2010). The inclusion of a parental voice in this chapter provides added research significance as queer youth, beyond their well-documented educational marginalization, must also often confront "the prospect of being outcasts in their own homes" (Goldfried & Goldfried, 2001, p. 684). After fifteen odd years of practising one-off approaches to tolerance and inclusion, we seek present-day guidance from past and current student voices alike, including those of contemporary parents, in order to "map [marginalization] trends over time and point out those that persist in the face of program or policy attention" (Tilleczek, 2010, p. 8).

Charged with "developing communities of creative and critical thinkers who value diversity" through problematizations (University of Prince Edward Island, Faculty of Education, 2009)—ongoing processes of submitting taken-for-granted assumptions to thought, questioning, debate, and discussion (O'Farrell, 2007)—we heighten pre-service teachers' exposure to changing: educational contexts, marginalization tactics, methods of resistance, and, ultimately, future possibilities. Upon compiling voices from the margins and infusing our academic endeavours with corresponding questions to, for, from, and about teachers, we imagine "stimulating disruptive inquiry" and loosening homophobia from current conceptual constraints framing it as a pedagogical problem adequately addressed through "trendy sideshow" approaches (Lipkin, 1999, p. 340). Through committing ourselves to "sustained and serious discourse" (Lipkin, p. 341), we hope to create space for pre-service teachers to imagine how late-twentieth and early twenty-first-century public schooling could be more equal and more just (O'Farrell, 2010) and to practice how to now make it so for all twenty-first-century students.

So when I was reading my speech [in class], the principal happened to walk in just as I admitted that I was, in fact, gay. As far as I can remember his chin hit the floor, he was so flabbergasted ... and called me to the office afterwards. Basically he warned me that if I didn't keep my sexual preference under wraps that I'd be suspended. And I said: "Well it's my business and if I want to share it with people it's up to me; nobody can tell me not to tell other people who I am ... 'cause I'm not afraid of it, so why should I be?" That's basically what my attitude was back then, and still is. I was suspended for being rude and insubordinate. (Unnamed high school student, quoted in Smith, 1998, p. 314)

In grade nine there was this big huge deal about my sexual orientation. A friend, [Monique], who stuck up for me because I was gay was taken by an administrator out of her gym class to a room and asked "are you gay?" She said "no." He then asked her: "Well is Katie gay? Can I talk with her about her sexual orientation?" Monique said: "No, you can't. It's none of your business." If he had pulled me into that room and questioned my sexual orientation I don't know what I would have said because I wasn't completely comfortable with it at the time. (Katie, quoted in Hilton, 2010)

Given the shroud of controversy enveloping classroom negotiation of sexuality as a legitimate educational topic (whether in PEI, Alberta, or any other Canadian province requiring advance parental notification and consent), just whose business is student sexualities? How is this business of sexuality to be enforced in schools? As with the guidance counsellors separated by time and the Vriend decision referenced at the outset of this chapter, again separated over time, we might deduce evolving school administrator positioning. From "keep your sexual orientation under wraps while at school" to "while at school please disclose to me your sexual orientation," clearly the principal threatening suspension in response to a high school student's coming-out speech in the mid-1990s and the active inquiry into a student's sexualities by a junior high school administrator in the mid-2000s reflect radically different pedagogical approaches towards the business of schooling and sexualities (Hilton, 2010; Smith, 1998).

Such an evolution might reflect school administrators discarding the traditional tactic of simply denying or, in this case, being "flabbergasted by" queer student's and queer people's existence in educational settings (Reilly, 2007). Resisting his principal's threats to "stay closeted at school or else," Smith's unnamed gay male student might be considered a harbinger of Wells' (2007, p. 18) "new generation of queer youth having the confidence and support to speak out and demand their human and civil rights be respected." The flabbergasted principal's order to remain silent was by then rendered impotent by "rapid and significant gains" in enacting gay-aware laws, policies, and programs throughout Canada and Canadian schools (Wells, 2007, p. 19). Disciplined for claiming his sexuality as "his business alone to share with others as he pleased" and suspended for rudeness and insubordination and apparently not for being gay, Smith's (1998, p. 18) research participant undoubtedly spread awareness of many queer youth's emerging unwillingness "to remain in the classroom closet." Likewise documented by Blount (2005), such denial tactics proved especially effective in keeping lesbian and gay teachers closeted lest they be summarily dismissed from employment as sick, dangerous predators.

Fast forwarding fifteen years from this student's resisting "do not disclose at school" tactics of marginalization, we encounter similar resistance employed by Monique confronting notably dissimilar "do disclose at school" tactics of marginalization. How could such seemingly polar opposite approaches, framed as active denial and active acknowledgement, both be framed as possibly discriminatory and as contributing to marginalization? Does not the inquisitive, seemingly non-threatening approach of Katie's junior high school administrator reflect present-day acknowledgement of, and sensitivity to, both queer youth's existence in schools and of their doing so at increasingly younger ages? Addressing these questions requires first contextualizing the administrator's actions within the "big, huge deal" surrounding Katie's perceived sexual orientation.

> [F]or an overnight trip in Grade 9 when I wasn't even out yet we had random room assignments and I didn't really know my two roommates. The two of them spread throughout school that they didn't want to room with me because I would probably try to rape them … that was the stupid, rude assumption they were spreading—and not just about me but about all gay people—and it made me feel bad about myself. The girls then went to school administration and said they shouldn't have to room with me. The administration allowed them a room of their own and chose to reassign me. That was how the administration handled the situation. (Katie, quoted in Hilton, 2010)

Despite PEI's policy of obtaining parental consent when addressing issues of sexuality, the school administrators followed up their "handling" of this situation by making it their business, without first having obtained parental consent, to confirm not only Katie's sexuality but also Monique's. From Katie's perspective, the impetus behind the administrators involving Monique in this "big, huge deal" was all too clear—stereotyping. However, following Campos (2005, p. 121), which of the many "sinister" stereotypes surrounding queer-identified or, in this case, queer-perceived individuals were in play? For Katie, the school administrators' actions reinforced stereotypes held by many of her peers that anyone, including teachers, defending perceived/identified queer youth must themselves be queer or, at minimum, probably queer (Lipkin, 1999). Given the context behind the administrator's investigating these two particular student's sexualities, what purposeful or inadvertent messages reverberated throughout school? Upon befriending and defending Katie, had Monique exposed the limits of tolerance and inclusion and, thereby, exposed her own sexuality to suspicion and necessary interrogation? The fact that the administrators responded by interrogating Katie and Monique's sexuality, choosing them as objects for scrutiny without addressing the integrity of the claims made against Katie and Monique, for that matter, is particularly instructive. Perhaps the lesson learned is that seemingly dissimilar approaches towards queer youth's existence in schools—"active denial" and "active acknowledgement"—are similarly employable for marginalizing all students, parents, and/or teachers committed to loosening themselves and schooling from the discriminatory constraints of homophobia.

Problematizing Katie's originally assigned roommates spreading throughout school that "Katie will probably try to rape us" and, perhaps most important from the pre-service teacher's perspective, problematizing the administrator's subsequent supportive intervention on their behalf, requires added contextualization from any of the multiple junior high school foundational documents. For example,

> [t]he social studies learning environment attempts to affirm the positive aspects of ... Canada's diversity in terms of social identity, economic context, race, ethnicity and gender ... and foster an understanding and appreciation of the multiple perspectives that this diversity can lend to the classroom. Regardless of their backgrounds, students should be given equal access to educational opportunities and can be successful at them.
>
> Students do come with different attitudes, levels of knowledge, and points of view, but rather than be obstacles, these differences should be opportunities to rise above stereotypes and to develop positive self-images. Students should be provided collaborative learning contexts in which they can become aware of and transcend their own stereotypical attitudes and behaviours. (Department of Education, 2006, p. 13 [emphasis added])

Considering the official weight of this document, we might therefore conclude that the "positive aspects of diversity" and "opportunities to rise above stereotypes" are limited to classroom activities only and inapplicable to extracurricular activities. Let us frame the issue somewhat differently in question format—whenever or wherever the presence of queer youth is perceived or known, ought overnight school trip sleeping arrangements be deemed a negative aspect of diversity, fair game for stereotyping, and negative self-imaging and, in sum, beyond reasonable limits of tolerant heterosexual/tolerated queer?

Despite school-based policies forbidding discrimination on the basis of sexual orientation, this limit of tolerance and inclusion is clear for administrators, teachers, and/or students who blindly accept, practise, and impose "one of the most circulated stereotypes about gay and lesbian persons"—the belief that queers molest youth (Campos, 2005, p. 122). Given this contextualization and returning to Vriend, were school administrators motivated by stereotype in imposing upon Katie and Monique a "burden or disadvantage not imposed on others and withholding of benefits or advantages which were available to others" on the proscribed ground of perceived or actual sexual orientation?[14] Under similar circumstances, must actions of all school administrators reflect such damaging stereotyping? No, at least not from the perspective of Ryan and Brenda, who encountered this same limit, at the same time, and in the same district. Most important from Ryan and Brenda's perspectives, however, was encountering this limit at a different school and with a different outcome.

> So right after Ryan's coming out in eighth grade, all of a sudden, out of the blue his teacher is threatening not to take him on the school trip to the Magdallen Islands. I remember meeting with administrators and asking: look, is this about Ryan's sexuality? Is he now not welcome on the trip because he's gay? Absolutely not, they replied. From their perspective, I think just by putting it out there Ryan was going on that trip, which he did, and everything worked out really well. Ryan has great memories of that trip and ... for the next year's trip to the Holocaust Museum, the first of its kind for kids on PEI, there was not a peep of concern from anyone in a position of authority ... that trip really opened up Ryan's and his classmates' eyes to history and issues of diversity and acceptance ... they came back so excited and inspired about everything they did and saw. But don't get me wrong, there was homophobia at Ryan's school, but it was decisively dealt with from the top ... School leadership set the tone that homophobia was an unacceptable basis for making decisions affecting students. (Brenda, quoted in Hilton, 2010)

Class travel to Quebec City for Katie and to the Magdallen Islands and the Holocaust Museum for Ryan were equally important educational opportunities for them, their classmates, and the entire school community. What then can be made of Katie recollecting: "I was unable to enjoy myself on that trip because of the way the whole sleeping arrangement situation was handled" (Katie, quoted in Hilton, 2010) versus Brenda recalling Ryan's entire class returned from school travels "wide-eyed ... inspired and excited about everything they did and saw" (Brenda, quoted in Hilton, 2010)? Had Katie, because of her perceived lesbianism, less right to enjoy herself and to learn from whatever opportunities the trip afforded? Might we consider Katie's disappointing extracurricular experience an extension of hostile school climates negatively impacting upon queer youth's academic achievement (Kosciw et al., 2010; GLSEN, 2009; Taylor & Peter, 2011)? As for the impact of this ordeal on Katie's classmates and school, how might having a wide-eyed, inspired, and excited Katie as a travelling partner have enriched their learning? Then again, how wide-eyed, inspired, and excited could anyone on that trip allow themselves to be lest somehow, someway, their sexuality be targeted next for interrogation? From this experience, Katie resolved that

> high school would not be a repeat of how difficult junior high was ... it prompted me to finally come out to my family ... what a weight off my shoulders that was. I decided to no longer worry about what others thought about my sexuality ... I made their thoughts their business, not mine. In all honesty, during the three years of high school I never experienced anything negative towards my sexual orientation. (Katie, quoted in Hilton, 2010)

Turning difficult schooling pasts into positive schooling futures by internalizing important life lessons from the "school of hard knocks"—is this, indeed, the limit of tolerance, inclusion, equality, and justice in Canadian schools for twenty-first-century youth?

From Ryan and Brenda's experiences, further substantiated by Kosciw, Diaz, and Greytak (2008), "when schools and educators take action, they can make a dramatic difference." We detect thereby the possible reality of school trip sleeping arrangements being otherwise than reflecting some pre-ordained limit of tolerance, inclusion, and non-discrimination in schooling. Sometimes, however, inaction is the best action that schools and educators can take. As captured by Ryan when discussing his "exploding out of the closet" in eighth grade just before the first of his two memorable and meaningful school trips:

> [L]ike somehow staff were "dialed" about gay issues. I figure either someone came out there before or else the teachers had really paid attention at some training seminar somewhere. The teachers knew that I knew they knew I was coming out of the closet (laughs) but they waited for me to come to them rather than them coming to me. They just let me do it my way because to them it didn't seem to matter. I know that was a problem for my friend Katie at her school ... where teachers tried to pounce on she and her straight friend, Monique ... they basically told the teacher to mind their own business. Whenever you're treated like that why would people ever expect you to be open with them? (Ryan, quoted in Hilton, 2010)

From Smith's (1998) unnamed research participant of yesteryear to the Katies, Moniques, and Ryans of today, the business of sexualities in school appears neither about "who is queer?" nor "when did they know?" In Canada's post-Vriend age of coast-to-coast-to-coast individual equality and justice on the basis of sexual orientation, the business of sexualities and schooling demands asking "what does sexuality matter?" and/or "how does sexuality matter?" Problematizing Ryan's relatively hassle-free access to the many benefits stemming from his junior high school's extracurricular school trips, we might assume that individual sexuality matters little in twenty-first-century Canadian schools. Including Katie's experiences in this problematization mix might lead to qualifying our conclusion by suggesting individual sexuality matters little in some but not all twenty-first-century Canadian schools. Remaining ever reluctant, however, to "draw simple conclusions about who is marginalized and how or what should be done" (Tilleczek, 2011, p. 3), and being that non-discrimination on the basis of sexual orientation in the public sphere applies equally to non-queer-identified persons, I close this chapter by problematizing one final school trip scenario implicating the rights of straight and queer students alike to equal and just treatment. Recalling his school trip experiences from high school, Ryan stated:

> Getting accepted for the canoe trip two years in a row was a really big deal because it was so super competitive. That first year I tented alone because I really didn't know anyone. Being that the trip happened in November when it was really cold I would wake up that first year and just be shaking because I was just so freezing … sleeping alone turned out to be a huge big deal. So the second year I go to the office and give them the list of my friends that I'll be tenting with, and all of our parents signed approval slips … we were all really excited. Anyways, they call me up and say you can't tent with these people because they are all girls. I was like what do you mean? I don't understand you already have our parents' approval. They [administrators] said well you guys could have sex [Ryan laughs]. I said well you know I'm gay and that I don't have sex with girls. If sex is what you're worried about, then isn't it riskier for me to sleep in a tent full of guys? I reminded them it wasn't safe to sleep in a tent by myself because of the cold issue plus I didn't want to tent with a bunch of guys that I didn't know if I was safe around … I didn't know their values and they could have been super homophobic. Administrators took the issue to district staff who apparently said they got where I was coming from but separate tents for boys and girls was district policy and they have to be fair with everyone.
>
> They basically told me that if they let me sleep in a tent with my girl-friends then straight guys will say that they want to sleep with their girl-friends, and then if they have babies the district could get sued. I know this is hearsay but a reliable source told me one of the teachers chaperoning the canoe trip said that because I was gay I really shouldn't sleep in a tent with either sex and that I should just be alone. My girlfriends and I were super bummed that I didn't go on that trip but I'm still glad I tried to make it happen. (Ryan, quoted in Hilton, 2010)

Covering as it does this complex of meanings about sex, sexual acts, sexuality, and sex roles (gender), Ryan's recollection of his high school travel experiences uncovers and, perhaps, summarizes the difficult balancing act confronting today's public school administrators—how to be fair to everyone without getting sued. While equality and justice might never be easily achieved anywhere in post-Vriend Canada, let alone in "consistently conservative PEI" (Robinson, 2006), the view taken in this chapter is that processes purporting to reflect these fundamental Canadian values must be submitted to the work of thought. So what thinking characterizes the experiences of Ryan, his girlfriends, their parents, and administrators chaperoning the canoe trip? How and what did sexuality matter in this specific scenario?

Notwithstanding parental consent and long-standing district policies that "parents know best" when it comes to matters of sexual health and wellness education, PEI school administrators overrode Ryan and his girlfriends sleeping together in the same tent (Department of Education, 2007). Paraphrasing Chrétien (1981), what important matters of school policy were at stake that required administrators, not parents, to have the final say on school trip sleeping arrangements? How had it come to be that the district's right to avoid pregnancy-related lawsuits outweighed Ryan's, his girlfriends', and their parent's right to determine, as had other campers and parents, individual sleeping arrangements? As in the case of Katie's junior high school trip to Quebec and of the school administrators leaving unmolested stereotypes of "queers molest youth," I suggest unquestioned stereotypes again guided administrator's actions. Returning to Campos (2005), Ryan's sexuality may have been disbelieved because of stereotypical beliefs that queer identification is a choice. Just as Ryan's real heterosexuality falsely occurred in eighth grade, therefore, it might now explode out of the closet if he was permitted to share a tent with the girls. Correspondingly, what knowledge of young straight females and/or males tenting together limits administrator's conceptualizations of them to pregnancies and lawsuits? Is it unnatural or inadvisable for girls and boys to develop platonic friendships? Incorporating gender stereotypes of "male equals active" and "female equals passive" are administrator's reinforcing beliefs that all young females submit to sexual advances and all young males are predators, unable or unwilling to take no for an answer? Or does the notion that "we have to be fair to everyone" really just provide tolerant, inclusive cover to school administrator's for enforcing "because you are gay, go sleep in the gay tent"? Such are the questions raised by voices from the margins when considering how the business of schooling, sexualities, and school trips intersect and are problematized by individual equality and justice in twenty-first-century post-Vriend Canadian public education.

Notes

1   All quotations of young people are demarcated with a pseudonym.
2   *Vriend v Alberta*, [1998] 1 S.C.R. 493.
3   *Individual Rights Protection Act*, R.S.A. 1980, c. I-2, s. 2; *Human Rights, Citizenship and Multiculturalism Act*, R.S.A. 1980, c. H-11.7, ss. 2(2), 3.
4   *Vriend, supra* note 1 at 6.
5   *Ibid.* at 90.
6   *M. v. H.*, [1999] 2 S.C.R. 3 at 6.
7   *Ibid.* at 3.
8   *Marriage Act*, R.S.P.E.I. 1988, c M-3, online: http://canlii.ca/t/lhgw.
9   *Act to Amend the Marriage Act*, R.S.P.E.I. 2005, c. 12 at 182.
10 *In the Matter of Marriage Commissioners Appointed under the Marriage Act*, 1995, [2011] S.S., c. M-4.1, 2011 SKCA 3 at 44.
11 *Reference re: Same-Sex Marriage*, 3 S.C.R. 698 3 2004.
12 *Canadian Charter of Rights and Freedoms*, Part 1 of the Constitution Act, 1982, *being Schedule B to the* Canada Act 1982 (U.K.), 1982, c. 11.
13 Bill 44, *Human Rights, Citizenship and Multiculturalism Amendment Act*, (2009), 27th Parl., 2nd Sess., 58 Elizabeth II.
14 *Vriend*, supra note 3 at 6.

References

Blount, J. (2005). *Fit to teach: Same-sex desire, gender and school work in the twentieth century*. Albany, NY: New York Press.

Bourassa, K., & Varnell, J. (2008). *Norway's expansion of human rights*. Online: http://www.samesexmarriage.ca/equality/nor170608.htm.

Britzman, D. J. (1995). Is there a queer pedagogy? Or, stop reading straight. *Educational Theory, 45*(2), 151-165.

Campos, D. (2005). *Understanding gay and lesbian youth lessons for straight school teachers, counselors, and administrators*. Lanham, MD: Rowman & Littlefield Education.

Canadian Broadcasting Corporation, News. (2009). *Alberta passes law allowing parents to pull kids out of class*. Online: http://www.cbc.ca/news/canada/edmonton/story/2009/06/02/alberta-human-rights-school-gay-education-law.html.

Cloud, J. (2005). The battle over gay teens. *Time* (2 October), 1-12.

Department of Education. (2006). *Atlantic Canada grade 7 social studies curriculum* (English programs). Online: http://www.gov.pe.ca/photos/original/ed_7socA_06.pdf.

Department of Education. (2007). *Health Curriculum Guides*. Online: http://www.gov.pe.ca/photos/original/ed_hea7_08.pdf.

Dickieson (1998). Prince Edward Island. Legislative Assembly. *Hansard,* 60th Parl., 1st Sess. (2 June 1998) at 5661.

Dieghan (1998). Prince Edward Island. Legislative Assembly. *Hansard,* 60th Parl., 1st Sess (2 June 1998) at 5662.

Eastern School District of Prince Edward Island. (1999). *Caring places to learn/Safe school environment* (Code: ADDA-R ed.). Charlottetown, PEI: Eastern School District.

Eastern School District of Prince Edward Island. (2011). *Race relations, cross cultural understanding and human rights in learning* (Code: IHAC-R). Charlottetown, PEI: Eastern School District.

Foucault, M., & Rabinow, P. (1997). *Ethics: Subjectivity and truth.* New York: New Press.

Goldfried, M. R., & Goldfried, A. P. (2001). The importance of parental support in the lives of gay, lesbian, and bisexual individuals. *Journal of Clinical Psychology, 57*(5), 681-693.

Grossman, A. H., Haney, A. P., Edwards, P., Alessi, E. J., Ardon, M., & Howell, T. J. (2009). Lesbian, gay, bisexual and transgender youth talk about experiencing and coping with school violence: A qualitative study. *Journal of LGBT Youth, 6*(1), 24-46. Online: http://www.tandfonline.com/doi/full/10.1080/19361650802379748.

Harris, S. (2008, April 3). Vriend at 10: Ten years after the watershed Vriend v Alberta decision. *VUE Weekly, 650,* 1.

Hehr (2009). Alberta. Legislative Assembly. *Hansard,* 27th Parl., 2nd Sess. (1 June 2009) at 1466.

Hilton, T. (2010). *Queering freedom: Schooling experiences of "out" youth and their families on Prince Edward Island.* (Paper presented at the annual conference of the Canadian Society in Education, Concordia University, Montreal, PQ).

Johansen, D., & Rosen, P. (2008). *The notwithstanding clause of the charter.* Ottawa, ON: Library of Parliament.

Kennedy, H. (2009a). *Alberta government supports making sexuality, evolution optional: Religious preference to trump in public education.* Online: http://egale.ca/.

Kosciw, J., Diaz, E., & Greytak, E. (2008). *The 2007 national school climate survey: The experiences of lesbian, gay, bisexual and transgender youth in our nation's schools.* New York: Gay, Lesbian and Straight Education Network.

Kumashiro, K. K. (2004). Uncertain beginnings: Learning to teach paradoxically. *Theory into Practice, 43*(2), 111-115. Online: http://muse.jhu.edu/journals/theory_into_practice/v043/43.2kumashiro.html.

Lipkin, A. (1999). *Understanding homosexuality, changing schools.* Boulder, CO: Westview Press.

Loutzenheiser, L. W., & MacIntosh, L. B. (2004). Citizenships, sexualities, and education. *Theory into Practice, 43*(2), 151-158. Online: http://muse.jhu.edu/journals/theory_into_practice/v043/43.2loutzenheiser.html.

Luther King, Jr., M. (1963). *Letter from Birmingham jail,* 16 April. Online: http://www.africa.upenn.edu/Articles_Gen/Letter_Birmingham.html.

O'Farrell, C. (2007). *Michel-foucault.com.* Online: http://www.michel-foucault.com/concepts/index.html.

Reilly, C. (2007). Making the invisible visible: Negotiating (in)visibility and transparency for LGBT issues in education. *Journal of Gay and Lesbian Issues in Education, 4*(3), 121. Online: http://www.informaworld.com/10.1300/J367v04n03_08.

Robinson, B. A. (2006). *Homosexual (same-sex) marriages in Canada, province of Prince Edward Island.* Online: http://www.religioustolerance.org/hommarbpei.htm.

Savin-Williams, R. (2005). *The new gay teenager.* Cambridge, MA: Harvard University Press.

Sedgwick, E. K. (1990). *Epistemology of the closet.* Berkeley, CA: University of California Press.

Smith, G. W. (1998). The ideology of "fag": The school experience of gay students. *Sociological Quarterly, 39*(2), 309-335. Online: http://www.jstor.org.rlproxy.upei.ca/stable/4121586.

Standing Committee on Social Development. (1998). Continuation of public hearings on the Human Rights Act (April 2). Charlottetown, PE: Legislative Assembly of Prince Edward Island.

Taylor, C., & Peter, T., with McMinn, T. L., Elliott, T., Beldom, S., Ferry, A., Gross, Z., Paquin, S., & Schachter, K. (2011). *Every class in every school: The first national climate survey on homophobia, biphobia, and transphobia in Canadian schools. Final report.* Toronto, ON: EGALE Canada Human Rights Trust. Online: http://www.egale.ca/EgaleFinalReport-web.pdf.

Tilleczek, K. (2010). Young lives as edge work for educational practice. *Education Canada, 50*(5), 3-3.

Tilleczek, K. (2011). Approaching youth studies: Being, becoming, and belonging. Don Mills, ON: Oxford University Press.

Tilleczek, K., Furlong, A., & Ferguson, B. (2010). Marginalized youth in contemporary educational contexts: A tranquil invitation to a rebellious celebration. *Education Canada, 50*, 6-10.

Turnbull, M., & Hilton, T. (2010). Infusing some queer into teacher education. *Education Canada, 50*(5), 18-22.

University of Prince Edward Island, Faculty of Education. (2009). *Mission statement, goals and history.* Online: http://education.upei.ca.rlproxy.upei.ca/mission-statement-goals-and-history.

Wells, K. (2007). Generation queer: Sexual minority youth and Canadian schools. *Education Canada, 48*(1), 18-22. Online: http://pridenet.ca/wp-content/uploads/generation-queer.pdf.

Wood, O. (2008). *Canadian pride legal history.* Toronto: Canadian Auto Workers.

Two Young Men, photograph by Elliott Tilleczek

chapter 10

Narrative Understandings of Lives Lived in (and out of) Schools

Vera Caine, Sean Lessard, Pam Steeves, and D. Jean Clandinin[1]

O ur scholarly and personal interests intertwine in our research in understanding lives narratively as unfolding, enfolding, nested compositions (Clandinin & Connelly, 2000; Clandinin et al., 2006). For many years now, following John Dewey's (1938) ideas on education as experience, we have worked with others to attend to lives in the making, lives in motion. In the project we describe in this chapter, alongside a group of other researchers, we became intrigued by the life composing of youth who had left schools (Clandinin et al., 2010). We worked alongside young people who had left school prior to high school completion so we might learn more about their storied experiences, recognizing that their lives in school were only part of their much larger life compositions. We were interested in learning of their lives, and, perhaps through learning about their lives, we wanted to learn more about our lives as educators and more about schools. Our overall intentions were, in part, to learn about what we call stories of school (Clandinin & Connelly, 1995) and about how we might begin to shape those stories. Our research explored how the youths' lives shaped their early leaving of school and how leaving school early shaped their lives.

Educators, policy-makers, and politicians are increasingly concerned about the complex and multiple costs of early school leaving—costs that include personal (i.e., poorer quality of life, compromised well-being), economic (higher levels of unemployment, lower income), and societal factors (increased demands for social services, increased crime, reduced community participation). Estimates of past and current school leaving rates fluctuate and are often inconsistent due to varied definitions and measurements of early school leaving.

Great variations are also found in the explanations for early school leaving, depending on the political, sociological, or philosophical framework chosen. Current understandings are shaped by the assumptions that it is advantageous for adolescents to be in school rather than out of school, that any education is superior to no education, and that there are explicit social and personal costs to early school leaving.

In the mid-1980s, there continued to be a philosophical shift in the understanding of early school leavers, which brought with it recognition that early school leaving comes from a process of disengagement, where early school leavers disengage themselves from the culture of schooling. Educationists generally agree that student engagement (e.g., time-on-task and participation) produces positive outcomes, but they noted that there is disagreement about what counts as engagement (Appleton, Christenson, & Furlong, 2008; Harris, 2008). Disengagement is seen as a non-linear process within a transition to adulthood. This term also pays attention to the relational impact of others and that youth engage with school based on kept or broken promises by others (Tilleczek, 2008). Student engagement or disengagement shows early school leaving to be a complex and often emotional process (Harris, 2008; Langhout & Mitchell, 2008; Tilleczek, 2008).

To this date, there is no universally accepted definition of early school leaving. Leavers are typically defined as students who leave school (not including transfers) before they graduate from high school with a regular diploma. Some students leave school before entering ninth grade (Tilleczek, 2008). There is also a general consensus that early school leaving is the result of a long process of disengagement (Archambault et al., 2009) and alienation that may be preceded by less severe types of disengagement such as truancy and grade retention (Tilleczek, 2008).

Although it is appealing to use the terms school leaver and dropout interchangeably, many researchers and policy-makers use the terms without paying close attention to the different philosophical and logistical underpinnings of the terms. No one framework has been developed that is able to capture the complexity of early school leaving. In general, students at risk of early school leaving are viewed from either an individual deficit perspective, which elaborates risk factors, or from disengagement perspectives, which take into account wider social inequities (Cassidy & Bates, 2005).

Research on risk factors that lead to early school leaving may represent a starting point for understanding the complexity of the dropout process (Lessard et al., 2008). Although individual deficit models continue to be explored, process theories of disengagement have become more common. These theories take into account that disengagement from school is a non-linear, partial, and fragmented process that is often contradictory, complex, filled with subversive forces and tensions, as well as a struggle for most students (Archambault et al., 2009; Tilleczek, 2008; Janosz et al., 2008). Hodgson (2007, p. 1-2) describes school leaving as "having complex historical antecedents that form and grow over time." Points of disengagement have been referred to as starting points, faltering points, and end points. At times, students "start from scratch," these are students who have multiple risk factors both at the family, school, and community level while others encounter "primarily protective factors" and, after leaving school early, they still see the possibility of negotiating their way back (Tilleczek, 2008).

Dropping out is not just an event but, rather, a process (Bradshaw, O'Brennan, & McNeely, 2008). It is not just a matter of deciding not to come back to school one day. According to Bowlby and McMullen (2002), many youth drop out and return to school several times before deciding to leave school completely. Since we were interested in the lives of the youth who left school early, we framed our study as a narrative inquiry working from the following definition:

> People shape their daily lives by stories of who they and others are and as they interpret their past in terms of these stories. Story, in the current idiom, is a portal through which a person enters the world and by which their experience of the world is interpreted and made personally meaningful. Narrative inquiry, the study of experience as story, then, is first and foremost a way of thinking about experience. (Connelly & Clandinin, 2006, p. 375)

In our narrative inquiry, our group of 11 researchers worked alongside 19 youth between the ages of 18 and 21 who left school before graduating and who had been out of school for more than a year. We selected youth whose life experiences were diverse. They lived in rural, urban, and suburban places. We included males and females; youth of diverse heritages; youth of different family constellations; youth of different socio-economic groupings, and so on. We met them in the midst of their complex, ongoing lives, lives that had not yet, at least, included high school graduation. We engaged with each youth in a series of conversations in 2008 and 2009, inspired by our overall research puzzles around how their lives shaped their leaving of school and how leaving school shaped their lives. We met in coffee shops, offices, cafés, diners, libraries— some of the youth took us back to their junior high schools. We framed the conversations by working within the relational inquiry space that we and each participant co-composed. As we talked together, we were attentive to asking about time, places, emotions, events, and other characters in their stories. We wondered about tensions they experienced as their lives bumped against social, cultural, institutional, familial, and linguistic narratives. We were mindful of attending to their lives in motion and not of focusing only on their experiences of schooling. Dropping out is seldom a clear choice of leaving school, yet a fair number of students are pushed out and simply fade away (Hattam & Smyth, 2003). Our field texts included transcripts of these conversations, our field notes on conversations, youths' artwork, and memory box artifacts.

As we first began to move from field texts to research texts, we composed narrative accounts of our unique experiences with the youth we had engaged in the conversations. In that first level of analysis, we worked within the three-dimensional narrative inquiry space shaped by temporality, sociality, and place(s) (Clandinin & Connelly, 2000). We wrote accounts and negotiated them with each participant. In the second level of analysis, we worked as an 11-member research team to look across the 19 individual narrative accounts to inquire into resonant threads or patterns that we could discern. We did so in order to offer a deeper and broader awareness of the experiences of early school leavers with an overall intention to open up new wonders and questions about early school leaving and, in part, to help us learn more about schools and how to shape them in ways that might be more responsive to the life composing of all youth. The following six fragments are taken from six of these narrative accounts.

Andrew in Relation with Jean

As I listened to Andrew tell of the place of sports in his life, he said: "*It has always been about basketball in junior high too, but, like the teachers in junior high, they seemed more caring and understanding so I kinda like got along with them, like really well.*"[2] Sports were the central thread in his life, and it was being able to play sports, particularly basketball, that kept him involved.

> *I'd just go to school and play basketball and I had good times in doing like school stuff, so, and in high school, it was a big change from how the teachers were in junior high to high school so then that's like when I was, I just like really focused on just wanting to play basketball.*

Andrew continued to play sports, mainly basketball, both in and out of school, during his junior high school years. He spoke of the support of his junior high school physical education teacher whose daughter he met while playing "club basketball." By the end of junior high school, he had to choose one sport and concentrate on it, and he chose basketball. He did, however, mention that when he was in Grade 11 he played some volleyball on the school team "for fun."

When it came time to choose a high school, Andrew selected the high school because of its interest in having him play basketball. As he said: *'Cause I just liked the, I had been talking to the coach since I was in, like Grade 6, so, kinda like had a bond there so I decided to go there."* He agreed when I said: *"So it's been about basketball for a long time."* Andrew's story of himself was composed around being a basketball player.

By the time he was in high school, Andrew was not particularly interested in any subject area. As he said:

> I was interested just 'cause I know I needed that to go somewhere else with basketball, but it wasn't really something, like I'd just make sure I'd get like a high percentage, I'd just make sure I'd get like the passing grade just so I could keep playing. So I wasn't really putting all my hard work into it [school work].

Skye Songmaker in Relation with Sean

"I didn't always understand my work and I am too shy to ask for help, I felt dumb." She told me often during our conversations that she struggled with the school work and that it was different than what she had learned on the reserve—the pace was too fast. She told me: *"Do you know that I am actually smart, Lessard? I was the class valedictorian in my Grade 9 class at the reserve."* I replied by simply saying: *"I know you are."*

She told me about her feelings coming to a new place and how she often felt low as a student. She told of one of her first days in class. The class went to a driving range to play golf. She was excited because golf was her favourite sport. However, she missed the school bus because she was not familiar with public transportation in this new city. She arrived late to the driving range having walked there by herself. The teacher stopped class and told everybody to *"look at who is late."* He asked where she was. She replied: *"I am not a city person, I got lost."* He laughed and said: *"Are you sure about that? Are you sure you didn't get lost at the mall?"* With everyone looking at her, they laughed. Skye did not remember many stories from high school, but this story stayed with her long after. She said: *"I felt like quitting right there and going home. But then he would have been right about me."* That day at the driving range: *"I felt like he thought I was just another dumb Indian."*

The girls (Skye and her sisters) recalled times in the past when their mom and dad had taught them sports, dancing, and culture. They laughed when they told stories and corrected each other along the way. As they told stories, they moved backwards in time to intergenerational connections they shared with their cultural roots. They told me they had been practising and learning about culture and traditional dancing since they were babies. I know by walking alongside them that their cultural roots come from a place. The passing down of knowledge through participation is a thread that weaves throughout their lives. The cultural stories and knowledge started before them, before their parents, as they told stories about their grandfather, a gifted man, a song maker, and singer. He was a very spiritual person with special gifts. The girls spoke proudly of their grandmothers and grandfathers and how culture had always existed in their family.

Christian in Relation with Vera

Christian was a very striking young man, quiet and soft-spoken. I was struck by some of his references to violence and the expression of the same in his drawings and tattoos. It was this tension between his demeanour and his told stories that drew me into his stories and his life.

Tattooed on Christian's arm are Chinese characters, characters that reflect what means the most in his life. I listen intently as he translated these characters for me: family, forever, friend(ship), companion. As he put all the words together, I heard him say: "*[F]orever family and friendship.*" As he said the words slowly, my mind returned to our previous conversations, and I could see that the tattooed characters are alive and embedded in all of his life stories. The leaving of school early was in part the story of longing to be with friends, of feeling isolated and lonely in a place that paid little attention: "*I stayed for 5 months in school just to prove a point to someone, yet I wasn't enjoying myself and I had no friends. Stuck in the same classroom, it made me miserable and I switched high schools because of friends.*" And I so strongly heard his family stories too, of the responsibility he carried from a very young age: "*In Grade 10 I had to go to the attendance board for the first time and I was really scared and afraid of being judged for my looks.*" In an effort to not be judged, Christian cut his hair. He had many questions about why he had such a strong sense of being judged. He thought: "*If they get to know me they are having no reason to judge me.*" He wanted to show them that he was serious about school; he attended school for five months without missing a day. He wanted to show them that "*people can work their way through school, that people can change.*" In the end, Christian realized that he was only attending school to prove a point to someone! He switched schools and, after being at a new high school for two days, his grandmother passed away, and he became very depressed and started to withdraw from school.

For now, the last picture in Christian's book of drawings that he shared with me is a Japanese half dragon and Koi fish:

> It is a Koi fish on a Japanese enchanted river; if the Koi fish is able to work itself over the waterfall, then it turns into a dragon. Koi fish become almost magic—overcoming certain paths, reaching goals, much like swimming over a waterfall. It is almost impossible to swim over a waterfall and perhaps it is symbolic of my life. It represents my life a lot.

Christian's life does reflect his effort and perseverance in the face of adversity, yet it also reflects wisdom, knowledge, longevity, and loyalty. In Christian's story, the Koi fish perhaps also symbolizes this courage and ability to overcome life's obstacles, a successful struggle against the odds, and a reminder that human suffering is part of life.

Kevlar in Relation with Pam

For Kevlar, turmoil "out of school" profoundly shaped his "in school" experiences:

> 'Cause in schools there's always the people who have the perfect lives, the perfect parents. And they rocket directly to the top. They're practically favoured by all the teachers because they get the best grades, because they're not even stressed at all. School is built for them. And it just doesn't work out well for anyone that's not in a perfect situation.

Kevlar's story was complex. "*In Grade 7 I learned how to play the saxophone and stuff. It was quite awesome. I loved the saxophone.*" Yet I soon learned he only barely passed Grade 9. "*They can't actually fail you in Grade 9.*" Whatever schooling gaps Kevlar had experienced, as he moved from place to place and school to school, he would not have to fail Grade 9. It seemed to be a second chance that could be taken advantage of when perfect situations are few and far between.

And then he said: "*I went to a group home. It was O.K. But I was practically traumatized. There's a probationary period. For the first two weeks there are chores, you have to follow all the rules and stuff. And if you don't, you are out. But I was like a 14 year old kid that just went through all this. So I ended up just a-woling from it. To try and go see my friends.*" Eventually, he ended up for a while "*going the homeless route.*"

> During this time, I started Grade 10 at George Wood. And I kept trying to do it as much as I could. Living in random places. But it's really hard to do school when you don't live anywhere. I could do the school ... It's just like after school. I would have to do my homework, figure out where I'm going to stay, figure out if I'm going to make it through the day.

He said Grade 11 was his best year, even though he attended two different high schools. But three-quarters through the first semester of Grade 12, he could not handle his roommates anymore, the parties until four and five in the morning, and he decided to move out. He tried to register for another year of Grade 12 at some other schools but he could not do it. Kevlar's understanding was that in Alberta (the province where he lived) "*it's almost impossible for a kid to get a 4th year at a public high school.*" When I asked Kevlar about support from friends, he told me that they were there but "*friends can only go so far ... because they're not in the same situation.*"

There were plans to register for virtual school: *"I've always known that education is the key to life and I think it's ridiculous to not get it."* He is planning to redo math and physics, taking Math 20 and 30 because they are pure and because he loves quantum physics. I wondered about resilience, and he agreed that he did seem to bounce back and if something did not work out, he *"would make something else work."*

Leanne in Relation with Sean

Leanne scrawled down the names of her family members from oldest to youngest and told me little stories about them in the process. She also wrote out the names of schools that she had attended. She pointed with her pen and tapped the paper, circling a school's name as she shared her junior high experience. She explained that this was where she felt the need to run opposite to what was going on. She did not always feel comfortable with the teachings and direction of her classes. They were different from what she wanted. I wondered what her picture of school would have looked like?

Leanne talked in great detail about her early school years and often described them as nothing out of the ordinary, *"just a regular kid going to school."* Once again, I wondered why she pointed out that junior high school experience and her memory of it. She explained to me that she had attended a local kindergarten in her neighbourhood and then went to a Christian school from Grades 1 to 9. Leanne reported that all she really remembered about the past were the sports stories. She reminded me that this was the time in her life that she first learned to play basketball.

She talked about this school of the past with feelings that were connected to how she had been currently feeling. I tried to inquire into this space and asked her if she felt negatively about this school while she attended or just then as she was reflecting on it. She described her junior high experience and the students with whom she attended school in the following way:

> It's not like we were oppressed, or maybe we were ... [laughs]. It's just that we (students) didn't have the experience of other kids, and many of us went counter to what we were always told to do, or told to act, we just went a little crazy when we were thrown into a big high school and given all these choices, we didn't know how to manage this. It's difficult going to high school.

I sat back and listened to Leanne on this day and wondered why it took so long for us to have this conversation. I have known her for many years and, through all of this time, our conversations had been largely on the surface. I wondered if we would have been able to have this conversation if we could have gone back in time or does the school landscape inhibit the possibility of sharing? Is there something about that high school space that defines roles and makes it difficult to have a conversation that is needed? When I think of my work as a high school teacher I often forget about the critical development that takes place for youth in elementary and junior high. My relationships with many students are often only sporadic interactions that take place in the hallway, changing only if I get an opportunity to connect through the classroom or extracurricular activities. These are the quick snapshots I see of many students. I only learn a small part of their stories in that high school place.

The conversation moved closer to the present and an area with which I was more familiar, the high school years. From my vantage point, I thought Leanne experienced many positive memories at this time in her life. I wondered if she would feel the same way? I thought about Leanne's position as a point guard on the basketball team. Was high school a blur? It may be like that point guard story, a basketball game, and how the way in which it is managed dictates success. The light bulbs on the score clock create numbers telling the fans who is winning and how much time is left in the game. The coach dictates to the players how the game will be played based on what is going on in that game during that moment or whether the team is winning or losing. Success in this game is so narrowly defined, and the choices made within can shape the outcome. What does a player do when the game does not turn out the way it is supposed to? How can we reimagine the story that takes place on the court? What happens when a player makes a mistake? Is there opportunity for redemption or does the game move on? I think of school stories, and not all of them have a happy ending. Some students have skills to navigate. They have an ability to negotiate changes in their stories. I think of the students who do not always know the right answers and desperately feel like they need to get away from that school place. I think they are just not interested in playing the game at the moment, but this does not mean they are not interested in the end result.

I wonder as I type this what Leanne will think when we read it together. Does this analogy fit the story that she told me? Does it make sense to her as she reflects on her school stories? I wonder what her new path will look like and if she will get back to playing the game that she loves? What stories will she create as she moves forward in time?

Many teachers knew Leanne quite well because of her presence in the hallway, involvement in sports, and high level of success in academics. However, she felt that she did not have close-knit relationships at school with her teachers. She said often during this part of the conversation that she felt that it was like "going through the motions, I can't really remember the classes at all or the teachers' names who taught me." She said that she really only "remembers the sports"—teachers "don't go that deep." When they talked to her, they seemed only concerned about the subjects they taught.

We talked about the process of going through Grades 10 through 12, and Leanne told me that *"there is so much more to me than what people think."* She explained how she viewed herself as different from many of her teammates in school, that she loved to paint, and play guitar. She asked if I remembered that. I replied yes, and I recalled the time I was surprised to see her board the bus with a guitar in hand, as we prepared for a week-long school field trip. I wasn't shocked because I didn't think she could play guitar. What did shock me was that she was the only member of the basketball team that went in her own direction. Many of the players often stuck together in classes and did not venture that far away from each other's company. Leanne reminded me during this conversation about how much grief she took from the other members of the team because she missed basketball games to attend the guitar field trip. This was an extremely unpopular choice in the eyes of her teammates. I wondered about the guitar story she was creating for herself and how it ran contrary to the dominant team story that existed in her life. I wondered if she still played the guitar and if she played to create her own individual stories, ones that were different than the collective.

Truong in Relation with Jean

Truong became a father to a daughter two and a half years ago. His daughter lives with her mother, but Truong and his mother have access to the child on the weekends. He describes his daughter as putting "joy in my life."

> When I see her laughing and playing around it's just like the greatest thing. So when she like, you know, she gives me like kisses and hugs and stuff, it's like it's a good thing to me, right, because I'm not used to it, like I've never kissed my mom in my life that I can remember. I've never, I've maybe hugged her once my whole life so I mean this kind of stuff is different to me. But she is my daughter, and I do love her. And she is, she is the joy in my life.

I wonder if his daughter has, in some ways, interrupted the stories he was living and telling. Did her arrival and his knowing he was a father shift the trajectory of his forward-looking story?

As we talked, Truong spoke of his experiences of leaving school. He had played on the volleyball team in Grades 10 and 11 and had experienced a great deal of success. However, Grade 12 was different:

> And then Grade 12 came around and there was no more volleyball ... and so I was like, whatever, I don't really feel like going to school anymore. I got kicked out second semester of Grade 12. Like I did go to my classes and stuff but I was more of, oh I'm late, forget it, I don't want to go anymore or, you know, stuff like that and I just didn't have motivation to go anywhere.

With regard to Grades 10 and 11, he said:

> *If I was late I'd still go to school, if I didn't have a ride to school I would bus to school, but in Grade 12 if I didn't have a ride I was, ah, I'm staying home today. If it's cold or like I bused to school in Grade 10 a couple of times during the winter and stuff, right, and, like, you know, but that's 'cause I had a game or practice or something after school so I wanted to be there.*

As Truong looked back over this time in high school, he said:

> *I didn't care about the teachers, I didn't do anything, I didn't really have motivation to go to school really except for when I had volleyball ... because my coach was my gym teacher that cared and he kind of kept me out of everything but ... the only things I really cared about in high school were basically my friends and volleyball.*

He had a "*distinctive hair style*" and was described as "*the Asian guy with the bangs 'cause I had like spiky hair with two long strands coming down the sides.*" He spoke of his teachers in high school in the following way:

> *Like a lot of teachers, I don't know if they liked me ... but a lot of coaches and teachers and stuff knew who I was. They knew me for, like the person that I was and stuff, but the principal or the student counsellor or whatever didn't really care, didn't, like, I've known a lot of kids that got so many chances, like they, they fought or whatever, they got kicked out of school and then they would come back and everything's good and stuff, right, but with me it was like, OK, come to the office, you're expelled because you skipped too much. And I'm, like, OK well, what am I going to do, I'm not going to cry about it right?*

As Truong told me these stories about not being given second chances as others had been, I sensed he had learned to accept such treatment and to not fight back. He described that he "*was like my own person with my own friends.*" Truong has tried to complete high school. He tried to register "*when I was about 18 or 19*" in order to "*finish up.*" He attributes his desire to complete high school to the birth of his daughter. He reported that he has

> *70-some credits, so if I finish my Grade 12 I know I can graduate, and I really wanted to when I was 19, but then money came into play and all that stuff, and I was thinking like student financing and stuff, but I went to do it and they were like: "No, you're one day too old." So they cut it off at September 1st and that's when my birthday is ... I didn't really try again 'cause money's still in play, like money's still an issue in my life, right.*

He started to work when he was about 15, at first with "under the table pay" when he "washed dishes and stuff for the restaurant" where his mom was the cook. The money he had earned then was to "*just kind of take care of myself and my mom didn't have to worry about me too much, right, like I'd have lunch money or whatever.*" He learned early to help out with the finances at home, to take care of himself, to save his mother from even more financial worry.

Truong has been a watchful big brother to his two younger siblings: "*I built the rep of people being scared of me and stuff like that so my little brother and my little sister can go through school peacefully.*" He learned to live and tell stories of himself as a tough guy, someone to be scared of, in order to provide his siblings with protection from harm. As he said:

> *I kinda lived the life that I lived basically for them to go through school and I've tried, I did everything that I can for them to graduate and stuff right, to go through school peacefully.*

Discussion: Resonant Narrative Threads

As a way to better understand the complexities of youths' experiences of early school leaving, we engaged in a second level of analysis across narrative accounts to identify six resonant threads. They are conversational spaces; relationships; identities; complexities over time; responsibilities; and cultural, social, and institutional narratives.

Conversational Spaces

The narrative accounts all speak clearly to the importance of creating conversational spaces that encourage youth to share their life experiences, including their school and school-leaving experiences. Off the school landscape and within the narrative inquiry spaces we composed with them, together we engaged the difficult conversations that allowed us to look backward and forward, inward and outward, to tell and retell life stories (Clandinin & Connelly, 2000). As we opened up inquiry spaces for conversation, we were moved and humbled by how quickly the youth began to tell their stories. Many of the stories seemed to have been resting with the youth and their families for some time, waiting to be told. We wondered about why the youth had not told these stories earlier and came to understand that they had not previously had spaces nor relationships, either in school or out of school, to tell these stories without interruption and to be able to open them to inquiry.

For many of the youth, the research conversations provided them an opportunity to reflect on their lives, particularly as students, and to begin to retell—that is, to inquire into the lives they were composing for themselves. For instance, as Christian told his stories, he spoke of losing the conversational spaces he had while he was in school. Christian wanted to live up to the expectations of his teachers and administrators of good school attendance. Yet when he needed to attend to his family's needs, he began to drift away from school, having no one to turn to.

We were also deeply impressed by the willingness of the youth to tell their stories when given an opportunity, in thoughtful, life-affirming ways. As he moved backward and forward in time, Kevlar saw a picture of himself emerging. He was amazed to think of *"tiny little moments that changed the rest of ... [his] life."* While negotiating the narrative account with us, he said it was good to see his story of leaving school on paper, adding *"reflecting on it with someone is different than reflecting on it yourself."* Some of these stories suggest that the youth were attempting to navigate complex institutional, social, and cultural narratives that were sometimes alienating and foreign.

Relationships

The importance of relationships to the youth became visible and multidimensional throughout our research. The participants' relationships with family, peers, school curriculum, and teachers, as well as the interruption of relationships through transitions, exemplifies the significance of relationship—connection and association—when we thought about early school leaving. In some cases, fragile and emerging new stories around being successful, being accepted, and belonging were interrupted when relationships changed, be it relationships with family, peers, teachers, or subject matter. For both Andrew and Truong, it was their passion for, and their excellence in, sports that kept them in school. For Andrew, his relationship with school was so interwoven with his membership on the high school basketball team that when he was no longer a part of the team going to school became impossible. Having lost his place on the team, he lost his relationship with school. Something similar happened with Truong. When the teacher who had coached the volleyball team was transferred out of the school and there was no longer the possibility of a volleyball team for him, Truong began to drift away from school. Being able to excel at sports had made school a place where he could belong. When that relationship vanished, he no longer felt that he belonged in school.

Often relational changes and interruptions create turmoil and confusion for youth as they struggle to make sense of, and recompose, new stories to live by while transitioning to newly reconfigured families, new homes, schools, or communities. Making the decision to leave school is part of the process of becoming someone. At other times, employment or caring for others is seen as choosing more adult-like identities (Archer & Yamashita, 2003). The performance of identities, expressed by fashion style and body image helped some students stay in school, while others were pushed out or excluded (Smyth &

Hattam, 2004). For other students, the process of success or even staying at school involved muting their voices (Smyth & Hattam, 2004). In particular, children from minority groups experienced the constructing of very limiting identities for themselves (Toohey, 2000).

Skye moved from the reserve to the city because her parents thought there were more opportunities there. However, Skye told stories of feeling too shy to ask about things that were different from what she was used to: "*I felt dumb.*" She remembered the story of missing a school bus for a field trip to the golf course because she was not familiar with transportation in the new city. Her story was dismissed. Again, we were struck by stories that do not describe schools as belonging places at times and places of transition. It has to be recognized that young people have a heightened sense of agency and are often not prepared to have their identities ignored or subordinated within the dominant school and policy framework. School trouble often stems from the interactive trouble between trying to become somebody and the narrowly defined identity that schools expect (Smyth & Hattam, 2004). School policies, teacher attitudes, and reactions as well as peer rejection all provide the message that those who leave school early do not belong (Lessard et al., 2008).

Identities

The youth were composing their identities on elementary, junior high, and senior high school landscapes as well as on complex home and community landscapes. Participating in the study itself was, for many, an act of choice that shaped a sense of authoring/authority in their lives. While they saw themselves composing who they were and who they were becoming, they did not tell their stories as school dropouts. A number of them actively resisted the label. They told their stories around plotlines of "*not in school for now.*" Their forward-looking stories included school. Kevlar, for example, even as he made it all the way to Grade 12 through extraordinary efforts ended up leaving school early because he was not in a situation that would enable him to do well. He identified himself as one who knew the value and necessity of education for pursuing his dream of attending a design college so he could someday become a creative graphic designer. Some early school leavers describe their experiences as a feeling of being trapped in a narrowly defined identity story. Others describe it as a dropout dance, a dance in which students both flex their muscles and perform, as a way to exert power over their own choices (Davis, 2006). Frequently, these students move in and out of school, and their school story is marked by repeated absences. The rhythms of moving in and out of school are filled with signifiers of rejection, even if the goals of school leavers and those who eventually graduate remain the same (Tanner, Krahn, & Hartnagel, 1995).

As the students chose to leave or return to school, we saw them as struggling to develop and sustain a sense of agency embodied in their unfolding lives. Their complex life stories showed a sense of them composing their own lives, sometimes in conversation with others, sometimes alone. Kevlar chose to *"get off the streets"* himself: *"I just decided to change things 'cause I was going to die if I didn't."* He started living in a group home. He chose to *"accept it for what it was."* Andrew also acted alone as he gradually drifted away from school. When asked if his mother had visited the school around the time he was kicked off the basketball team, Andrew said he did not think she could help. He chose to accept the coach's actions. For him, doing what seemed the *"right thing"* was his own decision.

Complexities across Time

Looking across multiple stories, we were struck by the complexity of stories lived when whole lives were considered. When early school leaving was seen as a complex set of storied events composed over time, the notion of a discrete decision or factor in dropping out of school became problematic. Complexity in composing lives over time became evident in the lives of the youths who left school early. Interwoven in their stories to live by were sometimes contradictory plotlines that led participants to leave school early. For Truong and Andrew, they were learning to live their stories as strong, highly skilled sports players. When they were no longer able to live out these stories of who they were in school, they drifted off.

Complexity, multilayered stress, and continuous tension resonated through many of the youths' stories when viewed over time. It is when we hear that education in Kevlar's words is the *"key to life"* and it is when we hear in his story that he loved courses in secondary school where he learned to play the saxophone and do computers and graphics that we begin to understand that Kevlar's leaving school at the beginning of Grade 12 was not a decision composed around a dislike for school. His eventual reason to leave school was bound up with his desire to do well in school. He could not do well in school with the living arrangements he had. He was not able to get a fourth year in high school when he tried in the months that followed. For Kevlar, his experiences represented an ironic contradiction when he was denied the opportunity to finish Grade 12 and to become the educated person he yearned to become. If we had not heard Kevlar's story, would we ever have come to understand his experiences over time? Would Kevlar simply look like a student with a transient, multiple school attendance record who ultimately quit school?

Early school leavers are impacted by the school context, structures, and norms, and their decision is often the end result of a long-standing struggle and various decisive moments along the pathway (Munns & McFadden, 2000). Sefa

Dei (2008) also draws our attention to schooling as community, where education must cultivate a sense of identity within community and culture.

Responsibilities

Relational responsibility threads were evident in many of the narrative accounts. Many of the youth were composing lives in which they struggled to balance conflicting responsibilities. At times, it seemed as though they were trying to compose lives that allowed them to shift between and across multiple responsibilities. The institutional, familial, and cultural narratives in which they were embedded shaped their experiences. They struggled to compose their own lives but did so in ways that allowed them to stay connected with one or more parents, siblings, and/or extended families and to remain responsive to cultural and familial narratives. Sometimes, these responsibilities were financial. Many of the youth had to make sense of these conflicting responsibilities on their own. Truong, for instance, was living out a story of being responsible in relation to his younger siblings and to his mother and now to his young daughter. Truong began to live out his story in his family early in his life as he got a job working in the same restaurant as his mother before he could be legally employed. Later, he contributed money to support the family and often provided physical protection for his mother and his younger siblings.

Christian was also composing his life attentive to a home life with a mother who had mental health issues and who struggled to find social support. Christian, with an absent father in many ways, also needed to support his family financially and, like Truong, began to live a story of oldest male in the family. Like Truong, he positioned himself in a place where he could support and encourage his sister to stay in school. The stories of Truong and Christian are nested within family responsibilities. Attending to family responsibilities at the heart of composing their lives outside of school often made it challenging for them to negotiate attending to the responsibilities they knew were important to composing a life in school.

Cultural, Social, Familial, and Institutional Narratives

All stories are embedded within social, cultural, institutional, and family narratives that shape, and are shaped by, individual's stories to live by (Connelly & Clandinin, 1999). As we attended to the cultural, social, familial, linguistic, and institutional narratives within which the youths composed their lives, we noted competing plotlines that shaped their stories to live by. The youths' stories spoke of, and to, contradictions between cultural narratives, familial narratives, and stories of school. Caught sometimes in these contradictions, youth were humiliated or embarrassed in front of other students and teachers.

Within the institutional landscape, composing an identity seemed to be more challenging than passively accepting one. Christian tried to reconcile his story of himself as being of Asian heritage with his story of being Canadian. He could not so easily follow the patterns of assimilation and multiculturalism. Cultural narratives and institutional narratives were often imposed on him. We wondered about Christian who was seen as the "Asian" kid and was stereotyped or Truong with his spiked haircut. How do these institutional narratives play out in some of the stories of how fast a particular youth is expelled or dismissed? What happens when children and youth do not fit easily into the story of a "good" student? Christian had tattoos, a different hairstyle, he always felt he was easily judged. The story of him was shaped by the place he lived, the inner city, with the underlying social narratives of gangs/drugs and so on, and where these narratives become inextricably linked. School is certainly not about being different or being given a voice or expressing opposition, as schools often legitimatize and reproduce large structured inequalities and silence students (Fine & Weis, 2003). Students can be explicitly or implicitly excluded from an education simply because they were made to feel that they did not deserve it, because they did not fit the perception of a "normal" or ideal student (Lessard et al., 2008). Expecting middle-class backgrounds also leads to a narrowly constructed identity story of children (Fine & Weis, 2003).

Similarly, the story Skye was composing of herself included being smart: "*You know I'm smart, Lessard.*" Yet when Skye and her family moved from the reserve to the city, Skye reported that she had little freedom in selecting classes. She registered late for school and was placed into classes that had room but that were also not popular. Within institutional landscapes, some of the youth's experiences were profoundly shaped by stories of school, particularly when the institutional plotlines were strictly adhered to, narrowing the educational opportunities. In the current era of high stakes testing, it has also been noted that educators and students are under great pressure to increase students' academic performance—failure on the students' part to perform well often leads to a feeling of deficit among "low"-achieving groups (Archer & Yamashita, 2003). Students not only are then exposed to an uninspiring pedagogy, but they are also made responsible for their failure. These discourses, practices, and policies indicate an area of new authoritarianism (Hodgson, 2007; Smyth & Hattam, 2001, 2002).

A Reflective Turn

These six resonant threads spoke to the complexities of the lives the youth were composing. Their lives awakened us to what might be possible if we engaged with their stories as a way to open up, or disrupt, current stories of schools to allow for the reimagining of schools. As we ended our narrative inquiry with the youth, we highlight three key understandings:

1. These youth did not see themselves as dropouts. They did not self-identify as school dropouts, but, rather, they see themselves as not being in school for now. Many imagined they would return to school when it was possible in their lives.
2. Each youth's life story was unique as they told it and did not fit into a pattern of behaviour that might be identified through factors and forces. We can, if we try, make them fit into those patterns. But we do not see that as being helpful to understanding early school leaving and, thus, not helpful to policy and program development.
3. The lives of the youth are complex, and when we began our research with asking about their lives we saw that they were all attempting to find ways to compose their lives. School is not the only life thread they are trying to compose.

The youths' stories call us, as Dewey (1938) wrote so long ago, to make the experience of youth in their life contexts the starting point not only for education but also for schooling. Could we begin to reimagine schooling as well as education as places where, as Greene (2001, p. 7) says,

> we are interested in openings, in unexplored possibilities, not in the predictable or the quantifiable, not in what is thought of as social control. For us, education signifies an initiation into new ways of seeing, hearing, feeling, moving. It signifies the nurture of a special kind of reflectiveness and expressiveness, a reaching out for meaning, a learning to learn.

Can we shift the stories of school in ways that might move us closer to education?

Notes

1   We acknowledge the support of the Alberta Centre for Child, Family and Community Research for undertaking this research.
2   The names of the youth and schools are pseudonyms. All of the individual conversations with research participants were undertaken in 2008-2009.

References

Appleton, J. J., Christenson, S. L., & Furlong, M. J. (2008). Student engagement with school: Critical conceptual and methodological issues of the construct. *Psychology in the Schools, 45*, 369-386.

Archambault, I., Janosz, M., Fallu, J., & Pagani, L. (2009). Student engagement and its relationship with early high school drop out. *Journal of Adolescence, 32*, 651-670.

Archer, L., & Yamashita, H. (2003). "Knowing their limits"? Identities, inequalities and inner city school leavers' post-16 aspirations. *Journal of Educational Policy 18*(1), 53-69.

Bowlby, J. W., & McMullen, K. (2002). *At a crossroads: First results for the 18 to 20-year-old cohort of the youth in transition survey.* Ottawa, ON: Human Resources Canada, Statistics Canada.

Bradshaw, C. P., O'Brennan, L. M., & McNeely, C. A. (2008). Core competencies and the prevention of school failure and early school leaving. *New Directions for Child and Adolescent Development, 122,* 12-32.

Cassidy, W., & Bates, A. (2005). "Drop-outs" and "Push-outs": Finding hope at a school that actualizes the ethic of care. *American Journal of Education 112*(1), 66-102.

Clandinin, D. J., & Connelly, F. M. (1995). *Teachers' professional knowledge landscapes.* New York: Teachers College Press.

Clandinin, D. J., & Connelly, F. M. (2000). *Narrative inquiry: Experience and story in qualitative research.* San Francisco: Jossey-Bass.

Clandinin, D. J., Huber, J., Huber, M., Murphy, M. S., Murray-Orr, A., Pearce, M., & Steeves, P. (2006). *Composing diverse identities: Narrative inquiries into the interwoven lives of children and teachers.* London and NewYork: Routledge.

Clandinin, D. J., Steeves, P., Li, Y., Mickelson, J. R., Buck, G., Pearce, M., Caine, V., ... & Huber, M. (2010). *Composing lives: A narrative account into the experiences of youth who left school early.* Online: http://www.uofaweb.ualberta.ca/elementaryed/CRTED.cfm.

Connelly, F. M., & Clandinin, D. J. (1996). Teachers' professional knowledge landscapes: Teacher stories, stories of teachers, school stories, stories of school. *Educational Researcher, 25*(3), 24-30.

Connelly, F. M., & Clandinin, D. J. (1999). *Shaping a professional identity: Stories of educational practice.* New York: Teachers College Press.

Connelly, F. M., & Clandinin, D. J. (2006). Narrative inquiry. In J. Green, G. Camilli, & P. Elmore (Eds.), *Handbook of complementary methods in education research* (3rd ed., pp. 477-487). Mahwah, NJ: Lawrence Erlbaum.

Davis, J. E. (2006). Research at the margin: Mapping masculinity and mobility of African-American high school dropouts. *International Journal of Qualitative Studies in Education 19*(3), 289-304.

Dewey, J. (1938). *Experience and education.* New York: Collier.

Fine, M., & Weis, L. (2003). *Silenced voices and extraordinary conversations: Re-imagining schools.* New York: Teachers College Press.

Greene, M. (2001). *Variations on a blue guitar: The Lincoln Center Institute lectures on aesthetic education.* New York: Teachers College Press.

Harris, L. R. (2008). A phenomenographic investigation of teacher conceptions of student engagement in learning. *Australian Educational Researcher, 35*(1), 57-79.

Hattam, R., & Smyth, J. (2003). "Not everyone has a perfect life": Becoming somebody without school. *Pedagogy, Culture & Society, 11*(3), 379-398.

Hodgson, D. (2007). Towards a more telling way of understanding early school leaving. *Issues in Educational Research, 17*(1), 40-61.

Janosz, M., Archambault, I., Morizot, J., & Pagani, L. S. (2008). School engagement trajectories and their differential predictive relations to dropout. *Journal of Social Issues, 64,* 21-40.

Langhout, R. D., & Mitchell, C. A. (2008). Engaging contexts: Drawing the link between student and teacher experiences of the hidden curriculum. *Journal of Community and Applied Social Psychology, 18*(6), 593-614.

Lessard, A., Butler-Kisber, L., Fortin, L., Marcotte, D., Potvin, P., & Royer, E. (2008). Shades of disengagement: High school dropouts speak out. *Social Psychology of Education, 11*(1), 25-42.

Munns, G., & McFadden, M. (2000). First chance, second chance or last chance? Resistance and response to education. *British Journal of Sociology of Education 21*(1), 59-75.

Sefa Dei, G. J. (2008). Schooling as community: Race, schooling, and the education of African youth. *Journal of Black Studies, 38,* 346-366.

Smyth, J., & Hattam, R. (2001). "Voiced" research as a sociology for understanding "dropping out" of school. *British Journal of Sociology of Education 22*(3), 401-415.

Smyth, J., & Hattam, R. (2002). Early school leaving and the cultural geography of high schools. *British Educational Research Journal 28*(3), 375-397.

Smyth, J., & Hattam, R. (2004). *Dropping out, drifting off, being excluded.* New York: Peter Lang Publishing.

Tanner, J., Krahn, H., & Hartnagel, T. F. (1995). *Fractured transitions from school to work: Revisiting the drop out problem.* Don Mills, ON: Oxford University Press.

Tilleczek, K. (Ed.) (2008). *Why do students drop out of high school? Narrative studies and social critiques.* New York: Edwin Mellen Press

Toohey, K. (2000). *Learning English at school: Identity, social relations and classroom practice.* Cleredon, UK: Multilingual Motto.

The Blue Brain Kid, drawing by Bria Dobson

Does Special Education Marginalize Young People?: The Need for Evidence-Informed Practices

Peter Chaban

Introduction

High school students do not like to be marginalized by their peer group, which is the high school community at large. However, high school special education programs unfortunately promote marginalization by institutionally segregating students through program practices, despite evidence-informed calls for inclusive education (Hehir, 2005). Recently, governments have complicated the picture by setting goals for graduation rates that inadvertently further exclude students in special education from being a part of the school community. For example, Ontario has set a graduation rate goal of 85% for its high schools. Yet, promoting a graduation rate that is not 100% suggests that 15% of the student population are not part of the strategy. A large portion of students represented in that 15% are in special education programs or are identified as special needs.

The last decade has seen concerted efforts to improve elementary school students' performance in literacy and math skills. Supported by the implementation of evidence-based practices and programs, there has been measured success. Provincial testing agencies have consistently shown year-to-year improvement in literacy scores and, to a lesser extent, numeracy scores. Initially, this success translated into improved high school scores, but over the last five years these scores have levelled out. A review of the last decade of scores on the Ontario Secondary School Literacy Test (OSSLT) supports this finding.

The OSSLT is a Grade 10 high-stakes literacy test that measures both reading and writing skills. It is also used as a graduation requirement for all Ontario high school students. Between 2001 and 2006, success rates moved from 75% to 84%. Since, 2006, success rates have flatlined at 84%, with the 2010 results coming in at 83% (see Education Quality and Accountability Office, 2011).

Special education students make up between 12-14% of high school populations (Bennett & Wynne, 2006). Over half of this group have learning disabilities and/or attention-deficit/hyperactivity disorder (ADHD). They have the intellectual competency to succeed, but they experience cognitive processing difficulties that undermine their ability to learn and perform based on conventional teaching and evaluation approaches. And for those who do graduate from high school, the possibility of post-secondary education is small. According to US data, high school students with learning disabilities enter post-secondary education at half the rate of their peer group. The percentage is believed to be even more negatively significant for students with ADHD (Gregg, 2009). Canadian rates are similar. Data from the Toronto District School Board shows that for students with learning disabilities, who do graduate from high school, only 31% pursue post-secondary education (Brown & Parekh, 2010.)

This finding has lifelong implications for this cohort both in employment and quality of life. Governments are rethinking successful educational outcomes beyond high school and into post-secondary institutions (Rich, 2010). Today, high school education is seen as only a transitional step and not the final stage towards participation in society. As the research shows, both the rates of employment and salaries increase with the number of years completed in post-secondary education (Curry & Stabile, 2004). In the United States, the federal agency responsible for education is now looking at 100% graduation rates for secondary education. As governments across Canada adjust their educational goals and expectations for high school, there is a good possibility that students with special needs will be excluded.

Special Education in High Schools

In the field of learning disabilities and ADHD, the goal has always been early identification and intervention (Gregg, 2009). Appropriate interventions and instructional practices can help students with specific learning difficulties show significant improvement (Kavale, 2005), but other learning problems may persist or begin to manifest themselves in high school, especially as the school demands change. Interventions that may have worked in elementary school can be non-productive or even iatrogenic in the high school context. More and more, evidence is suggesting that greater emphasis on compensatory strategies, and less on interventions, may make sense in high school (Gregg, 2009).

Compensatory strategies, which include accommodations, assistive technologies, and emphasis on learning strategies, have been shown to work with postsecondary students, and they make sense for high school settings. Yet, many high schools model their special education programs on elementary school models. Emphasis is placed on aggressive attempts to remediate core skill deficits rather than compensating for them. The consequence is usually having students fall further behind in accessing the academic curriculum, which is followed by an eventual transfer into non-academic subjects. This process, in turn, shuts out students with learning disabilities and/or ADHD from pursing university-based courses. Often, it also leads to disengagement from learning and finally dropping out altogether. Tilleczek and Clarke (2013) have shown that the youth who leave school early and also have a diagnosed special need find that the transition into high school often creates real gaps and problems. If they had been well cared for in elementary school, they felt angry and dismayed at the high school gaps. If they had poor care in elementary schools, high schools did much better and provided their first assistance—they felt it was too little too late but were pleased to have any assistance.

Another area of concern is the separation of special education departments from other subject area departments in most high schools. Special education departments generally offer two services. First, they offer training in study and learning strategies. These strategy programs are usually restricted to students in special education. They are not offered across the school community to all students. More importantly, these skills are taught as decontextualized from actual subject areas. Strategy training that is not connected to the expectations of a specific subject area tends not to be retained, and students who do remember do not generalize it across different subjects (Gildroy & Deshler, 2008). That is, they do not know how to adjust the strategy in different subject areas. When taught properly, learning strategies benefit all students. They should not be taught exclusively in special education. They should be integrated into the curriculum expectations of each subject area and reintroduced with each grade level. These strategies should include note-taking strategies, study skills, and reading comprehension strategies.

The second service offered through special education is the "resource room." It is a special class and time that is designated for subject-based tutoring services. Special education students receive help in areas where they may be struggling, or they are given time to work on their homework. Again, it is a good idea, but it should be made available to all students. As well, it should be designed in collaboration with subject area teachers. In isolation, mandatory resource classes only succeed in marginalizing students who are already struggling. Every student should access resource services to improve their grades, whether they are trying to pass a course or hoping to achieve honour student status. Allowing all students the opportunity to use the services of the "resource room" promotes an inclusive school culture and takes away one of the largest stigmas associated with special education. Both resource programs and strategy training make no sense in isolation. They do make sense when integrated into each subject and when made available universally in the school.

Finally, a general practice that has adverse consequences for students with learning disabilities and/or ADHD is the rigidity of subject requirements in Grades 9 and 10. Grades 9 and 10 function as bottleneck grades in a student's career, especially for students arriving in high school with learning difficulties. Students who arrive in high school from supportive and accommodating elementary school programs and are met with stringent course selection and beginning of "tracking" subjects for university, college, or general graduation. Flexibility around course selection does not appear until Grade 11. This rigidity around course selection can undermine a struggling student's transition into high school. Generally, movement in "tracking" is only in one direction. Students begin with academic selection and are moved downward based on performance. The system is not designed in the other direction. Students can take bridging courses but usually the knowledge gap is too great if this decision is made. Most students with learning disabilities and/or ADHD have already resigned themselves to non-academic outcomes. As a result of lower expectations, their motivation to work and succeed is greatly diminished.

What We Know about Successful High Schools

Administrators and education policy analysts should look at what works when reviewing high school special education, especially for students with learning disabilities and/or ADHD. Rumberger and Palardy (2005) reviewed six years of education data from over 14,000 high school graduates across the United States. This data included the year before they entered high school, four years of high school, and their first year of post-secondary education. They were able to extract four consistent themes from students who did well in high school and continued doing well in post-secondary education. Students identified their high schools as safe and caring; their teachers set high expectations for performance; their schools offered a high percentage of advanced placement courses; and, as students, they did at least 3.5 hours more of homework a week than the average. The students had identified two themes that run through the research literature of successful schools—positive learning environments and high expectations.

This finding supports the understanding that students who feel connected to their school and respected by teachers are more motivated to perform. Motivation in turn promotes deeper engagement in the process of learning.

This observation is evident in the general student population but also applicable to students with learning disabilities and/or ADHD. When courses are watered down or modified, students feel less valued and, in turn, less motivated to learn. In turn, engagement in the learning process becomes initially passive and then non-existent.

Recently, social and emotional learning has come to play a bigger role in how students learn. For teenagers, social and emotional learning is especially important. Adolescent development is marked by a disconnect between affect development (emotions and motivation) and cognitive control (Spear, 2000). As a result, emotions are very strong drivers of youth behaviour. We know that poor regulation of emotions has negative bearings on adolescent mortality rates (Dahl, 2004). However, within the context of safe school settings, with curricula that harness the passion and idealism of youth and teachers who understand how youth learn, students can thrive and engage in learning. This disconnect between affect development and cognitive control can be utilized to both promote cognitive development and a healthy sense of emotional well-being. This is especially important for students with learning disabilities and/or ADHD who often struggle with soft skills such as self-motivation, engagement in learning, interpersonal skills, and an understanding of how they learn (Biederman et al., 2006).

Challenges to Teachers

High school teachers receive limited training in adjusting their teaching practice according to student needs. As a result, high school teachers focus on delivering the curriculum more than on mentoring successful learning for each student. This point is not meant to blame teachers. They face many obstacles when it comes to changing practice. These barriers include the underlying beliefs and values associated with being a high school teacher and the institutional nature of the high school.

Many observers have pointed out that high school teachers work in isolation (Burney, 2004). They are isolated both within their own classrooms and from other teaching communities. As a result, they are unable to observe or share practices that work. Instead, they develop personalized and idiosyncratic teaching styles. Both in the popular media and within school communities, excellent teachers are seen as creative and autonomous. Unfortunately, what we really get is a large variation in teacher quality and effectiveness, without any knowledge base of what constitutes good teaching. It also promotes a culture that is resistant to change (Burney, 2004).

Without a solid understanding of what constitutes good instructional practice, it is often daunting when special education teachers try to promote new instructional practices or accommodations for students with learning disabilities and/or ADHD. Concepts such as the use of advance planners, shortening blocks of information, and using immediate feedback for lessons taught may not make full sense without a sound understanding of how learning occurs.

There is very little opportunity for high school teachers to share instructional information beyond their departments. Even within schools, sharing instructional strategies beyond individual departments is rare. When full staff development does take place, it is usually a one-day workshop and the topic is imposed externally. Ownership and opportunity for implementation are not brought into the process. As a result, the motivation to use different practices is not there.

The other problem is an institutional one. It is fair to say that high schools as institutions are struggling from an identity crisis. Historically, high schools have acted as gatekeepers, streaming students into tracks leading to either university, community colleges, or the workplace. Within this context, high school teachers have seen themselves as teachers of subjects rather than as teachers of students. Subject-based teachers often point out that they are trained to teach their subject area, not special education. As well, they identify that a student with learning problems can always be streamed into curricula that matches their ability. In fact, research has consistently pointed out that schools with low expectations can expect poor outcomes from their students (Grant, 2009).

Instructional practices, learning strategies, and accommodations that work for young people have been thoroughly researched. In fact, many of the instructional practices and learning strategies would benefit all high school students. As for accommodations, many teachers resist using them because they see an unfair advantage to the recipient of the accommodation (Gregg, 2009). Yet, the literature suggests that accommodations improve the performance of disabled students to a significantly greater extent than it improves the performance of non-disabled students (Gregg, 2009). High schools need to realize that much of what is resisted by them has been implemented in post-secondary settings.

Conclusions

The challenge to create a fully inclusive high school that sets a 100% graduation rate as its goal is daunting, but it is not an impossible task. Many of the pieces are already in place as many education jurisdictions have created multiple pathways towards a high school diploma. These pathways do not represent the old "streaming" model, which was based on the level of the learning. They now focus on facilitating various ways of acquiring credits towards achieving a high school diploma. Credit courses that reward experiential learning, dual-enrolment programs that allow students to experience college courses while working on their high school diploma, and alternative courses that appeal to student interests are all a step in the right direction. However, they are not enough because they still do not address how students with learning difficulties learn and how teachers can support this cohort to successfully learn.

The solution to expanding teacher knowledge around "learning and instructional practice" will have to come from bridging what researchers have learned and what teachers know about their school context. Such a solution will come when equal partnerships between schools and research centres become a reality. In these partnerships, research centres will become part of the school over extended years, helping teaching cultures to become research sensitive and researchers to recognize how schools work. Only as teachers and researchers share their knowledge and experiences on a daily basis over an extended time will teaching practices move beyond personalized style to standardized, evidence-based practices. It is only when this happens, that all teachers will know how to teach all students.

References

Bennett, S., & Wynne, K. (2006). *Special education transformation: The Report of the Co-Chairs with Recommendations of the Working Table on Special Education.* Online: Ontario Ministry of Education, http://www.edu.gov.on.ca.

Biederman, J., Monuteaux, M., Mick, E., Spencer, T., Wilens, T. E., Silva, J. M., & Faraone, S. V. (2006). Young adult outcome of attention deficit hyperactivity disorder: A controlled ten-year follow-up study. *Psychological Medicine, 36*(2), 167-179.

Brown, R., & Parekh, G. (2010) *Special education: Structural overview and student demographics* (Toronto District School Board Research Report). Toronto: Toronto District School Board.

Burney, D. (2004). Craft knowledge: The road to transforming schools. *Phi Delta Kappan, 87*(7), 526-531.

Curry, J., & Stabile, M. (2004). *Child mental health and human capital accumulation: The case of ADHD* (Working Paper no. 10435). Online: National Bureau of Economic Research, http://www.nber.org/papers/w10435.

Dahl, R. (2004). Adolescent brain development: A period of vulnerabilities and opportunities. *Annals of New York Academy of Science, 1021*, 1-22.

Education Quality and Accountability Office. (2011). Online: http://www.eqao.com/results/?Lang=E.

Gildroy, P., & Deshler, D. (2008). Effective learning strategy instruction. In R. Morris & N. Mather (Eds.), *Evidence-based instructions for students with learning and behavioral challenges* (pp. 288-301). New York: Routledge.

Gregg, N. (2009). *Adolescents and adults with learning disabilities and ADHD: Assessment and accommodation.* New York: Guilford Press

Grant, G. (2009). *Hope and despair in the American city: Why there are no bad schools in Raleigh.* Cambridge, MA: Harvard University Press.

Hehir, T. (2005). New directions in special education: Eliminating ableism in policy and practice. Cambridge, MA: Harvard Education Press

Kavale, K. A. (2005). Effective intervention for students with specific learning disability: The nature of special education. *Journal of Learning Disabilities, 13*(4), 127-138.

Rich, M., (2010). Factory jobs returning, but employers find skills shortage. *New York Times* (2 July), A1.

Rumberger, R., & Palardy, G. (2005). Does segregation still matter? The impact of student composition on academic achievement in high school. *Teachers College Record, 107*(9), 1999-2045.

Spear, L. P. (2000). The adolescent brain and age-related behavior manifestations. *Neuroscience Biobehavior Review, 24*, 417-463.

Tilleczek, K., & Clarke, J. (2013). *Narratives of special education and exceptionality: How and why do these young people leave school?* [manuscript in preparation].

Pieces of Me, multimedia collage by Andrea Bunnie

chapter 12

Using Visual Arts to Enhance Mental Health Literacy in Schools

Katherine M. Boydell[1]

Introduction

Mental health literacy refers to the knowledge and attitudes about mental disorders that help in their recognition, management, or prevention (Jorm et al., 1997). This definition has recently been more broadly defined as the knowledge and skills that enable individuals to access, understand, and apply information for mental health (Canadian Alliance on Mental Illness and Mental Health, 2008). Mental health literacy involves a range of skills and abilities that develop over time, within individuals and communities. As people gain more knowledge and become more adept at critically analyzing information, personal and social empowerment increases. Ultimately, this process builds a capacity for informed personal choice as well as collective action on the broader social and environmental determinants of mental illness and mental health (Canadian Alliance on Mental Illness and Mental Health, 2008, p. 8).

Worldwide mental health literacy is reported to be extremely low (Pinfold et al., 2005), thus representing a dominant barrier to help seeking and the receipt of services and supports (Cole, Coleman, & Heimberg, 2008). The goal of this chapter is to highlight the importance of enhancing mental health literacy in school settings and to describe our use of arts-based research projects to create awareness, understanding, and dialogue in secondary schools.

Background
Child and Youth Mental Health
Young adults suffer more from mental disorders than any other age group, but they are least likely to use resources (Canadian Community Health Survey, 2003).

Close to 20% of children worldwide have at least one mental health disorder (Waddell & Shepherd, 2002; World Health Organization, 2003). In Ontario, a similar proportion suffers from a mental health disorder, and only one in six receives formal treatment (Offord et al., 1987). Mental health problems are associated with higher rates of truancy, suspension, exclusion, school alienation and marginalization, and drop out (New Freedom Commission on Mental Health, 2003). Youth marginalization via mental health stigma and discrimination is experienced and perpetuated in the school system, making it an important setting to address the issue of mental health literacy (Rickwood, 2011).

Need for Mental Health Literacy

The general public is reported to have a poor understanding of mental illness (Pinfold et al., 2005). They are unable to properly identify mental disorders, do not understand the underlying contributory factors, are fearful of those perceived as mentally ill, have incorrect beliefs about treatment consequences, are often disinclined to seek and access help for mental disorders, and are uncertain how to help others (Jorm et al., 1997; Jorm et al., 2006). Evidence suggests that when mental health literacy increases, individuals have a better understanding of mental health and mental illness and are less likely to hold negative beliefs (Canadian Alliance on Mental Illness, 2008). The school setting is an ideal place to target mental health literacy efforts as mental disorders frequently have their onset in early adolescence (Jorm et al., 2010; Reavley & Jorm, 2010). It is reported that youth are hesitant to seek formal help for their mental health problems and prefer instead to turn to informal sources such as their parents, peers, and teachers (Jorm, Wright, & Morgan, 2007). Given the poor mental health literacy of informal sources of help, this is problematic for early intervention efforts.

Importance of the School Setting

Educators play an important role in the recognition and support for students with mental health problems (Collins & Holmshaw, 2008). They spend a great deal of time with students and are often the best judges of changes in cognitive and emotional behaviour, thus it is essential that they have the information they need to recognize problems early and get students the help they need (Pinfold et al., 2005). There is also documentation of their desire for further training in this area (Boydell et al., 2008b).

Much of the published literature on mental health literacy in school settings originates with Jorm and his colleagues in Australia (Jorm et al., 2006, 2010; Reavley & Jorm, 2010). They recognize that since mental health issues first manifest themselves in adolescence the school setting is an ideal locale to target awareness and education efforts. Their work focuses on improving the skills of teachers via a mental health first aid training course and demonstrates increases in teachers' knowledge, reduction in some aspects of stigma, and enhanced confidence in helping students and colleagues (Jorm et al., 2010).

Recent research identifies the preference of young people themselves to have mental health education and awareness available in the school setting for all students and their teachers (Boydell et al., 2008a, 2008b). Additionally, they are explicit in the ways in which this information should be delivered— for example, we were advised that students do not want a formal presentation made to them from behind a podium. Given this information, there is a need to explore the use of different strategies to create awareness and improve knowledge about mental health and illness in school settings.

Rethinking Mental Health Literacy in Schools: Use of the Arts in Education

The use of arts is supported by the World Health Organization, which recognizes that the arts can provide powerful health educational messages. Further, the current literature suggests that social scientists, artists, and health care practitioners recognize that arts-based methods elucidate human dimensions of health and illness in ways that augment our understanding of both health and social care (Pauwels, 2010). The arts are posited to offer alternative ways of producing and communicating research findings and best practices (Keen & Todres, 2007). Jones (2006) suggests that incorporating art forms into the research process results in evoking emotional responses, providing alternative forms of representation, and promoting dialogue and the sharing of stories. He also indicates that the use of artistic formats can inform and enrich the research process (Jones, 2006). Knowledge conceptualized in this way is demonstrated to be more accessible to diverse stakeholders (Colantonio et al., 2008).

Belliveau (2005) uses an interactive drama approach to address bullying in schools and finds that it enhanced student understanding of the problem. There is, however, very little research that uses the arts in school settings to create awareness and understanding of mental health issues. One study conducted by Roberts and colleagues (2007) used drama to teach students about the psychosis experience and encourage help-seeking efforts. Results of this initiative suggest that students and educators were profoundly moved by the performance, demonstrated clear evidence of increased awareness and understanding of psychosis, and showed enhanced knowledge of, and willingness to seek, help.

Three Exemplars

Three exemplars from our own work are used to illustrate the potential of using arts-based methods to enhance mental health literacy—to normalize mental health and mental illness and create environments where people can talk about mental health and seeking help freely. Two of the projects are specifically geared towards students and educators in secondary school settings. Project 1 describes a choreographed dance based on qualitative research on help seeking in psychosis; Project 2 focuses on a mural art installation project created by youth experiencing first episode psychosis; and Project 3 describes the use of digital storytelling to depict youth experiences of psychosis and cannabis use.

Project 1: Research-Based Dance

The dance project aims to contravene the conventional boundaries and forms of social scientific writing and includes a visual embodied representation (Boydell, 2011a, 2011b). Specifically, an arts-informed method (dance) is used to communicate empirical research about help seeking in first episode psychosis in inner-city secondary schools. A brief presentation outlining the research project and the findings was followed by the actual 15-minute perfor-mance and a post-performance talk-back session with students and educators. Audience engagement and dialogue were elicited via in-theatre observation of audience responses, moderated, post-performance audience discussions, audi-ence feedback in the form of Post-it notes, and researcher field notes. Analysis

The Anguish of Psychosis, performance by Dancing the Data for the symposium "Hearing Voices: The Utilizationn of Qualitative Research in First Episode Psychosis," October 2007. Photograph by Ashley Hutcheson. Image reprinted with the permis-sion of the photographer.

of this data suggests that dance is an effective way to disseminate empirical research results and to enhance awareness and understanding of the phenomena being studied. It also highlights the importance of the aesthetic qualities and visceral impact of the performance. Most importantly, many references were made to the need to continue to take this type of messaging to schools:

> [D]ances like this really create a better understanding to students in high school. (James)[2]

> It was amazing. They should come to our school. (Melissa)

> I recommend it for schools. (Noel)

> The dance was amazing. I thought that this was an amazing way to present information. It was very clear. I thought it would be a little boring if someone just spoke about psychosis, but this was more captivating. The dancers' facial expressions were outstanding. The message was well portrayed. (Beth)

> It was beautiful and moving, a creative and innovative way of expression and interpretation. Great job and please continue educating through dance. (Annie)

> Being someone at risk of psychosis, I found this piece moving and experienced something I would love to see again. The effects of psychosis are scary, but seeing this gives a sense of hope. The performance should not be changed; it is amazing as it is. The emotion and fears found in the piece are moving. (Sylvie)

> I thought that the dance was well performed and it has a bigger impact on young adults because sending a message through dance makes us more focused and aware than just listening to someone talk about it. (Charles)

> That was great. I think you should make the story in the dance clearer, otherwise I loved it. Maybe you should also let each dancer say who they are in the dance. (Francis)

Project 2: Mural Art

The mural project involves use of the arts as both process—in knowledge creation—and product—in knowledge dissemination. The first stage of the mural project is to involve young people who have experienced a first episode of psychosis in the creation of a mural depicting their experience of the pathway to mental health care and to document what they thought of being involved in this process. The second stage involves bringing the mural to secondary schools in urban and rural settings. This was done to create awareness and understanding of first episode psychosis, the process of seeking help, and, additionally, to document student and educator response to the mural installation.

Mural Creation

Eight young people, ranging in ages from 16 to 24 years, were recruited through first episode clinics in Toronto. The mural creation took place over eight consecutive days and was facilitated by a researcher/artist. This process was documented via a participant observer who took over 200 pages of field notes, a photographer who took more than 2,000 photos as well as daily journal reflections from the researcher/artist. The mural creation process concluded with a focus group with the mural artists to discuss why they chose to participate, what it was like to be part of the mural creation process, and what effect they thought the mural would have on other young people and educators in the school system.

Analysis of the focus group transcript reveals three main themes: empowerment, camaraderie, and expression. Young people talked about their involvement as being empowering in terms of breaking down stereotypes about their abilities (or lack thereof). The following example illustrates how one young man felt that being able to demonstrate creativity acted against the stigma of the side effects of psychotropic medication:

> People who have taken medication might be looked upon as being dull and not expressive. So, for that fact, that we were able to create something like this, and prove that we can ... have the creativity. (Steve)

An important consequence of working together to co-create the mural is the sense of camaraderie that develops among the participants. Participant observation notes document the interactions of the eight artists over the period of mural creation, particularly the side conversations and sharing of experiential stories. One participant commented:

> I liked coming out and talking to people who've had similar experiences because since my first episode I haven't really talked to anyone else who's had them within a recent amount of time. So, it was kind of neat to hear everyone else's stories and sort of see bits and pieces for you and find yourself relating. It was neat. (Leslie)

The opportunity to express the experience of help seeking in a visual manner was discussed by youth as being an important component of their experience. They highlighted their feelings of hesitancy at the outset of the project, particularly because they did not see themselves as "artists" and worried about their ability to contribute to an arts-based project.

They brought you together with whom experienced the first episode of psychosis and whatnot and also to have a venue where we can express our feelings and our thoughts of what happened to us and how we dealt with that—what triggered it … very beneficial and in a sense breaking us out of our shell. (Georgia)

The following young man describes his decision regarding the selection of images to portray his experiences:

I felt the Icarus and the man hanging from the chains were very much related to my first episode because it had a lot to do with a lot of metaphysical problems and a lot of delusions of extension and transcendence … trying to reach this higher point and just sort of having everything fall apart and fall back into the dark. I felt Icarus is good for that and the whole guy with the chains and stuff—he's more of the spiritualistic gains I received from going through this which is represented by the whole third eye thing and just sort of breaking free of all my, a lot of the problems that were present and just sort of coming to some understanding. (Tom)

Mural Dissemination

Three secondary schools in the Greater Toronto Area and six rural/remote schools in Ontario and Prince Edward Island were targeted for the installation of the mural. The mural installation has been displayed over a ten-day period in the Toronto schools to date. During this time period, students and educators had an opportunity to observe and engage with the mural. On the final day, a formal panel session and talkback was held to provide general information on first episode psychosis and the creation of the mural. Students and educators were also provided the opportunity to ask questions to the panel of researchers, the researcher artist, and the young muralists who had experienced psychosis. The data for the study consists of written feedback, which includes a public journal, a secure comment box, and a "graffiti wall" that accompanied the installation for on-going commentary. Following the panel presentation, the audience was invited to respond to the presentation and, more specifically, to the mural installation. This process was recorded via detailed field notes, and students also had the opportunity to write their comments on a Post-it note. Finally, two separate focus groups were conducted in each school study site, one with educators and one with students. Focus group participants were asked about the impact of the mural on their knowledge about psychosis and about the use of the arts as a knowledge translation tool.

The comments from the students indicate that the installation provoked the same questions that were later asked during the panel presentation. Responses

indicate that presenting mental health information in this manner helps to incite thinking about mental health issues and educate people about psychosis in particular. There was also a great deal of support for sharing this information in the school setting.

> *I think that you should go to other schools and teach them about psychosis.* (Patricia)

> *It was a very enlightening presentation, and I am very surprised of the facts about psychosis and it has been an educative presentation as well. And I would like to thank the people who came and spoke about their episode. Kudos to you all. And I suggest you keep on going. It is a very interesting workshop.* (Stephanie)

> *It's hard to differentiate between "quirkiness" and psychosis sometimes for me. Talking about that more might be good. Having people in who experienced psychosis is really helpful in a lot of ways—you can think people who experience mental illness aren't normal, or we should avoid them, or they can't be helped. Them coming in, although I'm sure super challenging, really helped me think about myself or my friends and mental illness and understand it—definitely the most meaningful part for me.* (Helena)

> *Best part by far was the young people's question and answer session!* (Katie)

Project 3: Digital Storytelling

This capacity-building and education development/knowledge-translation initiative focused on the experience of cannabis among youth with first episode psychosis. The capacity-building component was achieved via the education and support of youth participant-researchers who gathered qualitative data about the experience of cannabis use and psychosis among their peers. The education-development component utilized participant researchers to conduct focus groups and individual qualitative interviews with participant-subject youth treated for psychosis in four specialized treatment program sites across the country. The focus groups and interviews examine reasons for cannabis use or non-use, factors that may protect against drug use, and key messages for prevention programs. The ultimate goal of the project is to create awareness of the experience of cannabis use among youth with psychosis and the primary target audience is other young people.

In March 2010, 22 participant-researcher youth from across Canada gathered in Toronto for a three-day digital storytelling workshop.[3] Digital stories are short, first-person video narratives created by combining recorded voice, still and moving images, and music or other sounds. A digital story can bring to life the reality of how individuals experience a particular issue or problem day to day. During the workshop, youth were led through the process of creating short films based on their experiences and struggles with their mental health. As a result of the collective approach to storytelling, and the intensive nature of the process, the digital story workshop emerged as a valuable teambuilding tool. The product of the workshop—a series of powerful digital stories—were used to create awareness and educate others, opening up the opportunity to engage in a dialogue about mental health issues and thus enhance mental health literacy. The project team is now exploring the possibilities of sharing this work in school settings across the country.

Discussion

The projects described in this chapter demonstrate the potential of using arts-based methods to enhance the mental health literacy of youth in school settings. We know that previous research attempting to address literacy in school settings suggests that youth attitudes can be positively influenced by brief sessions to raise awareness (Pinfold et al., 2005). The work of Roberts and colleagues (2007) and Boydell (2011a, 2011b) suggests that many young people may be more receptive to receiving mental health messages in an arts-based form—a medium that may be more engaging to them. It raises a number of questions such as: Would such arts-based strategies be a helpful adjunct to more didactic methods of transmitting mental health messages? Why might they be more effective and under what circumstances? There is a growing commitment to using the classroom as a locale for promoting mental health and well-being and hope for longer term impact in terms of the reduction of stigma and discrimination among marginalized youth. This promising avenue can be capitalized on, and future research is required to address these questions. Such research could examine the influence of arts-based knowledge translation on the level of mental health literacy and its impact over time as well as the actual help-seeking behaviours of youth, with a longitudinal component of sufficient length to document help-seeking actions.

Notes

1   The dance project was funded by the Canadian Institutes of Health Research. The mural project was funded by Social Sciences and Humanities Research Council and Canadian Institutes for Health Research. The digital storytelling project was funded by Health Canada and the Schizophrenia Society of Canada. Sincere thanks to my core research team—Brenda Gladstone, Elaine Stasiulis, and Tiziana Volpe—whose contributions throughout all of the projects have been invaluable. Dance Project: Siona Jackson, Tim Isherwood, and the dance team. Mural Project: Theresa Ascencao, Natalie Baker, Bramilee Dhayanandhan, and the muralists. Digital Storytelling Workshop: Catherine Willinsky and the participant-researchers.

2   Pseudonyms have been given to all youth quoted in this chapter.

3   The digital stories produced in this workshop are available at http://www.canna bisandpsychosis.ca/.

References

Belliveau, G. (2005). An arts-based approach to teach social justice: Drama as a way to address bullying in schools. *International Journal of Arts Education, 3*(2), 136-165.

Boydell, K. M. (2011a). *Using performative art to communicate research: Dancing experiences of psychosis. Canadian Theatre Review, 146,* 12-17.

Boydell, K. M. (2011b). Making sense of collective events: The co-creation of a research-based dance. *Forum Qualitative Social Research, 12*(1), 5. Online: http://nbn-resolving .de/urn:nbn:de:0114-fqs110155.

Boydell, K. M., Stasiulis, E., Barwick, M., Greenberg, N., & Pong, R. (2008a). Challenges of knowledge translation in rural communities: The case of rural children's mental health. *Canadian Journal of Community Mental Health, 27*(1), 49-63.

Boydell, K. M., Volpe, T., Gladstone, B. M., Stasiulis, E., & Addington, J. (2008b). Youth at ultra high risk for psychosis: A comprehensive examination of pathways to mental health care. Ottawa, ON: Centre of Excellence for Child and Youth Mental Health.

Canadian Alliance on Mental Illness and Mental Health (CAMIMH). (2008). *National integrated framework for enhancing mental health literacy in Canada* (Final Report). Ottawa, ON: CAMIMH.

Canadian Community Health Survey. (2003). Ottawa, ON: Statistics Canada.

Colantonio, A., Kontos, P., Gilbert. J., Rossiter, K., & Keightly, M. (2008). After the crash: Research-based theater for knowledge transfer. *Journal of Continuing Education in the Health Professions, 28*(3), 180-185.

Coles, M. E., Coleman, S., & Heimberg, R. G. (2008). Addressing patient needs: The role of mental health literacy. *American Journal of Psychiatry, 165,* 399.

Collins, A., & Holmshaw, J. (2008). Early detection: A survey of secondary school teachers' knowledge about psychosis. *Early Intervention in Psychiatry, 2,* 90-97.

Jones, K. (2006). A biographic researcher in pursuit of an aesthetic: The use of arts-based (re)presentations in "performative" dissemination of life stories. *Qualitative Sociology Review, 2*(1), 66-85.

Jorm, A. F., Barney, L. J., Christensen, H., Highet, N. J., Kelly, C. M., & Kitchener, B. A. (2006). Research on mental health literacy: What we know and what we still need to know. *Australian and New Zealand Journal of Psychiatry, 40*, 3-5.

Jorm, A. F., Kitchener, B. A., Sawyer, M. G., Scales, H., & Cvetkovski, S. (2010). Mental health first aid training for high school teachers: A cluster randomized trial. *BMC Psychiatry, 10*(51), 2-12.

Jorm, A. F., Korten, A. E., Jacomb, P. A., Christensen, H., Rodgers, B., & Pollitt, P. (1997). "Mental health literacy": A survey of the public's ability to recognise mental disorders and their beliefs about the effectiveness of treatment. *Medical Journal of Australia, 166*, 182-186.

Jorm, A. F., Wright, A., & Morgan, A. J. (2007). Where to seek help for a mental disorder? National survey of the beliefs of Australian youth and their parents. *Medical Journal of Australia, 187*, 556-560.

Keen, S., & Todres, L. (2007). Strategies for disseminating qualitative research findings: Three exemplars. *Forum Qualitative Sozialforschung, 8*(3), Article 17. Online: http://www.qualitative-research.net/fqs/.

New Freedom Commission on Mental Health. (2003). *Achieving the promise: Transforming mental health care in America* (Final report no. SMA-03–3832). Rockville, MD: Department of Health and Human Services.

Offord, D., Boyle, C. M., Szatmari, P., Rae-Grant, N. I., Links, P. S., Cadman, D. T., ... Woodward, C. A. (1987). Ontario Health Study II: Six-Month Prevalence of Disorder and Rates of Service Utilization. *Archives of General Psychiatry, 44*(9), 832-836.

Pauwels, L. (2010). Visual sociology reframed: An analytical synthesis and discussion of visual methods in social and cultural research. *Sociological Methods and Research, 38*(4), 545-581.

Pinfold, V., Stuart, H., Thornicroft, G., & Arboeda-Florez, J. (2005). Working with young people: The impact of mental health awareness programmes in schools in the UK and Canada. *World Psychiatry, 4*(51), 48-52.

Reavley, N., & Jorm, A. F. (2010). Prevention and early intervention to improve mental health in higher education students: A review. *Early Intervention in Psychiatry, 4*(2), 132-142.

Rickwood, D. J. (2011). Promoting youth mental health: Priorities for policy from an Australian perspective (Supplemental material). *Early Intervention in Psychiatry, 5* (1), 40-45.

Roberts, G., Somers, J., Dawe, J., Passy, R., Mays, C., Carr, G., Smith, J. (2007). On the edge: A drama-based mental health education programme on early psychosis for schools. *Early Intervention in Psychiatry, 1*(2), 168-176.

Waddell, C., & Shepherd, C. (2002). *Prevalence of mental disorders in children and youth: A research update prepared for the British Columbia Ministry of Children and Family Development.* Vancouver, BC: Mental Health Evaluation and Community Consultation Unit, Department of Psychiatry, Faculty of Medicine, University of British Columbia.

World Health Organization. (2003). *Caring for children and adolescents with mental disorders: Setting WHO Directions.* Geneva, Switzerland: World Health Organization.

Moving Forward: *With, For,* and *By* Youth

Kate Tilleczek and Bruce Ferguson

> The true measure of a nation's standing is how well it attends to its children—their health and safety, their material security, their education and socialization, and their sense of being loved, valued, and included in the families and societies into which they are born. (UN Children's Fund, 2007)

E ducators, social scientists, and youth have long been concerned with the distribution and intersections of inequalities as they play out for young people: How are inequalities reproduced and/or resisted in schools? How are we to respond to them? Do we truly reflect the issues as youth experience them? John Dewey's (1938) clarifying work towards a theory and practice of education has long made us aware of the necessity of examining interactions between the lives of young people and a school's organization. Education based on knowing and valuing the experience of youth and creating continual educative responses was critical for Dewey. Any educational practice worth its salt thrives to reflect upon, and encourage, true educative experiences for meaningful democratic participation. What does this book suggest about how public education ow stacks up against this goal?

This book has demonstrated that there is a larger social context to equity in public education and to being marginalized at school. The authors and youth artists have provided both unique and similar expressions of the experience of marginalization. As more and more young people are being pushed to the margins of society and public education, how do we respond? It remains to be seen how growing income inequality and globalization will become further complicit and complicating in our often embarrassing and dishonourable treatment of marginalized young people at school. We must assess if young people are indeed becoming the new underclass as the Organisation for Economic

Co-operation and Development suggests. We must continue to work with, for, and by youth to assess, diarize, and resist these processes.

Knowing the experience of such marginalization is crucial to understanding. We must continue to map out and assess the empirical trends and their impacts on youth across countries, by region, by social class, by age, by gender, and by cultural status. However, we will not be able to tell how they matter for youth, families, communities, and schools without making visible what it is like to be marginalized in school each day. What does being marginalized in school tell us about how these trends are made, how they reproduce inequity, and how youth, families, and educators are negotiating and fighting back?

> I guess one of the things that I have become aware of is ... the lives of quiet desperation that more of them lead, that we're completely oblivious to. The single parent, no food, the abuse, the rape, the sexual assault, the issues with the justice system, the significant drug abuse that we're, we miss as teachers. But even last year [they were] in all the regular classes. And so most of them were written off as you know, they didn't do the work and they didn't attend. Not, why were they disengaged? And we never asked that ... But now there's still many of those kids within the school—And they survive ...—or they hide. Or they hide and they're, they're marginalized and they exist and they're the ones I think who've had a negative ... experience in grade school. (Jody, an educator, from Tilleczek, 2012)

The authors and artists in this book continue to strive for nuanced and critical understandings and collective responses. We have began to mobilize this work in many ways and places; in homes, schools, communities, and the streets. Best, however, to leave the closing (and opening) spaces to youth as we move collectively forward.

References

Dewey, J. (1938). *Experience and education.* New York: Simon and Schuster.

Tilleczek, K. (2012). Policy activism *with* and *for* youth transitions through public education. *Journal of Educational Administration and History, 44*(3), 253-267.

UN Children's Emergency Fund (UNICEF). (2007). *Child poverty in perspective: An overview of child well-being in rich countries* (Innocenti Report Card no. 7). Florence, Italy: UNICEF Innocenti Research Centre.

YOUTH POETRY AND PROSE

Marginalized

Mallory Goss

B it of an odd word, isn't it? At least, it's not word you hear every day. I'll admit that at first glance I wasn't exactly sure what it meant. I had a vague idea, but isn't the whole point of this piece to truly understand and express the meaning of marginalized youth? So I decided to dig a little deeper. Now, my mother always told me that in order to understand bigger words you needed to find the smaller words that were tucked away. The root words. After a quick examination, I decided that the root word had to be margin.

Margins? As in the small pink lines on loose leaf paper? Surely that can't be right. Another thing to think about when looking at language, however, is that you don't need to take everything quite so literally. Sometimes you need to look at things figuratively. With that in mind, I ran through a list of characteristics I would associate with margins. Margins are small. If you've ever looked at a piece of paper you'll have easily noticed that they are of a much more modest size than the main page. Being in the margins means being in the minority.

Margins are separate. The entire purpose of the small pink line is to divide. To create a barrier. To show where you should and shouldn't put your pencils marks. Being in the margins means being cut off from the rest.

Margins are overlooked. It's quite easy to not notice the margins at all. If you really looked they would be very obvious, but no one ever really bothers. Being in the margins means being forgotten.

Taking all of the above into consideration, I arrived at the conclusion that a marginalized youth must be a young person who embodies all of the above characteristics. A youth that is cut off from the main part of society through various factors, many of which likely aren't their fault. They are the minority, but they are there, and they need us to reach out to them. Unfortunately, as you can see in the previous paragraph, they are often overlooked.

The more I thought about marginalized youth, the more I thought of all the ones I knew who could fit the definition, and the more I wanted to find a solution. I hadn't even given thought to this particular issue until it had been brought to light by this contest, which is why I believe that the first step in solving the problem is awareness. We cannot solve a problem we aren't aware of. We need to let these kids and teenagers know that we are here and we care.

But what else can we do about it? We need to go beyond just acknowledging that these kids exist. After many years of schooling, I can tell you that margins will start to disappear when rubbed hard enough with an eraser. We need to erase the divide that separates the marginalized from the majority; we must cross the lines, we must break the barriers, we must take the factors that separate these youths from the rest of society and we must do away with them or at the very least find a way to work around them. Only then can we abolish margins and unify our society. I hope that with my new understanding of the problem, I can be a part of the solution.

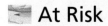

At Risk

Lishai Peel

The risk of being labelled "at risk"
is that youth will begin to see themselves
the way the world sees them
and eventually fill those prison beds
that were already made up for them

These Toronto streets are real estate
for the stateless wonders
who eat time while asking for spare change
but change has never been as simple as turning your head away
or reaching into your pocket for a few loose dollars

Change has never been as simple as writing poetry about poverty
or writing off policies to prevent poverty

or ignoring social issues that cause poverty
or placing all the blame on politicians
or politicians-
placing the burden on the health care system
the schools
the courts
the child welfare agencies
change is messy, but necessary
because there are youth who are living the truth of these words as I speak
like MCs making good of hip hop beats

When I first started studying at York University
Some person said to me:
"Lishai, be careful of the youth at Jane and Finch—
They are troubled and they never change"
As if to say that all they would be is where they come from
And all they would ever see
is the cycle of poverty
as if written into their biology

My silent tongue
Never told him what needed to be said
That poverty is racialized
and classified
by those who have class advantage
and privilege enough to say
that its ok to cut social funding—
just let the community take responsibility for the troubled youth

But so called troubled youth
Will remain troubled on or off the streets
If they are struggling in a system
That does not cater to their parents' inequality of income
Since their qualifications don't qualify them
For a piece of Canadian hospitality
Because they were educated in a third world country
It would seem that equal access to education
Is only valid if you are hailing from a first world nation

I don't know much about politics—
but I do know that things are looking messed up
when qualified immigrants are working low skilled jobs
when youth are finding different ways to adapt to their surroundings
them misconstrued by the media
termed "at risk"

packaged and sold for a dollar fifty
because the media knows what sells
so all they talk about is gang violence
resulting in the youth having to swallow their own silence
because they are stereotyped
without the type of analysis
that looks at what constitutes gang violence in the first place
and what conditions some youth are struggling with

there are folks in this city who are hungry for job security
    and affordable housing
youth who are hungry for movement and artistic expression
me—I am hungry for more than just words
because trust me, my words just don't pay the bills
but if I could shake off the tax man, the bill collectors and
    the voice in my head
telling me I'm caught in a trap
maybe, maybe my words would be enough.

Forgetting the Meaning of ...

Maryam Sharif-Razi

People classify us as deviant, lifeless criminals without power
But do they know our story or the slowness of each hour?
My mother died from AIDS when I was sixteen
Ever since then, life's been nothing but mean
I dropped out of school and turned to huffing
If I said it numbed the pain, I'd be bluffing
Because each day is a struggle for me and other youth of my type
It's not just mine but my best friend's tears I must wipe
Unlike most youth, we've never experienced the pleasures
Of having a shelter, family or any other treasures
I am not trying to imply that I am a victim of being
I know I am worthy, resourceful and I am foreseeing ...
A future filled with hope, aspirations and success
I know I won't be stuck forever in this mess
I have gone through so much and it has built up my immunity
Now I await some sort of change or just a single opportunity
To express my emotions, ideas and at last have a voice
Let the world finally know that this was never a choice

People should learn that not everything is as it seems
Just like them, we crave to accomplish our dreams
I know there awaits a future for both my friends and I
"Let society accept us," every night I propose to the sky
I want to get past the hardships and this ongoing confusion
One day soon, I hope to forget the meaning of exclusion

I Am from …

Alycia Fry

I am from the first grass that peeks through the snow in spring
The first blooming flowers and the birds return home
The bright warm sun's friendly warmth on my cheek again

I am from the first cool sweet glass of lemonade in the summer
Fresh cut grass and the smell of neighbourhood barbeques
Late nights and afternoon mornings
The cold plunge into my friend's pool

I am from the first autumn leaves that begin to fall
The smell of the turkey in the oven and apple pie in the fridge
Pumpkin carving, candy galore, a different identity for one night

I am from the first snow in winter
Snowball fights and slippery ice
The hope of a snow day, mom's making me go to school anyway
Hot chocolate in front of the fireplace
The happy feeling Christmas brings

I am from the endless laughs and giggles with friends
New beginnings and happy endings
Tears of sadness, tears of joy
Feeling alone, being in love

I am from many things; they all make me who I am
I wish life was just simple and we could all be able to express
    where we are from
But we can't, people shouldn't have to be afraid of where they are from
So one more important place that I am from is
It's ok to be different, be happy with who you are
Stand up for what you believe in, be the one that makes a change
That is where I am from …

index

A

aboriginal education, 4, 94, 108, 158, 171; in universities, 163; research about, 105, 171; and residential schools, 107
Afewerki, Agazi, 61
Anneke Rummens, Joanna, 115
art-based methods, 17, 229–31; examples of, 232–38

B

Blackstock, Cindy, 93
Boydell, Katherine M., 229

C

Caine, Vera, 197
Chaban, Peter, 219
Clandinin, D. Jean, 197

D

disengagement from education, 23, 123, 145, 198–99, 221

E

educational apartheid, 97, 105–06
Edwards, Chelsea, 93
engagement: community, 4, 68, 131, 133; immigrant, 124; student, 4, 131, 139, 147, 198, 222–23. See also disengagement
equity: Arts.For.Equity event, 28–29, 37; definition of, 117, 141; implementing, 131; for Indigenous children, 102, 104–05; in public education, 122, 125, 140, 164, 241
evidence-based practice, 219, 225

F

Ferguson, Bruce, 1, 241
Furlong, Andy, 137

G

globalization, 20, 76–78; education and, 75–76, 87; effects of, 43; income inequality and, 241

H

Hilton, Tom, 177
humanities-infused praxis, 17–20, 33–35; as engagement strategy, 22, 35–37, 131; liberal arts and, 18

I

identity, 2, 83, 127, 170; aboriginal, 98, 102, 158; formation of, 19, 34, 45, 79, 123, 182, 209–10; normalization of, 33–34
inequality: educational outcomes and, 4, 139; exposition of, 19–20; First Nations, 98–100; gender, 142; income, 4, 155–56, 169; international, 138, 141, 157–59

J

J. Sefa Dei, George, 115

K

King, Jennifer, 93
Kinlock, Karima, 17

L

language: aboriginal, 94, 99, 107, 171;
discrimination based on, 102–03,
129; marginalization based on, 116,
119–21; second, 26, 63, 66, 94, 121,
137
Lessard, Sean, 197
liminal: definition of, 14

M

marginality, 115; class and, 137–38;
communicating, 3, 21, 28–30, 168;
cultural, 146; inequality and, 143; in
schools, 36, 83, 117–18, 128, 156, 219;
normalization of, 77; place and, 80,
84, 126; policy and, 148; poverty and,
82; racial, 115; refusal of, 43–44; rural,
86; sexuality and, 178, 183; social, 19
mental health, 2–4; literacy, 229–38; in
schools, 231, 237
Mitchell, Jean, 75

P

poverty, 155–57, 244–45; distribution of,
157; in education, 163–64, 168; First
Nations, 94; marginalization and,
139–40, 158. See also inequality
public education: Canadian, 5; critique
of, 156; curriculum in, 155, 168;
humanities in, 17, 36; marginalized
youth in, 2

Q

queer theory, 177–90; in human rights,
180; in public schools, 181–82

R

rights: aboriginal, 94–95, 102–03, 107,
124; educational, 101–02, 132; human,
5, 85, 178, 184

S

Shafique, Mohammed, 61
Smyth, John, 43
socioeconomic status: effect on education, 148, 163; First Nations, 94, 119;
marginalization based on, 22, 120,
142, 168
special education, 219–25; First Nations,
99; funding for, 99
Steeves, Pam, 197

T

Tilleczek, Kate, 1, 17, 155, 241

Y

youth: aboriginal, 4, 96–98, 109, 119,
158, 163; immigrant, 26, 119, 124,
164; queer, 5, 177, 186; refugee, 119,
123–24
youth studies: limitations of, 21, 79; as
praxis, 19

**Titles in the SickKids Community and Mental Health Series
Published by Wilfrid Laurier University Press**

Hearing Voices: Qualitative Inquiry in Early Psychosis, edited by Katherine M. Boydell
and H. Bruce Ferguson / 2012 / 156 pp. / ISBN 978-1-55458-263-1

*Preventing Eating-Related and Weight-Related Disorders: Collaborative Research,
Advocacy, and Policy Change*, edited by Gail L. McVey, Michael P. Levine, Nina Piran,
and H. Bruce Ferguson / 2012 / 298 pp. / ISBN 978-1-55458-340-9

Youth, Education, and Marginality: Local and Global Expressions, edited by
Kate Tilliczek and H. Bruce Ferguson / 2013 / 264 pp. / ISBN 978-1-55458-634-9

*Understanding and Addressing Girls' Aggressive Behaviour: A Focus on
Relationships*, edited by Debra J. Pepler and H. Bruce Ferguson / forthcoming 2013 /
ISBN 978-1-55458-838-1